WAR AND THE SOUL

Praise for Edward Tick's
War and the Soul

Ed Tick not only provides a fascinating look into the minds and souls of veterans affected by post-traumatic stress disorder, but he also illustrates how healing the ailment can be achieved.

—GARY ACKERMAN, US Congressman

War and the Soul is a healing book that rises from the battle for the heart of this culture. Veterans' souls utter the anguish of wounds for which there is no medication. Ed Tick weaves the mythic background that alone can create understanding of these living tragedies. He offers both ancient and contemporary practices that can treat the loss of soul and the traumatic legacies of war and terror.

—MICHAEL J. MEADE, author, *Men and the Water of Life;*
Director, Mosaic Multicultural Foundation

This is no ordinary brilliant book. It is a document that leads us to the possibility of healing from the wars that devastate so entirely that no one is safe. This book can save our lives.

—DEENA METZGER, author, *Entering the Ghost River:*
Meditations on the Theory and Practice of Healing

Ed Tick has been my teacher for twenty-some years. Since the Vietnam War, he has been bringing his knowledge of healing cultures to bear on PTSD. These days the focus is too often on the strictly clinical, but Dr. Tick dares to bring in soul. If you are treating those suffering from deep trauma, or if you are a relative, a friend, or just an interested, caring person, you owe it to yourself and to your client or loved one to read this book.

—FRANK L. HOUDE, retired Lt. Colonel, US Air Force

As the world hangs in the balance, Ed Tick illuminates the path that could pull humanity back from the brink.

—KENNY AUSUBEL, Founder, Bioneers Foundation;
author, *Seeds of Change;* editor, *Ecological Medicine*

Dr. Tick brings to the task a deep compassion for the worldwide legion of war victims. Beyond that, he brings a scholar's sense of history, a visionary's gaze into the heart of darkness, and a poet's grace to make these poignant stories of personal agony somehow affirmative of the human spirit.

—STEPHEN LARSEN, Ph.D., Psychology Professor Emeritus, SUNY; author, *The Shaman's Doorway* and *The Mythic Imagination*

Americans need to understand the message from our men and women in uniform whom we have sent in harm's way. They are speaking to us in this pioneering book, *War and the Soul.*

—LOUISE CARUS MAHDI, Jungian analyst; author, *Betwixt and Between, Crossroads,* and *The Real St. Nicholas*

Silence perpetrates war and its consequences. Ed Tick pierces the silence around PTSD. With this book, the healing begins.

—LOUIE FREE, Founder, Free Radio Limited; radio host, WASN 1500 AM (northeast Ohio / western Pennsylvania)

Ed Tick shows us how war tears away at the soul of soldiers and how it impacts the collective soul of the world. If we all read this book it would change the face of war in our world and inspire us to find peaceful ways to create change.

—SANDRA INGERMAN, author, *Soul Retrieval*

Walking through hell with his heart wide open, Ed Tick takes us on a journey of transformative power. Using history, mythology, psychology, story, and insight born of years of helping veterans, Tick allows us to bear witness to the agony as well as the healing of those who have endured the horrors of war. It is a journey from darkness through shadow and, patiently, tirelessly, into the light.

—RICHARD GELDARD, Ph.D., author, *The Traveler's Key to Ancient Greece* and *The Essential Transcendentalists*

Also by Edward Tick

Sacred Mountain:
Encounters with the Vietnam Beast (1989)

The Practice of Dream Healing:
Bringing Ancient Greek Mysteries
into Modern Medicine (2001)

The Golden Tortoise:
Viet Nam Journeys (2005)

WAR AND THE SOUL

Healing Our Nation's Veterans from Post-traumatic Stress Disorder

EDWARD TICK, PH.D.

Quest Books
Theosophical Publishing House

Wheaton, Illinois ◆ Chennai (Madras), India

First Quest edition 2005

Quest Books
The Theosophical Publishing House
PO Box 270
Wheaton, IL 60189–0270

www.questbooks.net

Sitting Bull's song (in opening epigraph) reprinted from Stanley Vestal, *Sitting Bull: Champion of the Sioux* (Norman & London: Univ. of Oklahoma Press, 1989), 95. Fragment from *Erechtheus* by Euripides (epigraph to Part III) reprinted from Constantine A. Trypanis, ed. and trans., *The Penguin Book of Greek Verse* (London: Penguin Books, 1971), 256.

Cover photograph: Robert Ellison/Black Star

Cover design, book design, and typesetting by Dan Doolin

LIBRARY OF CONGRESS CATALOGING-IN-PUBLICATION DATA

Tick, Edward.
War and the soul: healing our nation's veterans from post-traumatic stress disorder / Edward Tick.—1st ed.
   p.   cm.
Includes bibliographic references and index.
ISBN-13: 978-0-8356-0831-2
ISBN-10: 0-8356-0831-X
1. Post-traumatic stress disorder—Treatment.   2. Post-traumatic stress disorder—Prevention.   3. Veterans—Mental health—United States. I. Title.
RC552.P67T53 2005
616.85'212—dc22   2005010810

      6   7   8   9   10   *   12   13   14   15   16

Printed in the United States of America

For my beloved children
Jeremy, Gabriel, and Sappho,
and for our future

Ye tribes, behold me.

The chiefs of old are gone.

Myself, I shall take courage.

—SITTING BULL,
Song on the occasion of becoming chief

Contents

Part III
THE LONG ROAD HOME

Acknowledgments

I express my gratitude and respect to all the veterans and survivors the world over who have entrusted me with their stories and their healing and have shared with me the love that is known only in one way: "except you share with them in hell."

I express my gratitude and respect to Sharron Dorr, senior editor at Quest Books, editor Carolyn Bond, and the entire staff at Quest. Sharron, Carolyn, and the staff have all believed in and labored over this book with exceeding skill and devotion. They share with me the hope that, with it, we can make a significant contribution to healing and peacemaking in our troubled world.

I express deepest love and gratitude to my wife, Kate Dahlstedt, and our children, Jeremy, Gabriel, and Sappho. They never falter on the lines of devotion and sacrifice; without them, I could not do this work and have a life.

All the stories told herein are true. If they come from sources not my own, I have provided an endnote for them. Any quotation I have not noted was received in personal communication with the survivor. Whenever a full name is given, it is a real name used with permission by a veteran, relative, or war survivor who wishes to stand in witness to his or her experiences. Where one name is given, it is to protect confidentiality.

When referring to Viet Nam and other places in-country, the Vietnamese spelling in monosyllabic words is used rather than Americanized combinations into single words. This small act helps return accuracy and respect to foreign places and peoples.

In Memoriam

Robert J. Ellison

The Quest staff and author Edward Tick honor Robert J. Ellison, the photographer of the soldier's face on the cover of this book.

Born in 1945, Robert took photographs of racial violence in Selma, Alabama, that were published in several magazines. As a photojournalist with the agency Black Star, he was with the marines at Khe Sanh, Viet Nam, in 1968. Some of his well-known images from that time appeared in *Newsweek*.

Sadly, Robert didn't live to see his pictures in print. The supply plane flying him back to the Khe Sanh base camp crashed, killing all on board. He was twenty-three years old. Robert posthumously received the Overseas Press Club award, and more of his work appears in the award-winning book *Requiem*. We honor him for his courageous dedication to serving the truth through his art.

Herbert Follis

We also honor Herbert Follis, whose face it is that graces our cover. When Robert Ellison took this picture, Herb was a nineteen-year-old marine returning to Khe Sanh after an exhausting three-day patrol. He also served at Camp Carroll, Camp Kolu, Phu Bai, and Quang Tri and received a Purple Heart.

Herb returned home to Cadiz, Kentucky, where he became American Legion Post Commander and Sergeant at Arms of the Marine Corps League. He founded and helped lead burial-squad details for veterans of all wars. "I don't feel guilty for having survived," he once said, "but I am determined that veterans and families get the honor they deserve."

Herb died on Veterans Day weekend, 2008. He is survived by his wife, Laura. "The memory of just holding her hand," he said, "was my best tool for getting through the war."

Introduction

The mortars have stopped falling. The tracers have stopped screaming. The mountains, jungles, and villages have stopped smoldering. But years later, veterans still have nightmares and flashbacks in which the old battles still rage. They still watch for threats and stand poised for danger. Their hearts respond to everyday situations as though they were vicious attacks and to ordinary relationships as though they were with long-gone comrades and enemies.

Though hostilities cease and life moves on, and though loved ones yearn for their healing, veterans often remain drenched in the imagery and emotion of war for decades and sometimes for their entire lives. For these survivors, every vital human characteristic that we attribute to the soul may be fundamentally reshaped. These traits include how we perceive; how our minds are organized and function; how we love and relate; what we believe, expect, and value; what we feel and refuse to feel; and what we judge as good or evil, right or wrong. Though the affliction that today we call post-traumatic stress disorder has had many names over the centuries, it is always the result of the way war invades, wounds, and transforms our spirit.

I have been working as a psychotherapist with war veterans and survivors for over a quarter of a century. I began in

1979, just a few years after the end of the Vietnam War. PTSD was not yet a recognized diagnostic category. Veterans my own age—some had survived combat, others had avoided it—were asking for help.

I sat with men whose souls seemed damaged and whose young lives seemed ruined. Scott, a helicopter door gunner, abandoned at night in the jungle, had killed in hand-to-hand combat. I had not seen him since we had played softball together in high school. Two hundred miles from our teenage neighborhood, he stumbled into my office stunned and wired, his life in shambles. I could not tolerate the idea that my old playmate and others like him would remain lost and without health, hope, or purpose.

For several years, I treated post-traumatic stress disorder in Vietnam combat veterans and in noncombatants and resisters. I spent four of those years directing a remote program for vets who could not reenter urban America even for a day. Over the ensuing decades, I learned of the prevalence and persistence of old war pain. My work expanded to include survivors of World War II, the Holocaust, the Korean War, the Gulf War, and the wars in Lebanon, Panama, El Salvador, and Ireland. I also treated Bosnian refugees from Serbian concentration camps, Iraq War veterans, and terminally ill veterans and their families from all wars. These struggling souls helped me learn that the traumatic impact of war and violence inflicts wounds so deep we need to address them with extraordinary attention, resources, and methods. Conventional models of medical and psychological functioning and therapeutics are not adequate to explain or treat such wounds. Veterans and their afflictions try to tell us so.

After a decade of the best psychotherapy I could offer, I went in search of more effective methods for healing our veterans. Through study, travel, interviews, and immersion in other cultures, I investigated warrior traditions worldwide and searched for holistic, experiential, and psychospiritual methods to use in healing vets today. These were my guiding questions: Does the wound we call PTSD result from violent combat in all times and places? Or is it unique to the Vietnam War and wars since? Does it result from American ways of fighting or of treating veterans? Does it result from modern technological warfare? Is it caused or exacerbated by the ways societies treat veterans upon return? Did other cultures, past and present, have effective ways of helping their wounded veterans heal and reintegrate?

One of the first things I learned is that we do not even know how to think about war. To be sure, the politics, economics, and history of particular conflicts are extensively documented. And it is true, as Abraham Lincoln said, that "we cannot escape history." But we can also become lost in it. In order to help our veterans, we need to go beyond the particular and understand what war is and how it works in all times and places.

Though people have not always fought for the same purposes or in the same ways, war is indeed universally traumatizing. Because of this inevitable trauma, our ancestors conducted war with far greater preparation, guidance, and restraint than we do today. Traditional societies required life-threatening service as a warrior of nearly all young males, but the potential destructiveness of that service was limited. One of the primary purposes of war was as a rite of passage into adulthood. Unlike our veterans today, warriors were reintegrated into civilian life with elaborate rituals that involved the whole community and imparted transformative spiritual wisdom. Though modern society has made such ancient beliefs and practices anachronistic, we are still ruled by and try to replicate them. And we are ruled by the mythic attraction to war itself.

History, anthropology, psychology, political science, mythology, world spiritual traditions — indeed, all lenses through which we peer — reveal that warrior classes and traditions are nearly universal aspects of human experience. As I discuss later, depth psychology calls a universal pattern innate to the human mind an *archetype*. Archetypes are inborn potentials for behavior and response. The presence of gods of war in all our root traditions — Jehovah in the Old Testament, Odin among the Norse, Ares and other combating deities in Greek mythology, the holy war and end-of-world stories in Christianity and other world religions — all demonstrate this universality.

Once we understand that war is a living archetype inherent to the psyche, we see that we will never end it through purely political or historical means. We are forced to ask then: is war inevitable? As long as we remain unconscious of the archetypal elements that drive us, we will not be able to escape from their pull. Our only chance for dissipating the archetypal force of war in our lives is to become conscious of how it works through us so that we do not remain possessed by it but rather can labor responsibly to direct its powers. Because of the ultimate nature of the effort, this labor is fundamentally a matter of soul.

War and the Soul reveals the universal substratum of all war as well as the universal dimensions of veterans' wounding and healing.

Part 1 establishes the traditional context of war in history, mythology, and religious and spiritual traditions. It examines what has happened to that context as civilizations developed more sophisticated weaponry and as during our modern era we have shifted to the practice of technological warfare. As we shall see, the more destructive war has become, the more one of its original functions as a rite of passage has been compromised, which is a major factor in the prevalence of PTSD among vets today.

Part 2 concerns the effects of war in terms of the symptoms that make up what we know as post-traumatic stress disorder, but with an important distinction: In my extensive work with vets, another thing I learned is that PTSD is not best understood or treated as a stress disorder, as it is now characterized. Rather, it is best understood as an identity disorder and soul wound, affecting the personality at the deepest levels. Traditional societies and some modern pioneers have held similar convictions. Part 2 describes in depth the aspects of understanding PTSD in terms of identity issues. We see why veterans' healing is so difficult to achieve and why conventional modalities often fall short. It took me decades to learn to negotiate the inner world of war survivors. One of my goals became to map this inner world so that veterans could find their ways through it and so that healers and loved ones could have an effective guide for facilitating veterans' homecoming.

Immersing in the universal dimensions of war also reveals wisdom that gives us hope for healing PTSD. Part 3 presents some of the ways I have practiced that can enable a disturbed vet to heal. Some of my sources for such practices are found in shamanic, ancient Greek, Native American, Vietnamese, and other traditions. Some are indicated in world mythological and spiritual records. Some are revealed when we listen deeply to what PTSD is asking of us rather than imposing our conventional ideas upon it. Specific techniques include purification, storytelling, healing journeys, grieving rituals, meetings with former enemies, soul retrieval, initiation ceremonies, and the creation and nurturing of a warrior class. I conduct retreats for men, for the Vietnam War generation, and for others whose generational experience was defined by any war. I conduct journeys for veterans, families, and communities across generations and internationally. These journeys help heal the rifts between vets and nonvets and between former enemies. They facilitate initiation as men and warriors and offer understanding, acceptance, and honor. All such efforts must be guided by principles consistent with our understanding of identity development and soul work.

This healing work means, in part, taking difficult action in the world and giving new meaning to old myths. For example, we still act according to the ancient belief in taking "an eye for an eye," seeking punishment and revenge on those who have hurt us. This ancient strategy continues the world's wounding in an endless recycling of violence. Instead, we can give new meaning to "an eye for an eye" by returning what we have taken and exchanging understanding and forgiveness. This is a necessary moral step even in "good wars," even if we believe we did no wrong. The work of restoration rebalances and heals the moral trauma at the heart of PTSD. Part 3 demonstrates how this works.

War teaches hard lessons. What we lose, we lose. After war or other traumatic loss, we are different forever. We can neither get the old self back nor return to a state of innocence. We have been through a psychospiritual death.

But like the mythological phoenix, from death we may attain a rebirth. When we reconstruct a survivor's identity from veteran to warrior, we open up dimensions of soul that modern society ignores, including those most painful and usually excluded from everyday life. Though conventional medicine and psychotherapy strive to be value neutral, in these healing efforts we must deal with our moral and spiritual dimensions. This is because warriorhood is not a role but a psychospiritual identity, an achieved condition of a mature,

6

wise, and experienced soul. By modeling warrior traditions worldwide in ways that are relevant and adapted to modern life, we can grow a new identity strong and compassionate enough to carry the wound and heal the soul.

War and the Soul holds forth the possibility that we can regrow the war-wounded soul in both individuals and cultures to nurture and educate a positive and affirming identity that surrounds the war experience with love, compassion, meaning, and forgiveness. When the survivor can accomplish this work, post-traumatic stress disorder as a soul wound evaporates. The survivor can truly come home and serve the causes of peace, justice, and healing. When nations can accomplish this work, in the words of the old gospel song, "We ain't gonna study war no more."

War is a mythical happening. . . .

Where else in human experience,

except in the throes of ardor. . .

do we find ourselves transported

to a mythical condition and

the gods most real?

—JAMES HILLMAN,
A Terrible Love of War

Part I

THE
SOUL
IN
WAR

One

WAR, TRAUMA, AND SOUL

Art burst into my psychotherapy office wearing a black leather riding jacket, tight jeans, and high black boots. His hair was cropped like that of a concentration camp inmate. I put out my hand and introduced myself. He stared at it and grunted, "Uh huh!"

He stomped through my office, looking out each window and behind each closed door. Then he moved his chair into a corner from which he could survey the entire room.

"That's better," Art said in a froggy voice. He looked over his shoulder and out the window towards the trees. "Yeah. Maybe I can relax a little here."

I stretched and said, "Well, I'm going to. I hope you can do the same."

He looked at me with wild eyes. "You are? You ain't afraid? You're not gonna scribble notes or nothin'?"

"No, this meeting is just for us to get to know each other."

"Okay, Doc. I'm in bad trouble. I need help."

The Veterans Administration had rated Art 50 percent

psychiatrically disabled. He worked part-time for the post office, where he experienced harassment, especially from his boss, who called him "the .38 killer." He had a hard time concentrating or restraining his rage and was afraid of losing his job.

"I have double vision," Art declared. "I'll be standing at the post office window selling stamps to an old lady, and at the same time, I'll be seeing NVA [North Vietnamese Army regulars] charging up the hill at my machine gun post. It takes all the control I can muster to stay at my window and just count out change."

Art trusted no one and was numb to all feelings but "staying on red alert." He had to distance himself from everyone or he'd let his guard down. He startled at every loud sound and could not sleep—or when he did, he had nightmares of combat. And he was plagued with survivor's guilt.

"I shouldn't be here. I should be dead a thousand times, the things I've been through. That's why I'm just waitin' for it. Death is chasing me. It'll catch up to me. Nobody could survive what I did and still be alive. Sometimes I'm convinced I'm not."

"You've been scared out of your wits," I said. "You've been through just about the most horrible things a person can endure. You must have been frightened down to your very soul."

"My soul?" Art's face turned white. He stared at me with pinpoint eyes. "My soul has fled."

"What do you mean?"

"It's gone. It fled my body. I felt it leave."

"Yes. Souls are alive. Souls can enter and souls can leave. Tell me how that happened."

He looked deeply and quizzically into my eyes. "You believe me?" he asked.

"Yes," I nodded.

He leaned forward. "I think you do. I'll tell you. It happened at Khe Sanh."[1]

"You were there?"

"The whole damn time! From the end of '67 till we pulled out in June of '68. You know how thick snowflakes fall in the middle of a blizzard?"

"Sure," I said.

"That's how we pounded the hell out of the enemy," Art said. "Day and night. Night and day. Air strikes. Heavy bombers. Fighter jets. Heavy and light artillery. I can still feel the earth shaking. In just nine weeks we dropped 75,000 tons of bombs. I'm tellin' you, Doc. A cockroach couldn't have lived through what we dropped on them."

Art leaned forward again, staring through me. "But each day, they charged up my hill again by the thousands. I was a machine gunner. I'd shoot and scream, 'You crazy bastards, don't make me kill you. Stop it! Go home!' They'd fall like flies but keep comin'. They must have lost ten thousand at Khe Sanh. But they wouldn't stop. It worked, too! We were stupid! Khe Sanh was just a blasted pile of mud that nobody wanted. But Westmoreland wasn't gonna lose. God, what we'll do to win! He brought everything we had to Khe Sanh while the Vietnamese spread out in the south and infiltrated everywhere. He fell right into their trap!"

I looked into Art's eyes, trying to keep him in the room. "That's enough to scare the soul out of anybody," I said.

"Let me tell you what it's like," Art went on. "You can feel the connection between your body and your soul when it starts to break. It's like a thread that starts fraying. I tried so hard during those long nights, the earth shuddering, my hands over my ears. I concentrated to keep that thread from snapping. But I could feel it getting thinner and thinner.

"One day, I had my breakfast in the mess. I sat in the

same blue plastic chair in the corner all the time. I felt safer there. Then I went to my post. I was at my machine gun. The same damn thing happened as happened every day. The gooks[2] were comin' up the hill. They were thick that day. They wouldn't stop. They fell by the dozens, but they just climbed over the bodies and kept comin'. God, I could see their eyes.

"Then mortars started fallin' on us. They must have set 'em up to support this charge. This time they were gonna get in. We had to hold the perimeter. I was shootin' and screamin'. I called for more ammo belts. I looked around. I was the only one left. I looked behind me and I could see my buddies running like hell toward the base. 'C'mon Art!' my sarge yelled. In front, the gooks were almost up the hill.

"God, I flew out of that foxhole like lightning. My feet were pounding the mud. I could feel the gooks behind me. I could hear their breathing. Bullets were whizzing by me. I was a goner for sure. That's when it happened."

"Your soul?" I asked, holding his gaze.

"I felt it, Doc. The cord snapped. My soul ran right out of my body. It ran faster than me, yards ahead of me. I was exhausted. I wanted to lie down and let them kill me. But it was like I was being pulled along in a jet stream. I couldn't stop. I guess my soul didn't want me to die yet. It saved me."

"Losing your soul is horrible. But it saved you. That sounds like the only good part."

"No. Wait. I got through our second line. What was left of my squad gathered where it was safe. But I couldn't stop. My soul kept pulling me. I kept running all the way to the mess. I ran in, like my blue chair could protect me. Then I stopped dead. My soul stood next to me. We looked. There was a huge hole in the roof over that section of the mess. My blue chair was blown to Kingdom Come. If I'd have stayed any longer at breakfast, I'd be in the other world. That was it."

"What?"

"It. The End. I saw my soul shake its head. There was no way it was gonna move back inside my body."

We both breathed deeply and sat in silence. Then I said, "Is it still out?"

"Yeah," Art said. "I don't ever tell anybody this, but it's right here next to me. It's sittin' here looking at you deciding if it's gonna trust you. It's like my twin. It's like there's two of me wherever I go. I can see it and feel it. I got to listen to what it says, y'know. You can't go against your soul."

Art stared out the window. "I can't believe I told you this. I don't tell nobody. So tell me, Doc. Is there any way to get your soul back into your body?"

"There is such a thing as soul work," I said. "Native Americans and ancient people knew just what you are talking about. Terror can make the soul flee the body. It's too dangerous to stay, so the soul leaves. But if you don't die, the soul gets stuck. It can't go to the spirit world because your body is still alive. But it's too scared to climb back inside."

"That's exactly it!" Art exclaimed. "I was afraid you'd say I'm crazy."

"I believe you, Art," I said. "What you're telling me isn't crazy. Your soul splitting from your body at that moment was sane."

Art allowed a tight-lipped smile.

"We can try to make your body and this life a safe place for your soul to move back into," I continued. "If we can get you off combat alert, if you can learn to trust a little bit, if we can find ways of talking, not just to you but to your soul over there, maybe we can bring you two closer together." I bowed in a gesture of welcome and respect to the air next to Art. He nodded, took a deep breath, and leaned back in his chair for the first time.

Art's experience occurred in 1967–68. "The End," as he described it, was also the title of a song the rock group The Doors was singing back home. Story and song both declare that war devastates not only our physical being but our very soul—for the entire culture as well as for the individual. In war, chaos overwhelms compassion, violence replaces cooperation, instinct replaces rationality, gut dominates mind. When drenched in these conditions, the soul is disfigured and can become lost for life. What is called soul loss is an extreme psychospiritual condition beyond what psychologists commonly call dissociation. It is far more than psychic numbing or separation of mind from body. It is a removal of the center of experience from the living body without completely snapping the connection. In the presence of overwhelming life-threatening violence, the soul—the true self—flees. The center of experience shifts; the body takes the impact of the trauma but does not register it as deeply as before. With body and soul separated, a person is trapped in a limbo where past and present intermingle without differentiation or continuity. Nothing feels right until body and soul rejoin.

Ancient peoples and traditional societies recognized soul wounding and soul loss as authentic conditions. Their shamans and spiritual healers practiced many forms of soul healing and retrieval. We will explore this phenomenon of soul wounding and soul loss, particularly in the context of war, in the chapters that follow. First, however, we must be clear on what we mean by the term *soul*.

The soul is at the center of human consciousness and experience. Yet we cannot see or measure soul directly. Rather, we "see it feelingly," to use Shakespeare's words from *King Lear;* we know soul through our experiences of its functions and traits. It is "the vaporization out of which everything derives," said Heraclitus.[3] It is not the body, explained Aristotle, but its originative principle.[4] It is through soul that we experience our human uniqueness and spiritual depth.

Throughout the ages, communities have made special efforts to protect or restore the souls of their warriors during times of war. Only in our postmodern, technological age do questions of the soul's veracity even arise. Not surprisingly, the soul's fundamental needs for well-being are often ignored nowadays. Yet survivors who will not otherwise talk about their violent experiences will engage when invited to speak in terms of soul. Often, they see no sense in talking of anything else.

The following are some of the ways the soul has been conceptualized historically:[5]

The soul is the drive to create and preserve life—that of our own, other people, our community, and the planet—as we participate in the endless creativity of the universe. Spinoza's dictum that every creature seeks to persist in its own being gives voice to this fundamental aspect of soul, which is at once biological and psychospiritual.

Needless to say, war threatens to the utmost this imperative to create and preserve. Consider, for instance, Bill, an eighty-year-old World War II veteran. At age nineteen, he had served as bombardier on a Flying Fortress dropping fire on Europe. Sixty-one years later, he cried as he trembled in front of me, "I went to war to save humanity, but ever since I've felt like a mass murderer!"

The soul is the awareness of oneself as a discrete entity moving through space and time. It is the part of us that contemplates our own existence. Epictitus defined the soul as the "me" at the center of our experience. Albert Camus said the soul is "myself, that is to say, this intense emotion which frees me from my surroundings."[6]

This separate but participating center is damaged in war as it valiantly struggles with gargantuan forces. The victim feels like an unwanted speck, a vermin to be eradicated. One Holocaust survivor said, "How would anybody feel after experiencing the entire world singling you out for annihilation?" And what about the agent of that annihilation? Combat veteran Gustav Hasford wrote simply, "What you do, you become."[7] Existentially speaking, the autonomous self, the "I," creates and defines itself by its actions and experiences. In war, that "I" redefines itself in terms of its capacity to cause pain or to endure the threat of sudden violent death, or both.

The soul is our intellectual power, that which thinks, reasons, and understands. Many philosophies consider reasoning the highest function of soul. Reason allows us to know ourselves—and to *know* that we know. It allows us to rise above our animal nature, to control our instincts, to shape our world, and to create things that did not exist before. Through reason, the soul contemplates the order of the universe and searches for meaning in our lives and in all existence.

But the distortions the soul undergoes in war reshape our cognitive functions and skew the ways our minds operate, including at the psychoneurological level. Our instinctive responses, having been evoked by battle, may remain unrestrained, and the ability to create and to find meaning may be stripped away.

The soul is what gives us our ethical sensibilities. It is the *spirit* behind the Ten Commandments, as distinct from the physical letters carved in rock. Soul is conscience. Socrates described an inner voice that told him only what *not* to do, stopping him only from taking an action that might hurt someone or lead to self-betrayal. Jiminy Cricket, Pinocchio's conscience, is a fairy-tale representation of this function. Jiminy clicked and croaked on Pinocchio's shoulder, attempting to guide his charge aright. It was only when Pinocchio respond-ed, discovering compassion and helping his maker, that he transformed from a wooden puppet into a live boy. When we act in accord with soul, we transform into real people; in dis-cord, we devolve and become like dead wood.

One veteran of the American invasion of El Salvador described his first kill. He had a defending peasant in his rifle sights, but he did not want to pull the trigger on an impover-ished farmer fearfully protecting his home. Meanwhile, his sergeant screamed in his ear, "Shoot, shoot, kill the bastard or I'll have you court-martialed!" He pulled the trigger. As he vomited and cried, his sarge slapped him on the back and said, "Don't worry. The first one is always the hardest. It'll never be so hard again." War survivors commonly report such situa-tions in which they felt forced to betray their moral codes. Afterward, they pass through life without feeling, like wooden puppets on strings.

The soul is our will, our individual volition. Plato said, "That which is moved from within has a soul." In contrast, when we are moved from without we are soulless.[8] Søren Kierkegaard declared that "purity of heart is to will one thing." Friedrich Nietzsche spoke of the will to power, William James of the will to believe. Will is the intention arising from within that drives us to think, feel, and act.

But in war, the gigantic will of the collective replaces that of the individual. For the military to function efficiently, it must run on a hierarchy of power, tradition, and discipline. Basic training curtails our personal will, and then brutal com-bat damages or destroys it as we are forced to act in ways that oppose our civilized natures and established identities.

The soul is our aesthetic sensibility, the aspect of ourselves that hungers for beauty and both perceives and appreciates it. As such, beauty is food for the soul. Ancient philosophers and modern scientists alike have described the soul as the expression of the universal principles of harmony and proportion. Plato named beauty as one of the perfect and universal Forms of which all creatures and things are less-than-perfect reflections. Beauty offers order, purpose, and grace. It reminds us of the inherent goodness of life and the creation.

Walt, a combat zone machinist, lived in the mud and gore of a besieged firebase in Viet Nam for a year. He declared, "Imagine what happens to your soul when it spends an entire year in a place of no beauty! It shrivels and dries up. It disappears. Without beauty your soul dies."

The soul is the part of us that loves and seeks intimacy. From ancient myths to modern movies and greeting cards, the soul is portrayed as attracted to others and fulfilled in relationship. The soul mirrors and is mirrored in the other. It knows and loves, or it fails to love and even hurts, the other.

Ironically, doing violence to another can be a profoundly intimate act. Larry, a captain in Viet Nam, said his life's most intimate encounter had been when staring into the eyes of a North Vietnamese officer as they grappled, their hands locked around each other's throats. Many veterans who have survived hand-to-hand combat talk about the erotic nature of the death struggle. The violence of battle can thus constitute a kind of reverse intimacy. In the aftermath of violence, vets sometimes find they have lost their ability to be intimate in a positive, loving way. The negative expressions of intimacy they are left with cause repeated loss and suffering, often for the rest of their lives.

The soul is the seat of the imagination, our image-making and image-interpreting functions. Our ability to create images is the way by which we organize our complex universe into fascinating and meaningful patterns—whether they were drawn on cave walls 25,000 years ago or as graffiti today. From poetic metaphor to fine art to blueprints and diagrams of the atom, we create images both to express the intangible and to help us manipulate the tangible world. We could say that the act of creating is one way we resonate with the Creator, no matter by what name we understand divinity. In this sense, the use of the imagination is inherently life affirming.

War, on the other hand, reshapes the imagination as an agent of negation. To create weapons and plan strategies that conquer and kill, the imagination must be enlisted in life-destroying service. Consider the Cold War, when the threat of possible attack put our country in a state of constant alert. One Cold War–era air force veteran had been a mechanic servicing bombers kept armed and always ready with nuclear weapons. He became an alcoholic as his means for tolerating his duty, his image for which was "the devil's work." In actual war, the raw power and brutal sensuality of combat so overwhelm the imagination that later the survivor can often see little other than destruction in dreams and daydreams. Veterans often recoil at portrayals of violence in films and on television as if they were the real things.

The soul is the great cry of I AM awakened in the individual. It is the seat of joy, the great affirmation, the inner breath that shouts "Yes!" to life, no matter what. From the soul comes the baby's first cry of life, the athlete's victory shout, the singer's house-shaking performance, the scientist's "eureka!" Every great spiritual teacher and religious leader has taught first not from doctrine but from this primal affirmation of existence.

In 1995, as Preston Stern lay ill with liver disease due to Agent Orange exposure during combat in Viet Nam, his family and friends begged him to find the will to survive. Though surrounded by a loving wife and children, Preston confided,

"War stole my will to live. I've only stayed alive this long for my family, but the truth is, I haven't wanted to be here since the war." He died soon after.

Perhaps our task during this dark time is to transcend our terror of annihilation with this affirmative cry I AM! In 1950, at the very dawn of the atomic age, William Faulkner declared in his Nobel Prize acceptance speech that though we live in a time when "there is only the question: when will I be blown up? . . . I decline to accept the end of man." [9] Without this singular inner grin and clench of determination, we may not be able to endure.

Finally, *the soul* contains what depth psychologists call the shadow. The contents of the shadow are those aspects of us judged unacceptable by society, religion, or ourselves. We cannot get rid of these aspects, so instead we carry them with us below our conscious awareness, often on an instinctual level. Every function of the soul has its shadow. We can do evil as well as good, create ugliness as well as beauty, do harm as well as give aid, be selfish as well as generous. While war can encourage certain positive traits to emerge, it also prompts us to project our collective shadow onto those we define as the enemy and then attack them.

Certainly, throughout history, war is the most destructive activity in which we human beings have ever engaged. Yet while ancient warfare could be exceedingly brutal, its impact was limited: It was fought hand to hand, as one warrior or one army against another. The effective range of the weapons— arrows, swords, spears—did not exceed the battlefield; the amount of destruction was limited by the strength of the individuals fighting. That fact began to change with the American Civil War, which, because of its advanced weaponry and massive casualties, is considered the first modern war. Ever since then, technology has multiplied war's destructiveness exponentially. Today, in our age of weapons of mass destruction, unpredictable terrorism, and up-to-the-minute news, the battlefield is everywhere. Entire populations and the ecological balance of the planet itself are at risk. The result is massive trauma—not just for combatants but also for civilians, who can suffer equally deep emotional and spiritual wounds from their losses. Listen to these people:

Notified that her husband's tour in the combat zones of Iraq was being extended by three months, a young wife cried out, "I feel bad, real bad, like I have a hole in my heart."[10]

Croatian journalist Slavenka Drakulic wrote during the Eastern European wars of the 1990s, "When you are forced to accept war as a fact, death becomes . . . a harsh reality that mangles your life even if it leaves you physically unharmed."[11] As a civilian struggling to survive warfare in Croatia and Boznia and Herzegovina, she experienced a "change in values, in one's way of thinking, one's perception of the world . . . a change that overtakes the inner self until one can scarcely recognize oneself any longer."[12]

A new widow said about the death of her young husband killed in Iraq, "Sadly, Pete's life was taken by an ungrateful people and for a cause that has lost all meaning."[13]

A mother who learned of the death of her son in Iraq cried out: "He did not approve of what the president was doing. . . . A mother's worst nightmare came true for me. . . . I'm very angry. It's senseless."[14]

Something can hurt so much it feels like it tears a hole in the heart. One's life is mangled. Devotion and service no longer hold meaning. The cause is no longer worth our sacrifice, and the senselessness of it all leaves one deeply angry. One scarcely knows oneself any longer. In these and countless similar statements, we hear the effect of war on the souls of people everywhere.

To begin to heal the damage, we must step into the eye of this destructive conflagration that has dominated human history to examine its nature and discover its truth. In particular, we must become aware of the spiritual dimensions of war, for therein lies its great power over us. For this effort, it is best to go back to the beginning, to the deepest and oldest places in human experience. We know these realms through mythology, for myth is always the story of origins and always takes place in the landscape of the inner self.

Two

The Mythic Arena of War

War is a mythic arena. In its noise and grandiosity, its manipulation of the forces of life and death, and its irrevocable shaping of history and destiny, war transforms the mundane into the epic and legendary. Rene, a marine, said that in jungle combat against North Vietnamese Army regulars he felt like a comic book superhero waging an intergalactic battle against cosmic enemies. The World War II correspondent Ernie Pyle wrote from the front lines of the North African campaign: "War makes strange giant creatures out of us little routine men who inhabit the earth."[1]

In war, as in myth, every action is definitive and the stakes are absolute. Any movement could be our last. During battle, the heart beats too hard. Adrenaline pumps too fast. Muscles and minds strain to perform beyond capacity. Sensations and feelings bombard too quickly to be processed. This extreme state might last seconds or hours, days or months. Then suddenly it stops. Though our system is still in overdrive, the world returns to quietude. We try to awaken as if from a trance. We look around. Where there was a forest, a village, or a city, we see fire and devastation. People, perhaps just scattered body parts, lie at our feet. We look away, remember our humanity, and search for our comrades. Some with whom we were just talking are groaning in pain. Some will never talk again. The world has returned to us, but it is different. We have helped make it so and we cannot repair it.

We, too, are different. But there is no time to figure out what we have become. The waiting and watching start anew. We become wakeful beyond the possibility of sleep. Bob Cagle said of his service in the Southeast Asian jungles, "I couldn't talk, curse, or groan out loud. For weeks at a time I couldn't go to the bathroom. Not even the most basic human functions were left to me." Yet though we are on permanent vigilance and cannot rest, days may pass with nothing to do but the most routine tasks. Boredom reaches the extreme and can be worse than battle. We long to break the tedium. Nervousness, grief, rage, and terror need outlets. The only means of release is the gun. We need an enemy. We crave battle.

This twin dimensionality of the war experience makes it surreal, almost hallucinatory. Horror is married to boredom, fascination to putrescence. Norman Mailer said of World War II: "War was odd. . . . It was all covered with tedium and routine, regulations and procedure, and yet there was a naked quivering heart to it, which involved you deeply when you were thrust into it. All the deep dark urges of man, the sacrifices on the hilltop, and the churning lusts of the night and sleep, weren't all of them contained in the shattering screaming burst of a shell, the manmade thunder and light?"[2]

In war everything is rendered ultimate, just as it is in myth. The tiniest event can be charged with intensity so overwhelming that it literally reprograms the central nervous system. We feel the breathing of the universe in our own labored breath as we strain to remain silent while those who would kill us walk mere yards away. We repress responses—words, cries of fear or grief, even bodily functions—with a force that can last a lifetime. We pour our attention into taking the next breath, choosing the next step, keeping the socks in our combat boots dry and the man guarding our back alive. The simplest act may be followed by death, as in this incident recounted by a veteran of the Vietnam War:

> I ask him does he want a cup of coffee. He nods and smiles. . . . I bounce over to the entrance to our bunker and duck inside. I grab our canteens, pull off the two cups, and fill them with coffee. . . .
>
> I carry the two steaming cups outside, cross over to Clyde, and hand him one. . . . He smiles and thanks me. We click cups. . . .
>
> He hands me back his empty cup. I say I'll be right back. He nods and smiles again. I turn and take a step. I hear a bang. My body clenches and stiffens. I spin. A bullet is crashing into Clyde's face. It is blowing apart. . . .
>
> I hit the ground as he does. I grab my rifle. . . . I want to kill. I have to.
>
> I crawl to Clyde. I put my hands on him. I try . . . to stop the blood and save his face. But there is no face. It is gone. There is nothing I can do. Nothing.[3]

Because the simplest matters—stepping away to refill a canteen—can be linked to such dire and unalterable consequences, they take on a transcendent quality. The glorified political causes that produced the conflagration do not matter, but the immediate and particular radiate a power that dims all else. The world is reduced to a crust of bread, a sliver of shrapnel, a dribble of blood, yet all creation is contained there. We "see the world in a grain of sand / and heaven in a wild flower," as the poet William Blake sang. From the trenches of World War I, Wilfred Owen countered that the "world is but the trembling of a flare, / And heaven but . . . the highway for a shell." He declared, "I, too, saw God through mud." [4]

What do we mean by *myth*? We do not use the word in the popular sense of a falsehood or superstition. Rather, we are speaking of myth as the universal stories that convey the deepest truths of human experience and repeat themselves in every generation and every individual. Since antiquity, whole cultures have told these stories to explain the meaning of life and to pass collective wisdom from one generation to another. Myths are the master templates for the patterns of our lives. All religion has its roots in myth. When our experiences of love, danger, challenge, quest, loss, calling, or adventure captivate us, when they glow so that they seem sent by the Divine, we know we are in the realm of myth.

Virtually every one of us, for example, experiences early love and dreams of a grace-filled life, and virtually every one of us is then wounded by the disappointing plunge into life's harsh realities. The story of Adam and Eve's expulsion from the Garden is a universal, mythic version of this drama. Our life histories fill in the particulars as this story unfolds through each of us and repeats in every generation.

Myth in this sense is not merely a prescientific explanation for facts about which we now know better, such as how the constellations of stars came to be in the sky. Though myth is often fantastic, it is not fantasy or make-believe. Rather, it is truth conveyed in fantastical metaphors.

When myths speak of gods and goddesses, kings and queens, warriors and wizards, they are revealing through metaphor certain universal role templates that depth psychologists call *archetypes*. These archetypes are living psychic forces. They are fundamental forms in the human psyche, innate to all of us. They arise spontaneously from the unconscious both in dreams and in myth, which we might think of as the "collective dream." Throughout the ages, these archetypal patterns have played themselves out again and again in all aspects of life, including how we organize government, pursue love and marriage, rear the young, heal the sick, and go to war.

Each culture manifests specific versions of these universal patterns. Each culture also creates its own version of how the universe is ordered and then claims that its version is correct and that its god is the true deity. Religions vary in terms of their particular collections of myths about ultimate concerns, but myth in the broad sense lies behind them all.

Myth thus underlies all rituals and rites of passage. When Jews practice the Passover Seder, Christians celebrate Easter, or Muslims make the *hajj,* the pilgrimage to Mecca, they repeat the foundational stories of their religions and cultures. They are meant, moreover, to *experience* the event through the ritual as if it were actually happening again—ritual being the enactment of a myth, and myth, as an expression of ultimate truth, always taking place in the eternal present. A Jew is meant to feel as if he actually left slavery in Egypt with Moses, a Christian as if she were present at Jesus's crucifixion and resurrection, a Muslim as if he were with Mohammed achieving salvation. All rituals are intended to evoke the sacred, connect our lives to eternal powers and themes, and repeat in us the formative dramas of our traditions.

Myth has a close relationship with the soul and the psyche. In fact, in ancient Greek *psyche* means "soul." Our modern scientific thinking equates psyche with mind, limiting the word to its psychological dimension alone and thus reducing its resonance and depth. Nonetheless, as every ancient and modern tradition avers, we are on a spiritual journey through this life and, if we are to travel well, it is important to understand the concept of psyche in this fuller sense of soul. Mythology can be a great guide, for myth always takes place in the landscape of the psyche and reveals the journey from the soul's perspective.

Myth has tremendous power to drive human behavior and beliefs. This is especially true regarding war. War is an eternally recurring theme in myth and history, and nearly every culture has had its version of the warrior. Throughout history, warfare has provided both the container and the means of expression for war's mythic themes: doing God's work, undergoing rites of passage by which boys become men, and realizing the full expression of the warrior archetype.

The *Iliad* and the *Odyssey,* the twin epics by the ancient Greek poet Homer, are full of mythological figures and motifs that reflect perennial truths about war and the warrior archetype. The *Iliad* tells the tale of the decade-long war between the Trojans and the Greeks, one of whose heroes was Odysseus. The *Odyssey* recounts Odysseus's adventures on his way home from the war, which spanned another decade. It is one of the greatest works in all of literature and has served as a model of the hero's journey and the warrior's return ever since. Along the way, Odysseus had to survive many ordeals. Every soldier is Odysseus, in that the soldier's journey home from war is always long and complicated; his body often arrives long before his mind readjusts. We gain the most from myth when we unravel its particulars. Odysseus's resisting the enticement of the beautiful Sirens, steering his way through dangerous instinctual forces, wrestling with homesickness and despair, encountering the dead, and feeling alienated and displaced from wife, son, and home are all storied versions of the challenges returning veterans must endure.

When we examine mythologies, ancient and not so ancient, the world over, we see that war's mythic power has *always* affected the psyche and that people have always spoken of war in mythic terms and justified their engagement in it thereby. To better comprehend the mythic foundations of our own relationship to war, let us consider the mythologies of the civilizations that lie at the roots of Western culture—the Greek, the ancient Judaic, and the northern European.

Two and a half millennia ago, the Greek philosopher Heraclitus declared, "War is both father and king of all."[5] Observing the eternal juxtaposition of opposites—hot and cold, up and down, conflict and repose, life and death—and the equally eternal force of change, he concluded that opposition, and thus competition and strife, are built into the very nature of the cosmos. It is the nature of opposites to clash and contend, and it is natural that only some survive the confrontation. Nothing lasts; everything, whether human or natural, eventually disappears through either death or transformation.[6] To quote Heraclitus again: "It should be understood that war is the common condition, that strife is justice, and that all things come to pass through the compulsion of strife."[7] War was thus understood as part of the natural order of things. Moreover, by naming war as father of all, Heraclitus also meant that all new things are born out of this conflict.

The ancient Greek word Heraclitus used for both war and strife is *eris*. *Eris* as strife is an elemental force of the cosmos; *eris* as war is the same force playing itself out in the human arena. This same revelation about the cosmic source of war is embedded in other European languages. The words for war—*guerre* in French, *guerra* in Spanish, and our English word *war*—all derive from the Old High German word *werra.* Like *eris, werra* meant strife.[8] Some sources trace *strife* to the Old French *estrif,* or *strive* in English. Both clashing and striving are contained in the power called strife. Both can be used for good or ill, for or against self or other. Both can inspire us either to excel or to destroy. And both dwell in the soul of war.

The ancient Greeks personified the archetypal forces they observed in the human and natural worlds as gods. Their gods were, fundamentally, *what is.* The Greeks imagined their deities not as necessarily kind and loving but as embodying all forces, values, emotions, and behaviors we experience in our lives. Thus ancient mythology was a psychology of the cosmos.

The Greeks conceptualized the force they called *eris* as a goddess, and they described her in images and stories that demonstrated how this god force worked in the human world.[9] In early stories, Eris was the sister and companion to Ares, the god of war; she was the force behind the resentments and possessiveness that lead to rivalry and, at their worst, to violence and wanton destruction. "Insatiable," Homer called her as he recounted her movements across the battlefield at Troy next to her gore-steeped brother: "She sowed ferocity, traversing / the ranks of men, redoubling groans and cries." [10]

One myth in particular reveals this power at work at the origin of war. The story goes that Eris was the only divinity not invited to the wedding of King Peleus to the nymph Thetis. Swearing revenge, Eris tossed a golden apple labeled "for the fairest" into the gathering. Each of the three goddesses Hera, Athena, and Aphrodite—representing marriage, wisdom, and beauty—believed she was the fairest, and competition ensued. The goddesses asked the king of the gods, Zeus, to choose between them; he referred the contest to the mortal Paris, a prince of Troy. Paris rejected Hera's bribe of dominion over Europe and Athena's of victory against the Greeks. Instead, he chose Aphrodite for her promise to procure him the most beautiful woman in the world. This woman was Helen, wife of King Menelaos of Sparta. Paris abducted her and the Greeks joined the Spartans in pursuit, leading to the Trojan War—ten years of slaughter that ended with the destruction of a great city.

The king-gods of early civilizations, from which we inherit our modern beliefs about God the Father, came into dominance around six thousand years ago with the decline of the goddess cultures and the establishment of sedentary agricultural and urban civilizations. Early civilizations saw these king-gods as concentrating three main functions—the civic, priestly, and military—in their one being. Zeus for the Greeks, like Jehovah for the Israelites, Baal for the Canaanites, and Horus for the Egyptians, was lawgiver and protector, the source of the sacred, and lord of war. These king-gods were often connected with high dwelling places—mountains and heavens—just as Zeus ruled the Greek gods' home on Mount Olympus. And they were especially associated with their powers—storm, thunder, and cataclysm—even as Zeus was with his lightning bolt of wrath and destruction. Thus Heraclitus declared, "War and Zeus are the same thing." [11]

The Greek pantheon also included two specific deities of war. The first was Ares, the god of slaughter. Homer called him "bane," "the whirlwind," the god who "is blood-encrusted . . . and knows no dignity." The second was Athena, who, in contrast, used war consciously and rationally for the protection of civilization. As the maiden of power and wisdom, Athena was the unvanquished strategist. She did not delight in battle's horrific ecstasy. Rather, in her upraised palm she held Nike, winged victory, the triumph of spirit. In the Acropolis Museum in Athens, a unique bas-relief portrays the goddess leaning on her spear in contemplation, her head bent in sorrow over the many sacrifices and losses necessary to protect her city. We never see Ares this way. Ares and Athena are the two poles between which our relationship to war forever swings—greed and restraint, frenzy and strategy, bloodlust and grief—two deities serving the best and worst of one great antagonistic force.

Hero myths of all traditional cultures portray the supernatural powers as favoring particular warriors who serve them and carry out their hidden purposes. The Greek gods and goddesses appeared in the midst of war and tried to influence its outcome. In Homer's *Iliad,* Hera and Athena aided the Greeks because of their enmity toward Paris. Aphrodite intervened to save Paris and her wounded son, Aeneas. The god of the sea, Poseidon, whipped the armies into a berserk state. The sun god, Apollo, confronted the hero, Achilles. Hermes, the messenger god, guided the Trojan ruler, King Priam, through enemy lines. Athena counseled the Greeks and protected Odysseus. In the frenzy of possession by their favored gods, the warriors at Troy became savage and irresistible, filled with "passion to do battle . . . that joy of battle which the god inspired." [12]

The battlefield is an arena for the Divine in the Old Testament as well, which depicts war as Jehovah's instrument and method of punishment. Among endless examples, we can cite the prophet Habakkuk, who cried out to the Lord, "You march through the earth in indignation / You thresh the nations in anger";[13] or Isaiah, who declared, in a series of oracles against his people's enemies, that God would dishonor them and lay waste their countries, for he is one who makes "the city a heap, the fortified city a ruin."[14]

The mythology of the ancient Middle East tells us that great gods contended for the loyalty of the local tribes and, through the conflicts between those tribes, competed for the title of Creator and for sacred dominion over the land as King and Conqueror. The gods warred through their people. The people warred for their gods. Each god power was believed to lead his people into conflict and to inspire and protect them in battle. If his people were victorious, it was a victory by and for the god.

Thus Jehovah battled for the Israelites, who worshipped and served him. Jehovah, like Zeus, was originally a mountain and sky god claiming supremacy over competing deities. On the battlefield he was the Lord of Hosts, the cosmic warrior-king before whom mountains trembled and cities crumbled. When the Israelites escaped slavery in Egypt, it was their warrior god who overcame their enslavers: "The Lord is a man of war; the Lord is his name. Pharaoh's chariots and his host he cast into the sea . . . thy right hand, O Lord, shatters the enemy."[15]

When the newly freed Israelites crossed the desert and arrived at foreign borders, their god granted them dominion over the lands of heathen peoples and, as war chief, led them into conquest: "Hear, O Israel, you are to pass over the Jordan this day, to go in and dispossess nations greater and mightier than yourselves, cities great and fortified up to heaven. . . . Know therefore this day that he who goes before you as a devouring fire is the Lord your God; he will destroy them and subdue them before you; so you shall drive them out, and make them perish quickly, as the Lord has promised you."[16]

It was not because of their great goodness that the people were given dominion but rather because it was God's plan. Those against whom God and his chosen people warred were evil, and the binding loyalties between God and the tribal ancestors had to be maintained over the generations: "Not because of your righteousness or the uprightness of your heart are you going in to possess their land; but because of the wickedness of these nations is the Lord driving them out before you, and that he may confirm the word that he swore to your fathers." [17]

Over a period of five centuries, Jehovah and his armies contended against the Egyptians, Canaanites, Philistines, Moabites, Edomites, and many others. The Jewish people evolved from a small nomadic tribe to a nation that was proud, free, and aggressively in pursuit of its unique identity and destiny. The first kings of the people, Saul and David, were chosen by God through his prophets and ruled and conquered only as long as they pleased God. Through the unfolding of history, early belief averred, God revealed the divine plan. The God who created "the earth and all its host" also wished his people to conquer and to multiply. When the people and their rulers were good, just, and loyal to their God and his traditions, they triumphed. If they sinned or strayed from God's rules or purpose, they were defeated. Victory was God's triumph over false gods and their followers; defeat was God's punishment of his chosen people for their own moral failures. In either case, war and its fortunes emanated from God.

In the somber countries of Northern Europe, the pagan era lasted into the eleventh century. The mythology of the early Norse people also expressed the belief that war is built into the nature of the cosmos. Their king and war god was Odin. He, too, like Zeus and Jehovah, was the supreme sky father. Just as in Greek mythology Zeus overthrew his father

Chronos, in the Norse myth Odin slew Ymir, his own grandfather, and then created the heavens and earth out of his body. Warfare began with an act of Odin's: "Odin took aim and shot into the host / that was the first war in the world."[18]

Odin needed his warriors, and they needed him. Not only did Odin choose those who would fall and enlist them in the final battle. He also drove his fighters *berserk.* This Old Norse word, meaning "bear sark," or "bearskin shirt," evoked the ritual donning of a wild animal skin that magically transformed the warrior into "a wild beast-warrior, irresistible and invulnerable."[19] Our English word derives directly from this term. When berserk, warriors "were frantic as dogs or wolves . . . bit their shields . . . slew men . . . but neither fire nor iron could hurt them."[20]

Other spirits aided Odin, too, and completed the link between the heavens and mortals. In imagery reminiscent of the Greek furies or the Biblical Horsemen of the Apocalypse, the Valkyries were portrayed as fearsome female spirits, armored and riding on horseback. They carried out Odin's wishes during battle, granting victory and guiding slain warriors to Valhalla, the hall of devoted and aristocratic warriors killed in combat.

Among the Norse, for whom life was short and difficult and whose unstable societies were used to violence,[21] war reflected the ultimate battle of the forces of the universe. The good and favored warriors aligned themselves with those forces that preserved life. They fought for them, even if it drove them berserk and shaped their characters for life, even if it was finally a hopeless battle that would end in defeat. For the Norse also believed in a race of Giants who were eternally at war with the gods. In Norse, as in Judeo-Christian and other beliefs, the end of time would come. The last day, known as Ragnarok and comparable to Armageddon, was truly the

End. In that battle, rather than the world being purified and souls saved, the Giants would triumph and bring the divine palace and entire world order crashing down. Warriors served the gods and people in staving off this end. Every warrior was such a hero, and every battle was such a final effort against annihilation.

All of these early mythologies—Greek, Hebrew, and Norse—proposed that human war originates in the impulses of the Divine and reflects cosmic strife: violence and creation are inseparably linked. The gist of it goes like this: In the beginning, the gods contended for dominion and the people for survival. Just as the Greeks viewed Zeus as the lord of war and granter of victory, so did the Norse view Odin and the Hebrews, Jehovah. For the early Israelites, the God who created the universe was the same deity who led them in battle. The God whose people triumphed was the true deity and had the most righteous followers. Whomever they warred against and defeated were unholy; their kings were false and deserved to fall. God was obviously not on their side, for only the divinely inspired and sanctioned were allowed to succeed.

This belief has shaped the evolution of cultures everywhere—including the Asian, African, and Native American—and is at the very roots of our compulsion for war making. Enduring to the present day, it is the essential religious foundation of all our wars. When any country goes to war, it does so in the name of what it holds most sacred. And when any country claims victory, it does so in the name of that holy cause and as proof that it represents the truth.

The concept of Holy War as we know it evolved out of this early religious history. As the Bible portrays them, Holy Wars tend to follow a characteristic pattern, and divinely sanctioned wars in other traditions are no different:[22] They begin with a call from or consultation with the god and with signs or alarms calling forth assemblies of warriors. The warriors are blessed; the god himself is their leader and requires their complete devotion. During battle a divinely inspired terror overtakes the enemy, who then crumbles before the god and his army's onslaught. Then follows victory; the distribution, destruction, or incorporation of the spoils; and finally, the disbanding of the campaign. Myths and sacred texts the world over preserve this pattern. Though actual events reflect it only imperfectly, they are often interpreted in its terms—as sacred history unfolding in the human dimension.

By the early Christian era, the concept of war as the expression of divine will was well established. Paul in the New Testament preached to the Romans that God chooses mortal rulers and that, as his chosen servants, they can do no wrong. Therefore, we should follow their will as the definition of "doing good." But if any of us, individuals or nations, "do wrong," then we must "be afraid, for he does not bear the sword in vain; he is the servant of God to execute his wrath on the wrongdoer."[23]

Over time, the belief that war derived from God's will developed into the Just War argument. Augustine declared in the fourth century: "The natural order conducive to peace among mortals demands that the power to declare and counsel war should be in the hands of those who hold supreme authority."[24] He exhorted that war was just if it was declared by a legitimate authority descended from God, was waged for a just cause, and was guided by good intentions "of securing peace, punishing evil-doers, and uplifting the good." On the other hand, wars were "rightly condemned" if fueled by "the passion for inflicting harm, the cruel thirst for vengeance, an unpacific and relentless spirit, the fever of revolt, the lust of power."[25] Nearly a thousand years later, during the Middle Ages, the Crusaders' battle cry was "God wills it!"

The Just War reasoning behind the American Civil War's carnage was to end slavery and preserve the Union. In World War I, it was "to end all wars"; in World War II, to defeat Hitler and save civilization; during the Cold War and in Korea and Viet Nam, to save the world from Communism. The Iraq War, Americans are repeatedly told, is a war to defeat terrorism, cleanse the world of savage dictators, and protect ourselves against imminent dangers. And lest we think that the concept of God operating through the characters and forces of history is archaic superstition, consider these words the president of an American technology corporation wrote to me: "Was Mr. Bush appointed by God? Yes, as with every king, president, dictator, judge, CEO, and other type of leader, God himself sets people in power for his reasons, not ours."

Human history seems to demonstrate that we cannot, or will not, collectively surrender our devotion to the practice of warfare, given our inherited belief that God is at the center of it. Almost every culture that has ever existed has brought forth models of both war and the warrior in its mythology and history. The absence of warfare in a culture is so rare as to suggest that war is endemic to human experience.

Is descent into savagery, then, our inevitable portion? Our forebears acknowledged war's powers as cosmically driven forces, and their storytellers personified these forces as deities and exalted them in myth. Do we know better today? Are we more rational? Can we understand war as merely a collision of contemporary political issues? Are we intelligent or diplomatic enough to resolve these historical conflicts nonviolently and thus make war obsolete?

We may hope so. Yet when we look at war closely, the gods and god forces do still contend. We must understand that war's arena is always cosmic, always mythic, for only in that way will we understand that we cannot possibly stop a particular war or the suffering it causes by rational argument. War is almost never truly about the particular. Rather, war is an archetypal force that creates a larger-than-life arena into which we are irresistibly pulled. In war we embody and wrestle with god powers. The politics and hostilities of warfare rise from the gut of the war god. War evokes in us an altered state of consciousness. Odin, Ares, the Lord of Hosts, Lord Krishna possess us. We are their servants.

We thus arrive at a terrible conundrum. A devout person might argue that since war has been associated with God (or Allah, or any other expression of the Divine) for a long, long time, it is demonstrably true: war really is God's work on earth. Yes, the argument might go, war has become terribly technological and destructive; but by heading us toward Armageddon, we are fulfilling God's will. What is most difficult to see, however, is that all sides make this same claim and that *everyone's* beliefs are manifestations of the same universal myth. One God, one belief system, is not more or less true than any other; all, including our own, are versions of the same archetypal story working itself out in the human psyche. We cannot escape the mythic dimension. We can only awaken to it and decide how we will live it out.

We do not hate the altered state of war. Though we may suffer during and after it, and though we may deny its damage, regret its aftermath, and refuse to acknowledge its pain, as a people we do not hate it. To the contrary, we crave the state of being war offers us. We are aroused by, addicted to, and in love with the archetype of war. As journalist and war correspondent Chris Hedges declares, war gives us meaning by fulfilling our "passionate yearning for a nationalistic cause that exalts us" and by plunging us into a "mythic reality." [26]

Describing ourselves as civilized people, we claim to believe that war is, or ought to be, a final strategy chosen by society only under the most extreme conditions when all other options have failed. Clearly, however, war is rarely such a last resort. Scholars have determined that during the 5,600 years of written history, 14,600 wars have been waged, that is, two or three wars for every year. [27] War is an activity used more often and more handily than we would wish. Rather than the exception, it is the rule.

In every war, up to and including the present one in Iraq, politicians and military leaders have sought to mobilize their people by reminding them that they are engaging in war under divine order and protection. War must appear so for the citizenry to judge it as worth the sacrifice of husbands, sons, and daughters and the assumption of the burdensome roles of avenging angel and mystic warrior. Announcing the beginning of the Iraq War, George Bush declared that his purpose was "to defend the world from grave danger," [28] to "wage a war on terror," and to confront "the axis of evil." Echoing him, Lt. Col. Tim Collins said, "The enemy should be in no doubt that we are his nemesis and that we are bringing about his rightful destruction." On the opposing side, rallying his people to resist the American invasion, Saddam Hussein sounded equally mythic as he declared, "Strike them and strike evil so that evil will be defeated. With Iraq will our Arab nation and mankind also triumph."

The belief in Just War has shaped the violent unfolding of history. Every war is the Trojan War; every war is Armageddon. Every war is a contest between civilization and barbarism, a contemporary reflection of the final mythic battle. All survivors of conflagration know intimately war's mythic nature from their experience—tiny souls struggling to endure in the midst of brutal and devouring forces. Homer declared, "To meet destruction or to come through: these are the terms of war." [29]

We suffer war's aftermath generation after generation, yet from that suffering we fail to correct our mythologizing. We rush to engage in war, to report its triumphs and losses, and to celebrate it in our histories, yet we fail to discern our idealization of it. We continue to believe that war is divinely sanctioned, that is it God's instrument, that it is one god's way of contending with another for dominion over the earth and its inhabitants. We revel in war's meaning and elevate our lost loved ones to heroic status while denying its true costs to our antagonists and ourselves. It seems as though we are compelled to create and participate in the horror of war in order to live out its mythology.

Three

WAR AS A RITE OF PASSAGE

As far back in history as we can see, human societies have marked the transitions between the stages of life—birth, puberty, adulthood, marriage, death—with rites of passage. When societies provide ritual guidance through such life-stage transitions, they and their members tend toward health, wholeness, and harmony. But when they fail to provide meaningful rites for these passages, they and their members alike suffer confusion, dysfunction, and disarray.

Rites of passage are *necessary* for healthy human development. We need them to prepare for, demarcate, and celebrate our changes through the life cycle and in relation to our society. They are not just leftovers from primitive eras; they are archetypal, so they show up in substitute forms when ignored. When we reach one of life's thresholds, it always challenges us to grow, change, and deepen. Simultaneously, we let go of our old identity and the accoutrements we no longer need. Most of us eventually give up our childhood toys, leave home, and become independent. We start and complete schools and jobs,

join the military, give up our single lifestyle to become partners or spouses and then perhaps parents and grandparents.
Eventually, we stop working, suffer illness, and face death. In
each major transition, we undergo a transformation, even
though our present culture provides little formal ritual for
doing so.

In contrast to modern society, traditional peoples celebrated major life-stage transitions in clear, often communal,
and sometimes elaborately staged ceremonies. A rite of passage is much like a passage down a long corridor where we
are put through training and ordeals that prepare us for a
rebirth as a new person, with new status and new wisdom. We
enter the doorway at one end of the corridor, in one life stage,
and exit at the other end, transformed. We are considered to
have a new identity and may even be given a new name. In our
new state, we have become an adult of the people, a husband
or wife, a warrior serving the greater good. As Mircea Eliade
tells us, "Initiation is equivalent to a basic change in the existential condition; the novice emerges from his ordeal endowed
with a totally different being from that which he possessed
before initiation; he has become *another*" and experienced
"a ritual death followed by resurrection or a new birth." [1]

Especially relevant to the topic of war are rites of passage for adolescents as they transition into adulthood. During
these initiations, traditional societies often separated boys and
girls from their families and playmates. They might take them
into the woods, the desert, a cave, a temple, or an underground
chamber. Elders might teach them the secrets of the tribe's
sacred history or their own sexuality. They might put them
through ordeals of ritual decorating, wounding, or scarring,
such as circumcisions for boys. The initiates might undertake
a vision quest or other adventure in nature. Many societies
trained boys for war through their entire childhood. The boys

wished and expected to become warriors, and their whole focus was on preparing themselves for this role. They understood achieving it as desirable and necessary in order to be accepted as men.

All traditional rites of passage include certain components: creation of sacred space; training by elders; ordeals that test and prepare the initiate; rituals that symbolize the transformation sought. These components were often enacted in the presence of peers, community, and, it is believed, divine powers. If the initiate endured the ordeal successfully, it was believed these powers had blessed and guided him in ways that would stay with him all his life. The concluding celebrations, during which typically the initiate was renamed, were an essential part of the rite. Members of the community served as witnesses to the initiate's transformation, and it was dishonorable to be absent. We must witness for and initiate each other. Our transformations are not completed in solitude; they are honored in public and integrated into the culture as its shared history.

Once the initiates had passed the ordeal and been publicly celebrated, they gained the privileges of their new status as men and warriors. They also assumed its responsibilities, inheriting the understanding that the history and destiny of their people was now dependent upon how they served.

Contrast this scenario with the lack of meaningful rites of passage for adolescents today, which psychologists and sociologists are recognizing as the cause of many of the problems of our youth. Some formal rites do still exist—rituals such as bar mitzvahs and bat mitzvahs, first communions, confirmations, graduation ceremonies, and the taking of a military oath. Less formally, the milestones our teens instinctively invest with the importance of puberty rites are getting a driver's license or becoming of age to drink.

These rites, however, lack many of the essential components of traditional rites mentioned above: training by elders, life-changing ordeals, blessing by the community, and the handing over of symbols of spiritual power. In their absence, today's adolescents try to create their own rituals of danger through drugs and alcohol, hazing, vandalism, belonging to a gang, or other wild behavior designed to prove their courage.

The point here is not to idealize the past. Transition to a more mature life stage has never been easy, and, in traditional cultures as well as today, some youth did not accomplish it successfully. Sometimes an adolescent died during the ordeal. Sometimes a young person was not called to a rite. That person might then have had to seek an alternative identity. Shamans, for example, did not always become warriors. Sometimes, too, individuals could not meet expectations and failed the test, in which case they might have lived as though fixated at an earlier stage of development and social status. In traditional cultures, if one could not complete the initiation well, though the community grieved, it considered that soul unable to meet the demands of the next life stage.

Nevertheless, evidence from anthropology, depth psychology, cross-cultural studies, and the endurance of traditional societies shows that traditional puberty rites worked most of the time. Because they were complete, containing all the elements we have discussed, they were usually successful in transforming young initiates into adults who were psychologically healthy and socially well-integrated into their culture.

Since time out of mind, human societies have used warrior training and warfare in this initiatory way. Indeed, war has perhaps always been the most compelling initiation into adulthood. This may be because war replicates all the physical, emotional, intellectual, and spiritual challenges of life in their most intense and threatening forms. Beginning with basic training, as Robert Jay Lifton explains, war is an "initiation process, a symbolic form of death and rebirth . . . [wherein the] civil identity, with its built-in restraints, is eradicated, or at least undermined and set aside in favor of the warrior identity and its central focus upon killing." [2]

The study of worldwide mythology and the work of historians, anthropologists, and archaeologists show us that cultures in almost all times and places have deemed it necessary to have a warrior class of citizens. The formula is simple: the preparation is specialized training; the proving ground is battle. Risking death for the protection of one's people transforms a boy into a warrior. Successful completion of the transformation makes him a man. This pattern is so universal that in the portrait of the human psyche evolved by depth psychologists the warrior is a recurring motif recognized as an archetype.

When war is the initiatory rite, it is as if the transition to adulthood were instigated by shock therapy. The shock propels us suddenly and immediately, in a survive-or-die manner, out of innocence and into the biting realities of experience. Traditionally, those who had the skill to survive and grow from the experience then took their place in society as warriors. The simple conviction was that "war, to those who understand it, shows forth the man." [3]

The philosopher William James reflected on the value war has as a preparatory ordeal for the rigorous demands of adulthood:

> War and adventure assuredly keep all who engage
> in them from treating themselves too tenderly. They

49

require such incredible effort, depth beyond depth of exertion . . . that the whole scale of motivation alters. Discomfort and annoyance, hunger and wet, pain and cold, squalor and filth cease to have any deterrent operation whatever. Death turns into a commonplace matter. . . . With the annulling of these customary inhibitions, ranges of new energy are set free, and life seems cast upon a higher plane of power.[4]

James concludes: "War is a school of strenuous life and heroism; and being in the line of the aboriginal instinct, is the only school that is as yet universally available."[5]

But a crucial distinction exists: In traditional societies, unlike those today, war was a mythic arena in which death was possible, certainly, but its chances were limited. Among New Guinea tribes, for example, war "was less war than ceremonial sport, a wild, fierce festival. Territorial conquest was unknown. . . . There was enough land for all. . . . A day of war was dangerous and splendid, regardless of its outcome; it was a war of individuals and gallantry, quite innocent of tactics and cold slaughter. A single death on either side would mean victory or defeat."[6] Likewise, "Indian warfare on the Plains was simply a gorgeous mounted game of tag. Public honor, social privilege, wealth, and the love of women were its glittering prizes: its forfeit, death."[7]

Of course, traditional warfare sometimes served to protect or increase tribal lands or hunting rights, carry on age-old feuds, and reinforce social solidarity by seeing one's tribe as bordered by enemies. But its main purpose was testing and honing rather than conquest. For young men, war was school and initiatory ritual. For mature men, it was the means to measure their prowess and reinforce their position. Among North

American Plains and Forest peoples, the warrior's main objective was to gain trophies, by which he increased his tribal status, proved his character, and demonstrated his spiritual potency. Such qualities were critically important in these cultures where life was conceived of as "an ordeal, a proving, and above all a proving of courage and patience and endurance on the warpath."[8]

The great warrior and chief known as Tatanka Iyotake in his native Lakota language and as Sitting Bull to the world had not always displayed the heroism and leadership for which he is famous. As a child growing up in the Hunkpapa tribe of the Teton Sioux, he was deliberate and awkward. For this reason, he was nicknamed Slow. By age ten, Slow had killed his first buffalo. But in Plains society he would remain a boy until he achieved his first success in battle through a courageous act witnessed by his peers.

Slow's father was also named Sitting Bull after an initiation of his own when he had encountered a talking buffalo on a hunt. The buffalo was sacred to his tribe, so this meeting signified his connection to the community's guiding divine power. The old bull that wandered into the hunter's camp had recited the names of the four stages of the buffalo's life, after which Plains people modeled their own lives. The sitting bull was the first and youngest stage. At the time, Slow's father had been called Returns Again, a warrior name of honor earned by going back to the battlefield to strike at enemies a second time. After the encounter with the buffalo, however, he threw away his old name and took for a new one the first words the sacred bull had spoken to him.

When Slow was fourteen, he watched restlessly while his father rode off with others to make a raid on the warriors of their traditional enemies, the Crow. Slow was still small and too young to be skilled in the use of weapons, but he was anxious to win the respect due to a warrior. Determined to join the foray, he jumped on his pony and rode in pursuit, announcing his intention when he reached the war party. Not wanting to dampen his son's spirit, his father welcomed him, gave him instructions on bravery and wisdom in battle, and handed him a coup stick with which he might strike an enemy and gain honor.

The Sioux warriors set up an ambush. As the Crow war party approached, Slow charged out in front of his comrades. The surprised Crow retreated. Slow was the first to reach the slowest warrior, who dismounted and aimed his bow and arrow. But Slow's fast pony carried him to the enemy. He struck the man with his stick, thus counting coup on an armed adversary, and knocked him over. The other Sioux warriors killed the man and routed the enemy.

Upon returning to camp, Sitting Bull the father mounted his son Slow on a tall, strong bay horse. He paraded him through the camp, crying out, "My son has struck the enemy! He is brave! I name him Sitting Bull!" Warriors applauded, women sang, and Slow's friends and the girls stared in awe. His father gave four poor men good horses in his son's honor. From that day on, Slow was the Sitting Bull we know from history. He was considered a warrior and a full man, with all the rights, privileges, respect, and honor thereby. Giving away his name to his son, his father took the new name of Jumping Bull, the second of the buffalo's life stages named in his vision.

All the elements of war as a rite of passage are present in this story. The battlefield becomes the sacred space in which the initiate is tested and where he can prove himself and achieve transformation. Ritual elders are in attendance throughout the ordeal. Combat itself serves as the test. The community has abiding values, demanding expectations, long traditions, and elaborate rituals for the initiation. It is highly invested in the outcome and participates as witness and then in celebration when the test is passed. Upon completion, the initiate gains a new name and new tribal status with concomitant roles, rights, and responsibilities.

Also, the story of Slow's transformation into Sitting Bull reaffirms the values of the Plains culture in which he lived. The people believed that their buffalo god had spoken to Returns Again through a vision; and his name, Sitting Bull, reinforced the lineage, both his own and his people's, back to the tribe's protective deities. The elder Sitting Bull and his son Slow, like their companions, assumed that these deities would assist them in battle. In this story, in fact, two sacred tales overlap—the father's vision and the son's initiation. The tribe now has not one mystic warrior but two, not one cultural hero but two, not one sacred name given by the buffalo god through the sacred bull but two.

Modern cultures, like traditional ones, seek the initiation of their boys, the renewal and reaffirmation of society, and reconnection to divinity through war. In effect, joining the military is the closest thing we have today to a traditional adolescent rite of passage. "Be all you can be," American youth are told. "The Marines are looking for a few good men." And "Be an Army of One." Advertisements variously show warriors in dress garb complete with swords and soldiers conquering impossible obstacles, celebrating their brotherhood, or transformed into mythic warriors slaying dragons. Youths are promised the psychospiritual transformation from ordinary citizens into noble warriors.

Young men and women reenact the frame of military service as a rite of passage even when many components such as elders, sacred space, and spiritual presence are missing or differently shaped. In basic training, recruits are stripped of their civilian identities. They are shaved, renamed, reclothed, and retrained to behave according to the belief that loyalty to the group matters above one's own life. Their value system is transformed; they are indoctrinated with the group's higher purposes they are now meant to serve. They are taught that they are no longer individuals; their autonomy no longer matters and in fact can be dangerous. They are led by decorated elders whom they respect, salute, and address honorifically. These elders serve as role models; their higher status is a goal recruits are taught they might attain if they are man enough, good enough, devoted enough. They are expected to be willing to make the "supreme sacrifice" for ideals beyond themselves.

Young soldiers today are instinctively aware that warfare is such a rite, and they can suffer great psychological pain if they perceive themselves as having failed.

John, a Korean War veteran, sat across from me. Beneath his bald scalp, his eyes and face looked haggard. His body slumped in his chair. He spoke in a monotone, as if dragging memories out of his dark and dusty inner basement.

John had served in the navy off the coast of Korea. His ship had helped supply soldiers fighting on land, but, he was convinced, he had never been in serious danger himself. He had served well and was honorably discharged. John believed in our country and its ideals, had thought the Cold War threats were genuine, and while serving did all that was asked without question. None of his personal actions had been morally objectionable, nor had he felt political or moral conflict over the war.

However, since Korea, John had felt separate from his generation and the flow of history. He declared that only combat troops were really tested and that therefore they were the only real men. He considered himself unworthy in this respect. "What kind of manhood test is it," he asked, "to unload supplies on a safe ship while guys my age are killing and dying in the snows?" When he looked in the mirror he saw only an empty shell. "Can a man," John asked with sudden anguish, "go from adolescence directly into old age and miss all the life in between?" His negative self-judgment reflected not the judgments of his contemporaries but his own sense of having failed to pass the test war had presented as the proving ground.[9]

I told this Korean War vet that rites of passage could occur throughout life and it was never too late. I invited him to seek initiation now in ways that were relevant and meaningful to his current life stage and value system. He left our meeting hopeful that his dream of manhood was not dead. But he did not come to see me again, and I do not know if he accepted the challenge.

Both Slow's experience and John's by contrast illustrate that the true initiatory task is to face and defeat an armed foe. John felt he had not become an initiated man in Korea largely because he had not survived a life-or-death encounter. This is a common issue among veterans. Noncombatants like John often see themselves as failures and idealize those who saw combat. The distinction concerns not so much whether one has killed but whether one has faced danger. Medical personnel who served in the battle zone, for instance, are usually highly honored by their peers as combat veterans, even though they did not wield weapons themselves.

The importance of proving oneself in the ultimate test is evident in the very slang soldiers use. American soldiers refer to their initial combat encounters as "breaking the cherry" or "baptism by fire" and to the first time they kill as their "first blood." These names evoke the rite-of-passage dimension of combat while disguising its brutality and show that combatants believe these acts mark true life-stage transformations. Their peers value or devalue them accordingly. Jack, a marine reconnaissance squad veteran, narrated:

> Over in Nam, you weren't shit 'til you proved yourself in the heat. When you were new, nobody wanted to know you. They sat you on top of the hooch doing rocket watch. But if you stood up under fire, they asked where you were from and who your people were. They showed you how to operate the radio. You became part of the family. At first I thought it was cruel. But it wasn't. The right kind of guy helped you survive. The wrong kind could get you killed in the blink of an eye.

Jack arrived in Da Nang, Viet Nam, in October 1968 and was assigned to a reconnaissance company short of men near the demilitarized zone. Within a few days, he was flown by helicopter with his patrol of seven others into the bush.

Jack and his team were walking through thick jungle when, without warning, AK-47s opened fire. The squad dived behind fallen banana trees and returned fire.

"The AK-47s cracked like whips," Jack said. "The fire came from spider holes. Bullets whizzed over my head like hornets. When I peeked to return fire, I saw my log being chewed away—chunk, chunk, chunk—before my eyes. I screamed for the guy next to me to pass me his grenade launcher."

"Why?" I asked. "Were you trying to prove yourself?"

"Hell, no," Jack said. "We could have stayed pinned down for hours. I couldn't just lie there and watch my log being chewed away splinter by splinter. I figured if I'm gonna buy it my first time out, better do it fast."

"That was brave," I said.

"Bull," Jack said. "I was scared shitless. Any vet who tells you anything else is full of it."

Jack grabbed two grenade launchers, dove over the log, and belly-crawled through the brush, inch by inch, toward the holes. Bullets buzzed over his head and pummeled the dirt around him.

When he was within range of the holes, he extended the muzzle of his first tube, pulled the grenade pin, got up on both knees, and fired. He dove back into the dirt and repeated the moves. Then, again on his belly, he crawled back under his buddies' fire. By the time he rejoined his team, the enemy had broken off contact.

"That was my first time out," Jack said. "That was the way I broke my cherry. From then on, I was part of the family."

Jack shook his head. "Funny thing was, those launchers were single shot, only one charge each. I had shot my wad. I was out there unarmed and helpless. Good thing they broke off." [10]

Like Sitting Bull's story, Jack's demonstrates the initiatory dimensions of modern war. But it also exemplifies the ways in which modern conditions differ from the far more ritualized warfare of traditional cultures.

Jack's experience was like that of a traditional youth in that he had grown up in a rural village indoctrinated with the established values of his society. He had enlisted as soon as he was able, immediately upon high school graduation. He believed in traditional dimensions of manhood that include physical prowess and military service. He wanted to be initiated as a warrior in his country's service. He successfully went through the intensive marine training that transformed him from a civilian into someone who knew how to kill and how to survive in combat.

Upon arrival in Viet Nam, Jack was a novice, ready to be tested but still a "virgin." He was not yet a warrior but only the FNG ("fucking new guy" in GI slang). Until he had proved himself as an asset to the mission and his fellows' survival, he was treated as a nonperson—"fresh meat," as GIs say.

Immediately upon exposure to danger, Jack "showed forth the man." He did not deny that he was frightened; nevertheless, he behaved, as Ernest Hemingway defined courage, with "grace under pressure." When ambushed, he did not hide and unduly protect his own life. Rather, he believed it was better to die quickly and honorably. He lived up to the Plains ideal whereby a man charged into danger, declaring, "It is a good day to die," or singing as one Crow warrior did:

> Sky and Earth are everlasting!
> Old age is a thing of evil!
> Charge![11]

After the action, Jack's peers welcomed him as a warrior. They applauded and respected him and treated him differently from then on. Eventually, he was considered a very good marine, someone whom others felt lucky to be around. He was given a nickname and decorated, receiving further modern versions of traditional warrior accoutrements.

Yet here the similarities end, for even when initiation appears to be successful, modern war as a rite of passage is woefully incomplete. Jack's experience lacks significant elements of a traditional initiation.

For one thing, no one blessed his field of combat, turning it into sacred space. Though war is inherently a mythic arena, the modern battlefield is not a ritual proving ground. Moreover, in traditional warfare wholesale slaughter was not the means for achieving political, social, or religious goals. Rather, slaughter was minimized while manhood trials, though not the central purpose, were important elements. Jack, on the other hand, was on a search and destroy mission. On the modern battlefield, in both small- and large-unit action, groups armed heavily with high-tech weapons try to inflict as much death and destruction on each other as possible.

Initiatory elders are also missing from Jack's experience. In traditional cultures, war chiefs led the way into battle. Sometimes elders no longer able to fight would watch over the fray and call it off when casualties became too high. Among some tribes, a medicine-pipe carrier would accompany the warriors, not to fight but to guard the pipe and pray while the others fought. In the Western tradition of soldiering as well, up through the American Civil War, it was the senior officers who led their men into battle. Only in the modern era, when war has become so massive, complicated, and deadly, have the seniors retreated to the rear lines to command in safety. Now the only elders on the battlefield are more experienced peers, often only a few ranks or years older than the initiate, trying to get their missions accomplished while losing as few of their men as possible. They can hardly be considered ritual elders overseeing a sacred transformational process.

In its ancient and ritual forms, warfare was often personal. Enemy combatants often knew each other by name, and the victor's status was partly based upon the status of the enemy he had defeated. Homer's *Iliad* records numerous tales of individual combat between contending champions whose families, histories, and reputations were well known to each other. But modern war is impersonal. Whom you fight, what their battle experience and status in their culture is, and how they are armed are all matters of chance. Jack had no idea of the identity of the soldiers whose spider holes he grenaded. In fact, he identified them as Viet Cong only by assumption.

Our modern-day reasons for being in war are also often impersonal—because we are ordered to do it, or because we are poor and unemployed, or because we are fighting for vague, universalistic ideals. In the American experience, it has rarely been because our families and food supplies are directly at risk. Even when our leaders preach that our homeland is threatened, as they have done during the Viet Nam and the current Iraq wars, we do not experience the threat directly, and belief in it becomes a source of division rather than of unification. And rather than discovering the battlefield to be a personal proving ground, a soldier finds he is just one more participant. Ed Bloch, who fought as a marine in the Pacific theater during World War II, said, "Sure it was my rite of passage. I went to war to show Hitler that Jews did have guts, that we are men. What I didn't know before the slaughter is that it didn't matter. Not Hitler or any leaders on either side cared what happened to me."

Finally, modern war is fraught with symbolism, just as it was in traditional societies—but, again, with significant differences. Traditional rites commonly included the awarding of symbols representing ordeals endured, wisdom and status gained, and divine or natural powers that became personal sources of aid. Thus Slow became Sitting Bull, his elder awarding him the name of an animal sacred to his people. He wore upright eagle feathers to demonstrate his successful achievement of battle feats, and he painted depictions of his most famous exploits on his teepee and personal effects. Today, military elders award much symbolism—medals, battle ribbons, and promotions—that connects modern soldiers to the warrior tradition of their cultures. But the quality of sacredness is usually missing.

Nevertheless, spiritually meaningful symbolism often arises spontaneously on the modern battlefield—demonstrating again that the need for the elements of rites of passage is "hard-wired" in us and that they will express themselves naturally under conditions that evoke them. Mel Suhd, for instance, dreamed of a protective Indian spirit before entering the Battle of the Bulge. Pat and his best friend spontaneously donned colorful over-the-shoulder sashes in their jungle unit in Viet Nam. They had no idea they were emulating the tradition of the Sash Wearers among Lakota warriors. Keith Forry found wolf teeth in the Vietnamese jungle and made a protective spirit necklace of them, at the time unaware he was emulating ancient warrior behavior.

In contrast to some modern vets who reject their officially awarded medals, Mel, Pat, and Keith highly valued their mystical warrior experiences, as though they had indeed encountered divine presence through the symbolism. But dreams, sashes, and animal teeth are clearly not recognized parts of modern military accoutrement, and we rarely hear of animal totems, helping spirits, or visionary experiences in modern war stories. However, it is probably more because they remain secrets in a society that does not recognize them than it is because they do not occur. Many modern soldiers wear crosses, stars, or other religious symbolism; carry mementoes or Saint's cards; and pray deeply during combat. Most soldiers know the truth of the adage, "There are no atheists in the foxhole."

To return to Jack, at first it might seem that he experienced a successful rite of passage: He proved himself to his peers, was initiated into the society of warriors, received a nickname, and was counted a lucky and effective warrior. And he did survive a thirteen-month tour of duty in the marines.

But as we have seen, Jack's exemplary modern initiation, an argument in blood, did not include such traditional components as participation in sacred time and space, the witness and blessing of ritual elders, personal reasons for the fight, the belief that he triumphed due to his own admirable qualities, and the evocation of spiritual dimensions. Any rite of passage missing these elements will be partial and incomplete. The resulting identity achieved will thus also be incomplete and misshapen.

Ultimately, Jack's service led to post-traumatic stress disorder and neurological disease related to Agent Orange exposure. He retreated for a time to ramshackle motel rooms on the edges of civilization. He suffered chronic nightmares and flashbacks. He felt alienated from society and participated in its activities only occasionally. He had an unstable employment history and was unable to form lasting intimate relationships except with other wounded veterans. He came to be dependent upon his disability payment to support a meager, on-the-edge lifestyle, finally ending up in a wheelchair. Though honored by his soldier and veteran peers, Jack was not ultimately able to become a mature warrior serving his tribe and, in his turn, nurturing the next generation.

Jack was a good man whose lifelong worth was lost to our society because of his military service. His story, like that of many others, demonstrates that though modern warfare seems to replicate the pattern of a rite of passage, its conditions tend to be inimical to rather than encouraging of initiation and maturation. Modern warfare promises transformation, but it ultimately fails to deliver.

Four

ANCIENT MYTH AND MODERN WAR

A s we know from mythologies the world over, traditional warfare provided for expression of the warrior archetype and served as a container for the initiatory process. Combat among traditional warriors of the Great Plains, for instance, was largely a display of manhood and spirit. As such, it was considered most honorable as a one-against-one competition. It sometimes resulted in death, of course, but other times in merely counting coup, as Slow did. Though driven by the need to protect the tribe and its lands, war functioned largely as a rite of passage.

During the last decades of the traditional Native American warrior cultures, these motivations collided sharply with the industrialized form of war making introduced by Euro-American settlers. The result was often poignant events such as this one:

One day a band of Plains warriors watched from a hill-top while a large, heavily armed detachment of cavalry—an escort for a group of miners and their supply trains exploring the territory for gold—set up camp in a fortified circle. To the Plains warriors, the whites' way of camping in a thick huddle seemed cowardly. And for the warriors to remain watching from afar while their home territory was invaded would have been not only dishonorable but dangerous.

Soon a single warrior rode out of the feathered grouping. Galloping on his fast war pony, he drew close to the crowd of soldiers and miners and began to circle them. He cried his challenge: Was there a warrior of courage among the whites? Who would step forward and meet him in single combat? In quick response, dozens of guns exploded, blowing the warrior off his horse and killing him instantly.

This story epitomizes the clash between ancient and modern ways of making war. As previously described, many ancient cultures melded martial and spiritual traditions into one path toward warriorhood. Tribal warfare was a personal matter. War being a proving ground for manhood, traditional warriors were willing and eager to challenge one another directly. Enemies frequently knew each other by name, reputation, lineage, and even protective spirits, the symbols for which were frequently displayed on war gear. The destructive capacity of weapons was limited in range, scope, and speed; individual intelligence and prowess were thus significant factors in determining the outcome, and a warrior could feel proud of his success. He could also feel socially purposeful and justified, since his one-on-one combat often decided the fate of his family and entire community. Since everyone's future was at stake, everyone was involved: Elders and spiritual servants prepared the warrior for battle and were often present during it. Sometimes parents, spouses, and children viewed it from nearby. Upon the warrior's safe return, the entire community celebrated, elevating him to the status of hero and revering his exploits in songs and poems.

In contrast, and as the Plains story forecasts, modern warfare is characterized by enormous numbers of soldiers firing high-tech weapons en masse. No personal dimension exists. Enemies are unknown to one another; individual enemy soldiers merely represent an abstract group of politically defined antagonists. Uniforms make them indistinguishable from their fellows. They rarely display symbols of personal or spiritual prowess; officers may even discard their rank insignias to be less desirable targets. The outcome is determined not by individual combat between champions but by which side inflicts the most damage upon the other. The community of the threatened group, instead of viewing the battlefield from a safe distance, may be very involved and directly in harm's way. The community of the *invading* group, on the other hand, remains distant. Its commanding elders tend to stay in the rear lines, where they direct operations in relative safety, and its citizens themselves are often continents away. These distant citizens experience threat primarily as the danger to someone they know in the service. Surrealistically, they can engage in life as usual, even while loved ones struggle to the death on the other side of the planet and their country is defined as in a state of war. If and when soldiers do return, after perhaps some initial fanfare they are expected to reintegrate into mainstream consumer culture with little or no help. In the worst-case scenario, far from being celebrated, they are shunned or marginalized, as many Vietnam War veterans were.

And in the progression from ancient to contemporary warfare, the human psyche itself has often been blasted, even as the Plains warrior was by the soldiers' rifles. While traditional warfare in its limited nature facilitated transformation on spiritual as well as social levels, in this day of broad-scale destruction, war's potential as a rite of passage has begun to break down. The psyche becomes overwhelmed, as we saw with Jack. His story is exemplary in that, even though he became a successful marine, as a veteran he was not able to make a successful transition to a new life stage. Instead, he became one of the countless psychospiritual and medical casualties of modern war.

Nevertheless, war's archetypal elements continue to try to play themselves out. We see that certain aspects of the human psyche and society require them in order to mature, whether we consider ancient or modern forms of warfare. Societies need people to serve in preserving them—people who can tolerate risk, threat, or danger without backing down or running in fear. Children, vulnerable mothers, and oldsters all need strong and wise people who are able to keep them safe. And civilization needs the sensitivity and valuing of life that one who knows its fragility can develop. Psychologically, spiritually, and culturally, we need mature warriors.

Moreover, the archetypal aspects of war as expressed in myth are not optional. They will work in, on, and through us whether or not we are aware of them. We can no more ignore them than we can the principles of physics. We must somehow support the manifestation of the warrior archetype and live the myths. But in the interest of the well-being of our soldiers and our society, we can have some control and choices. We have choices in *how* we engage these archetypes, how consciously we repeat them, how we direct their energies, and what types of outcome we seek. These decisions, as we shall see, have bearing on how we heal our veterans and how we shape our human future.

The correlation between the advancement of war technology, the decrease in war's efficacy as an initiatory rite, and the resulting increase in psychic disturbance is clear when we look at the development of war historically.

That warfare was originally often conducted more for proving manhood than for actual slaughter we can surmise by looking at traditional tribes that have survived into the modern age. For some peoples of New Guinea, for instance, war into the modern era was still a great ritual panoply to be called off with the first casualty.[1] Other than for its initiatory value, traditional warfare was also waged for land and sustenance; early tribes often just wanted food and water. The oldest form of warfare we know about is represented by the Plains people's attempt to halt the incursion into their hunting and camping grounds. When climates shifted and fertile land or waters dried up, tribal groups warred on their neighbors for better territory. Weaker tribes sometimes offered little resistance, but might have migrated to find new lands or do battle with still weaker peoples.

Of course, not all indigenous practices regarding war were the same. Some peoples were significantly more war-directed than others. Anthropologists have uncovered a few cultures that seemed to have no war or warriors, such as on the island of ancient Crete or deep in difficult jungle terrain even today. Being largely isolated from potential enemies, these cultures have not had to worry about protecting their lands and food supplies. But in general, evidence shows that most early peoples seem to have used limited and ritualized warfare as a rite of passage for their young men, a form of social definition and cohesion, and a means of providing self-protection and meeting basic needs.

When humans learned to make bronze, their first metallic alloy, around 3000 BCE, they applied the discovery to the development of new weaponry. Bronze swords, battle-axes, shields, and knives replaced earlier stone weapons. Since the advent of that first manmade material, scientific and technological progress has remained linked with warfare and weaponry. Through the Bronze Age, as the early urban civilizations of Asia, the Middle East, North Africa, and Europe developed and populations increased, technology, weaponry, the sizes of armies, and the extent of casualties all grew together. And while the aim was not to exterminate an enemy's civilian population, the goal could be to wipe out all their men and their royal line and raze their cities so that they could not become a threat again.

Homer's ninth-century-BCE account of the Trojan War, which itself occurred around 1240 BCE, testifies to tens of thousands of men locked in mutual slaughter, culminating in the destruction of the city of Troy. The Bible is likewise full of accounts of the complete destruction of city-states. This form of warfare continued through the classical era. The Romans and the Crusaders of the Middle Ages used aggression as a political tool. War involved great numbers of troops, and weapons and strategies were so advanced as to cause extensive damage. And as the destructive capabilities of warfare evolved, its ritualistic dimensions shrank.

The true era of modern warfare began with the American Civil War. While we did not yet have weapons of mass destruction, the Civil War was characterized by highly destructive weaponry, masses of soldiers available for slaughter, and significant destruction of civilian property. In part, it was a war between the new world and the old. The rural population of the South, with limited manpower and resources, modeled its culture on agrarian and chivalric values and ideals. Its officers were often gentlemen, ruling plantations like fiefdoms, owning slaves and controlling local politics. These gentlemen warriors were pitted against hoards of fighters from the urban culture of the North, stocked with newly arrived and unemployed immigrants available for service. The northern soldiers were well-equipped and heavily armed with the most advanced weapons of the times. They were willing to destroy everything in their paths and to cause and suffer massive casualties to gain victory. And gain victory they did. Although the chivalric myth of the noble warrior did not die with the Civil War, it was greatly brutalized.

The Civil War, along with the European conflicts of that era, represented breakthroughs in the kind and extent of technological weaponry and the amount of slaughter society would tolerate. Since then, the technology for deadliness has increased with every war and during peacetime as well. The advent of aerial bombardments had first occurred in 1849, when Austria sent time-bomb laden balloons over Venice. That technology took a quantum leap after the historic occasion when the Wright brothers flew their first successful airplane in 1903. Despite Orville Wright's objection, the invention was drafted for service as a deadly weapon shortly thereafter. By 1907, the U.S. Army had organized an aeronautical division, and by 1909, it had a plane called the Wright Flyer. That same year the British, French, and Germans bought their first military aircraft. Bulgarian pilots were the first to use airplanes as bombers, dropping explosives on Turkish troops during the Balkan Wars in 1913.

In World War I air combat, the antique pattern of ancient ritual combat persisted; pilots jousted in the skies one on one, like gentlemen and lords in their flying steeds. Yet they also strafed and bombed the cities on the earth below, moving us toward the mass destructiveness of today. Machine guns had become a decisive factor. Developed in primitive forms in the 1500s, they were first made brutally effective in the Civil War, but only became fully automated in 1889. By World War I, numerous types were available, with such deadly results that they accounted for 90 percent of military casualties. Field officers flung muddied and exhausted foot soldiers by the tens of thousands against machine gun emplacements, in yet another clash between the noble charge of the heroic warrior and the murderous realities of modern military technology. Mythic meaning and an entire generation were slaughtered in the encounter.

The tank was first used by the British in 1916. Rather than hastening the end of the war, it prompted the Germans to develop tanks of their own, as well as land mines to stop the British. Other forms of advanced weaponry first employed on a large scale in World War I—including blimps, bombs, poison gas, mortars, heavy artillery, and submarines—have similar histories. And here is the consequence: In four years of war there were 9 million military deaths, while civilian deaths due to military action, massacre, starvation, or disease totaled at 12.4 million. An additional 22 million people were wounded, and 10 million became refugees. The U.S. cost for fighting in World War I was $35.5 billion. If the Civil War had been a giant leap into modern warfare, World War I proved an even greater one. It constituted a massive exercise in technology-driven slaughter wholesale to the point of meaninglessness. One World War I veteran said, "The older I get, the sadder I feel about the uselessness of it all."[2] And from the trenches, Wilfred Owen lamented the slaying of "half the seed of Europe, one by one."[3]

World War I was named "the war to end all wars" because of the technology employed on such a massive scale for the first time. Surely, we believed, such destructive weapons resulting in so much death would finally end the human scourge that has accompanied civilization since the beginning of recorded time. But, of course, rather than end all wars, World War I helped usher in the endless arms races that proceeded through the Spanish Civil War and World War II into the Cold War, the nuclear arms race, and then Korea, Viet Nam, and countless other arenas. Each conflict has been characterized by increased development of military technology—ships, planes, tanks, artillery, bombs, guns, and rockets of all kinds—causing ever-greater human and ecological damage. At the present time, our weaponry is so advanced that it impacts a society's infrastructure and natural environment to an unimaginable degree. Modern techno-war constitutes a major source of disease and pollution; its physical as well as psychological damage manifests for generations after the hostilities have ceased.

Its economic consequences are equally disastrous. According to the Center for Defense Information, in order to participate in the Cold War and its nuclear arms race, the United States alone spent a total of $13.1 trillion in military expenditures from 1948 through the collapse of the Soviet Union in 1991.

Perhaps the most thoroughly documented example of techno-combat is the Vietnam War. We all know about the 58,000 names of the American dead on the Wall in Washington, D.C. But what were the full costs to Americans and to the Vietnamese and their land? Over the past quarter of a century, a thorough portrait has emerged. In the stories my first combat-veteran patients related to me decades ago, they confessed they had killed not just enemy soldiers but children and mothers, pets and livestock, and had destroyed homes, gardens, schools, and food supplies. The following numbers testify to the costs of the war to both sides:

CASUALTIES OF THE VIETNAM WAR [4]

The People	American Troops	Vietnamese People
In country	2.5 million	est. 1970 pop. 41 million
In combat	1.5 million	unknown
Killed in action	58,178	2.5 million
Wounded	300,000+	4 million
	(includes U.S.: 74,000 quadriplegics/multiple amputees)	
Missing in action	2,000+	250,000
PTSD	1.5 million+	unknown
Suicides	100,000+	unknown
Homeless	150,000 nightly	unknown
Boatpeople	0	1 million (V.N., Laos, Cambodia)
Lost at sea	0	500,000
Disabled street people	unknown	3 million
New Agent Orange birth deformities	unknown	35,000/ year
Peacetime deaths due to unexploded bombs/mines (1975–1998)	0	50,000+ (V.N., Laos, Cambodia)
Maimed by bombs/mines	0	67,000
Reeducation camps	0	400,000 in 100 camps

The Vietnamese Land

Total herbicides used	19.4 million gallons
Agent Orange sprayed	11.7 million gallons
Mangrove forests destroyed	60% of country
Forest & jungle destroyed	4.5 million acres, 20% of country
Cultivated land destroyed	585,000 acres, 8% of country
U.S. Bombing	8 billion + pounds; (4 times more than WWII total, equal to 600 Hiroshima-size bombs)
	23 million bomb craters
	2,257 U.S. aircraft lost

Destroyed Vietnamese Infrastructure

Villages	Over 4,000 bombed, 150 completely destroyed (of 5,778 total villages)
Dykes	10 million cubic meters
Hydroelectric works	815
Lake embankments	1,100
Forestries	8
Agricultural research centers	48, with 6,000 agricultural machines and 46,000 water buffalo
Factories	400
Power stations	18
Boats	13,000
Bridges	15,100
High schools & universities	2,923
Hospitals	350
Maternities	1,500
Churches	484
Pagodas	465
Thatched huts	240,540

Total cost to the U.S.: $925 billion

We might think the Vietnam War was an anomaly, so long and fiercely contended that its statistics were uncharacteristically high. Today, we are told we live in an era of "smart weapons"—that our precision-guided munitions and other new precise technologies ensure "minimal collateral damage." But, in fact, the only possible reduction in casualties is to our side, the side with the astronomically expensive weaponry, the side whose cities, agriculture, and civilian populations are not at risk. In our era, mass slaughter of the other and destruction of the enemy's ecology continues to increase. The realities are just not reported by the U.S. media or government, whose account of casualties, though disturbing, routinely appears modest.

For example, the Gulf War (1990–1991) was lauded as an operation causing little loss to U.S. forces. During hostilities, the United States suffered 148 combat deaths, 235 other deaths, and 467 wounded. However, this low casualty rate comprised only what was immediately suffered during the short period of active combat. As of May 2002, more than a decade later, the Veterans Administration had recognized a total of 262,586 veterans disabled due to Gulf War duties and 10,617 dead of combat-related injuries and illnesses since. That raises the casualty rate of American forces in the Gulf War to the rather substantial figure of 30.8 percent.[5]

In that war, the United States estimates that 100,000 Iraqi military were killed and 300,000 wounded. Human rights groups claim much higher figures. Civilian death estimates range up to 200,000 killed. Smart bombs accounted for only 7.4 percent of all bombs dropped. Others included the deadly cluster bombs, which break up into smaller bomblets, and daisy cutters, 15,000-pound bombs that demolish everything within hundreds of yards. Eyewitness reports from oil well employees claim that 700 oil well fires burned for nine months after the Gulf War, severely polluting people and landscape before they were finally extinguished.

During the 1999 U.S. bombing of the Balkans, I happened to be traveling in neighboring European countries. Accounts of that military action—air strikes with the deployment of "smart bombs" and no ground war—vary greatly in their estimates of civilians killed. The Yugoslav government claims 1,200 to 5,000 nonmilitary deaths and the Human Rights Watch verifies 500, while the Pentagon claims only 20 to 30 such incidents.[6] The European media, however, delivered directly from the war zone and uncensored, revealed a different story that did not appear "smart." While at home we bragged about "minimizing collateral damage," I saw footage of the bombing of apartment complexes, bus and train terminals, civilian vehicles, schools, hospitals, embassies, bridges, roadways, and water supplies.

In the 2001 war in Afghanistan, the United States used cluster bombs so extensively that it became an international controversy. In the first week of that war alone, B-1 bombers dropped 50 cluster bombs, scattering 10,100 bomblets.[7] According to the United Nations—as the cumulative result of the U.S. military presence in 2001, the Soviet Russian wars in the mid-1980s, and recent ecological crises such as a severe regional drought—Afghanistan has suffered a 40-70 percent loss of its forest cover, almost complete loss of all wetlands, and the compromise of its entire urban water supply, resulting in open sewage seeping into drinking water.[8] The mortality rate for children under age five is one in four, double the U.S. rate and due largely to diarrhea, respiratory infections, malnutrition, and vaccine-preventable diseases. Afghanistan has 2 million war widows and tens of thousands of deaf-mute and disabled children and adults peddling on the streets. A total of 6 million people—one-third of the population—had to flee the country during the wars.[9] Meanwhile, in 2001 in Afghanistan, the United States suffered only 936 military deaths.

Worldwide, 3.6 million people have been killed in wars since 1990, many in the fifty-five civil wars during that period. Nearly half of the dead have been children, "reflecting the fact that civilians have increasingly become the victims in contemporary conflicts." Carol Bellamy, executive director of the United Nations Children's Fund, witnesses "the many ways conflict affected the lives of children—in Ugandan villages where they are abducted by rebels; in Congo, where they are systematically raped as a weapon of war; and in Iraq, where school enrollment has increased but so has malnutrition."[10]

In a personal communication, Vietnam War air force veteran Jim Helt writes:

> For me "collateral damage" is one of the most insidious phrases in the English language. At first brush it seems rather innocuous, but it means dead and wounded noncombatant women, children, men, elderly. It sanitizes death. I imagined the terror a typical family living in an apartment in Baghdad would experience. They awake at night to the sound of bombs falling on their city. They see fireworks in the sky, but not friendly fireworks! This goes on night after night. This so-called attack for liberation angers them. It will foster anti-American feelings and it will breed a new generation of terrorists.

The technology of destruction has progressed so far that, even if a combatant or civilian survives physically unscathed, he or she is bound to be gravely impacted by the terror it evokes. Richard Gabriel, a former intelligence officer in the

Pentagon's Directorate of Foreign Intelligence and an expert on combat psychiatry, states, "War has simply become too stressful for even the strongest among us to stand for very long."[11] Every participant in modern war inevitably experiences some degree of psychological, moral, or spiritual breakdown. William Manchester, a marine veteran of the Pacific theatre in World War II, comments regarding combatants in particular, "No man in battle is really sane. The mind-set of the soldier on the battlefield is a highly disturbed mind, and this is an epidemic insanity which afflicts everybody there, and those not afflicted by it die very quickly."[12] Gabriel says bluntly:

> The simple fact is that men are crushed by the strain of modern war. . . . All men are at risk of becoming psychiatric casualties and, in fact, most men will collapse given enough exposure to battle stress. There is no such thing as getting used to combat. . . . Studies of World War II soldiers revealed that about 2 percent [did] not collapse. But these men were already mad, for most of them were aggressive psychopathic personalities before they entered battle. It is only the sane who break down.[13]

The archetypal dimensions of war—legends of heroic deeds, divine mentoring of the warrior inspired by elders, and battle conditions where these patterns could be lived out sufficiently to shape the soul—have been handed down through the generations to our present day. Yet modern conditions make the realization of these ancient and proven archetypes anachronistic, if not impossible. In modern war, combatants cannot become larger-than-life heroes. Rather, they are miniscule globules of armed protoplasm hurled at enemies in uncountable numbers. Massive death numbers, a scorched-earth policy, and the technological weaponry to accomplish both are the hallmarks of modern war.

In the moral and spiritual vacuum caused by this much destruction, the only meaning that remains is mere survival. And survival, now reduced to an accident in the midst of global carnage, is laden with a sense of unworthiness and guilt. As Manchester said about the battle for Okinawa during World War II, "The fact remains that more than seventy-seven thousand civilians died here during the battle, and no one comes out of a fight like that with clean hands."[14] Under such conditions, the ancient mythic heroism, spirituality, and initiatory values of warfare are canceled out.

Yet the mythic dimensions of war remain very much with us as universal patterns in the human psyche that we attempt to replicate in every epoch of history. Young men, and now women, too, still march off as individual combatants striving to live out the model of the mythic warrior-hero. Whether enlisted as recruits for official or paramilitary, military or insurgent, guerilla or terrorist forces, they are taught, and still believe, that their wills, values, and small arms can stand as Excaliburs against evil. But into what kind of arena do they carry their patriotism and their impulse for heroism and initiation? We are trapped in a terrible tension between the soul's craving for realization of the warrior archetype and the realities of a warfare that devastates the soul who seeks it.

Five

THE SOUL IN SLAUGHTER

"A single death is a tragedy," said Joseph Stalin. "A million deaths is a statistic." To Stalin, bent upon the world triumph of Communism, depersonalization and terror were not problems; they were tools for achieving his goals. Individuality was a danger to be eradicated. He knew that, under the bombardment of state-sponsored terror, individuals become numb and eventually allow the state to control their lives. Responsible for the murder of millions, both his own people and others, he once said, "Death solves all problems—no man, no problem."

More than half a century later, we are in danger of a similar kind of numbing. The overwhelming death statistics delivered through the media—where millions, for instance, watched the endlessly repeated broadcasts of hijacked planes slamming into the World Trade Center—sets our defenses in motion. We feel helpless faced with deaths of such magnitude; we become apathetic. We turn the radio or television channel to something funny, mindless, relaxing. We put down the newspaper that causes us discomfort. Rationalizing that violence is necessary for our security, we turn away, hoping it does not touch our loved ones or us, distancing ourselves from others' losses. We adopt an absolutist worldview that declares our side good and the other side evil so that we can view our victims as deserving of punishment and thereby ease our guilt.

George Orwell strove to warn of the dangers of state and corporate power not just in Communist countries but around the world. In *1984,* his novel about the anti-utopian future we seem to be living now, his protagonist, Winston Smith, was conditioned to tolerate the bombardment of statistics, propaganda, "disinformation," and "eternal war" around the globe issued by the state to assert control. When Smith finally began to emerge from his stupor, "He fell asleep murmuring 'Sanity is not statistical,' with the feeling that this remark contained in it a profound wisdom."[1]

And so it does. We do violence to ourselves in emptying death of personal meaning, in relying on statistics as a substitute for truth. This kind of depersonalization is what led to Stalin's abuses and the body counts of the Vietnam War. It supports the current belief that we can win any war if we just kill enough insurgents—if we can succeed at "making war against another country's birth rates," as political analyst Prof. Steven Leibo puts it. We begin to recover our sanity when we brush aside the statistics and apply ourselves to restoring quality of life to the real people we have dehumanized.

Stalin's observation is pregnant, not just because it acknowledges how violence reduces real people to statistics, but also because it heralds the loss of tragedy. The response to tragedy is not just sorrow but deep grief; it is a profound condition of the soul. Tragedy depicts what is most noble in us as we struggle against our own dark fate. It demonstrates, as

Shakespeare says in *Julius Caesar*, that "the fault . . . is not in the stars but in ourselves." Embracing tragedy—crying over our grievous but inevitable losses—keeps our hearts alive.

When Goethe's protagonist, Dr. Faust, protests as his beloved is dragged to hell, Mephistopheles, the devil, simply says, "She is not the first." Faust cries out: "O woe, woe which no human soul can grasp. . . . The misery of this single one pierces to the very marrow of my life; and thou art calmly grinning at the fate of thousands!"[2] Indifference to individual suffering projects us into Mephistopheles' realm, the realm of the diabolical. Recall Madeleine Albright's rejoinder, while serving as secretary of state, to the United Nations report that one-half million Iraqi children died as a result of the U.S.-led embargo against that country: "Well, this is a price that we feel we are willing to pay."[3] Consider also Specialist Charles Graner's defense in response to his conviction for torturing Iraqi prisoners at Abu Ghraib: He was only following orders, doing his job as a good soldier, and had no regrets. When we hear government leaders and military officers, as well as priests of various convictions, terrorists, and the common person on the street all justifying the mass killing of innocent civilians—including children—for political ends, we know it is time to restore the moral vision of Faust: One person's suffering should truly be enough to make us doubt and stop.

In simple terms, the process of making war comprises two parts: First we dehumanize the people involved, both our antagonists and our own population; then we place "them" and ourselves in a kill-or-be-killed situation.

In order to create soldiers willing to kill and a citizenry willing to tolerate it, we must first depersonalize and demonize the other. To depersonalize portrays others as anonymous and less than human. To demonize is to take the process a step further by making the other a carrier of evil, an incarnation of the devil. Terms conveying such demonization are familiar: During World War II, the Germans were called krauts and the Japanese, nips. The Vietnamese were called gooks and dinks. Now, in Iraq, American troops call Iraqi people towelheads, ragheads, and hadjis.

The process of depersonalization begins long before combat, and political leaders of all persuasions have used the same techniques. Nazi leader Hermann Goering explained that the imagination of a people must be reshaped in order to prepare a reluctant citizenry for war: "Naturally, the common people don't want war. . . . It is the leaders of the country who determine policy, and it is always a simple matter to drag the people along, whether it is a democracy, or a fascist dictatorship, or a parliament, or a communist dictatorship." His prison psychologist, G. M. Gilbert, answered that a democracy is different; people have a say through their vote, and in the United States only Congress can declare war. Goering responded, "Voice or no voice, the people can always be brought to the bidding of the leaders. That is easy. All you have to do is to tell them they are being attacked, and denounce the pacifists for lack of patriotism and exposing the country to danger. It works the same in any country." [4]

Jean-Paul Sartre rightly stated that war begins as soon as we *conceive* of another as hostile to us. The United States went to war in Iraq, not when George Bush ordered our troops to invade, but as soon as he invoked his "axis of evil." Whether or not Saddam Hussein actually did evil is secondary here (clearly, he did). Rather, the point is that what we believe about another people enables us, even forces us, to go to war. War is first and foremost an act of the imagination, a psychic, cultural, and spiritual action that breaks apart the human community and renders part of it as the "other"—that is, as different from us. Every side does this. It is a necessary step preceding violence. Among Native American peoples, some tribal names translate into "human beings" or the equivalent. Members of competing tribes were something else. For example, *Cheyenne* comes from the Lakota term for that tribe meaning "red talkers," or "those who spoke an alien language."[5] It is reminiscent of the origin of the word for "barbarian" in ancient Greek—*barbaros*—signifying the incomprehensible dialect of the Persians that the Greeks judged uncivilized and inferior. The Cheyenne name for their own people simply meant those who are alike or of a similar breed, "Us."[6] Anyone else was "them." Another tribal name, *Absaroka*, may signify "chosen people,"[7] suggestive of the phrase the early Jewish people used to signify a special destiny but also separateness.

In our modern era, the Nazis not only believed but attempted to document scientifically that the Jews were less than human, just as European settlers in South Africa had made similar attempts toward the natives there. From the recent Balkan Wars, journalist Slavenka Drakulic observed that "someone is always a Jew. Once the concept of 'otherness' takes root, the unimaginable becomes possible."[8] She continues, "Once excluded, [people] become aliens. Not-me. Not-us. You still feel responsible but in a different way, as towards beggars. . . . The feeling of human solidarity turns into an issue of my personal ethics. . . . You are no longer obliged to do something for their sake."[9] This is true of anyone we place in special categories—refugees, veterans, victims, and survivors, as well as enemies—even though they may be our neighbors. In the British movie *Pretty Dirty Things*, one migrant shouts at another, "I'm a certified refugee. You're an illegal. You have nothing. You are nothing."

In nineteenth-century America, similar thinking under-girded the attempted genocide of our indigenous peoples in order to seize their lands. General Sherman once sent a tele-gram to President Grant stating, "We must act with vindictive earnestness against the Sioux, even to their extermination, men, women, and children. Nothing less will reach the root of the case."[10]

Except under extraordinary conditions, creating such otherness is necessary in order to kill. At his trial for the My Lai massacre, Lt. William Calley declared, "I was ordered to go in there and destroy the enemy. That was my job on that day. That was the mission I was given. I did not sit down and think in terms of men, women, and children. They were all classified the same, and that was the classification that we dealt with, just as enemy soldiers."[11]

Calley did not see people. Once we have labeled a group as "other," it is a short step to render them "enemy." This, too, is an act of the imagination. The word *enemy* derives from the same source as *inimical*. Both come from the Latin *inimicus*, literally, *in amicus,* or "not friend." The word carries the connotation of the oft-repeated threat, used by anyone from feuding children to world leaders, "You're either for us or against us."

This black-or-white thinking of "for or against" is imma-ture. It does not allow for the real-life fact that someone can fail to be a friend and yet not be an enemy. Child development studies show that the skill of learning to think in grays—see-ing the world as complex and full of ambiguity rather than in terms of either/or—typically emerges between the ages of four and five.[12] Reverting to a toddler's black-and-white think-ing is a defensive response to an otherness that may be a threat. We can see this reversion clearly in the records from Calley's trial:

Q: What were you firing at?

A: At the enemy, sir.

Q: At people?

A: At the enemy, sir.

Q: They weren't even human beings?

A: Yes, sir.

Q: Were they men?

A: I don't know sir. I would imagine they were, sir.

Q: Didn't you see?

A: Pardon, sir?

Q: Did you see them?

A: I wasn't discriminating.

Q: Did you see women?

A: I don't know, sir.

Q: What do you mean you weren't discriminating?

A: I didn't discriminate between individuals in the village, sir. They were all the enemy, they were all to be destroyed, sir.[13]

The dehumanization of the other necessitates the dehumanization of our own people as well. The state and the press, says Chris Hedges, are "the chief institutions that disseminate the myth."[14] Barraged by the media, over time the citizenry hardens into accepting killing as necessary for its own protection, as a fitting treatment of the other and as the proper moral choice.[15] Regarding the fomenting of the Balkan

Wars, Hedges explains: "It took Milosevic four years of hate propaganda and lies, pumped forth daily over the airways from Belgrade, before he got one Serb to cross the border into Bosnia and begin the murderous rampage that triggered the war." [16]

The similar work of removing our soldiers' civilizing inhibitions begins at boot camp. Stripping recruits of most vestiges of civilian identity, having them practice techniques of killing until they can repeat them unconsciously, working them to exhaustion, intimidating them with demeaning nicknames and tasks, and punishing those who resist indoctrination are just a few of the common strategies. One veteran reported that his first psychological trauma occurred not in combat but during basic training, when his drill sergeant forced his squad to crush kittens to death in their hands. He cried, declaring that it was wrong and he couldn't do it. He was shamed until, near breaking, he killed his kitten. He reports that he cried over the kitten's death but later was able to kill people without remorse.

The impact of basic training cannot be overstated. There is a direct relationship between the dehumanization of our troops and what happens in the combat zone. As Tim O'Brien explained, "To understand what happens to the GI among the mine fields of My Lai, you must understand something about what happens in America. You must understand Fort Lewis, Washington. You must understand a thing called basic training." During bayonet training, O'Brien's drill sergeant bellowed in his ear, "Dinks are little s---s. If you want their guts, you gotta go low. Crouch and dig." [17]

Erich Maria Remarque described his training in boot camp for World War I: "I have remade his [the drill instructor's] bed fourteen times in one morning . . . kneaded a pair of prehistoric boots that were as hard as iron for twenty hours . . .

scrubbed out the Corporal's Mess with a toothbrush . . . clear[ed] the barrack-square of snow with a hand broom and dustpan . . . stood at attention in a hard frost without gloves . . . run eight times from the top floor of the barracks down to the courtyard."[18]

Lest it be thought these practices are anachronistic, I will add that I recently observed combat training of young National Guardsmen preparing to go to Iraq. Their drill instructors pushed the "girlies" to the side, grabbed training rifles from shaking hands, and turned them on the trainees to show how quickly they could be killed. They screamed, "You wanna be dead? Then you gotta kill first!" And, "Troops, you're not thrusting. You're thinking of them as people! They're not! They're towelheads!" Arthur, one of my students, is a gentle young man mobilized for Iraq. As I wished him luck and safety, he answered, "I'll be all right as long as I don't think of them as human beings. If I stop and think about what I'm doing, then I'll be in trouble."

After dehumanization, the second essential component for making war is constructed around one very simple rule: kill the other before he kills you. Combat propels people by the millions into this predicament. Almost universally, when people experience their own lives as threatened, they will strike back. Under such conditions, as poet Nguyen Duy, veteran of the North Vietnamese signal corps, declares, "It is easy to kill."[19] On the front lines, war is not about politics, it is about staying alive. And it is a situation from which there is almost no way out.

Jack—the Vietnam War marine squad leader we met earlier—had over two hundred confirmed kills. He explained, "You don't kill 'cause you want to hurt somebody. Only sick people do that. It isn't a killing rage really. It's just a rage to save your own life. You're trying to stop the other guy from killing you at the same moment he's trying to stop you from killing him. In the bush you don't kill from rage. You kill from fear."

Participants in wars the world over corroborate Jack's words. An Austrian mountaineer fighting with the Germans in the Battle of Crete remarked: "Here it is a matter of life and death. You do not have time to think clearly, because you are just trying to avoid getting killed." [20] From the Balkan Wars, Drakulic explained, "They attacked us, we responded. Here, war is a simple matter. There are no politics any more. No dilemmas. Nothing but the naked struggle for life." [21]

In the Cambodian genocide youthful relatives were forced to become the torturers and executioners of their family members, friends, and neighbors. They cooperated because "they didn't have any choice, and that is why they didn't think about morality when it came to obeying orders." The desire to survive superseded all else. [22] Jasmin, a refugee I treated who was an inmate in the Serbian concentration camps, described the way he and other Bosnian Muslim inmates were tortured. The men and boys of his village were arranged into pairs; friends, fathers and sons, cousins were placed face to face. One of each pair was given a pistol while Serbian guards held guns to their heads. The men with pistols were ordered to shoot their partners. If they did not do it by the count of ten, they would be shot themselves. Tearfully and in a choking voice, Jasmin told me that his own partner, his uncle, had looked him in the eyes and ordered, "Do it! You have to! I forgive you!" Those were his last words.

But there is another motive to kill that can be even more compelling than the will to survive. Countless veterans and survivors have declared it is loyalty to friends, families, and foxhole mates that can most impel people, whether the aim is to protect one's comrades or to avenge them. William Manchester observed, "Men do not fight for flag or country, for the Marine Corps or glory or any other abstraction. They fight for one another."

As much as war depends on the creation of otherness, it also fosters an intimacy based upon sameness: We are of the same unit, nationality, and cause, and we share the same threat to our lives. This intimacy under the constant threat of death engenders for some the deepest love they ever experience. As infantry veteran Bob Cagle says, "The greatest honor I can give you, the greatest love I can express, is my willingness to die for you." This love lasts a lifetime and beyond death. Robert Reiter, a combat marine and veteran's service counselor, has maintained this kind of love for his best friend, who was killed beside him during a jungle mission. For Reiter and many vets, such love translates into a lifetime of advocacy work—"my calling to serve my brothers," as Reiter puts it.

Mythology and history are full of stories in which the loss of cherished friends impels one to kill. In the *Iliad*, Achilles had quit the field of combat after having lost faith in the cause—as soldiers have done from mythical Troy through modern Iraq. But when his beloved companion-in-arms, Patroklos, was killed, Achilles returned to the battlefield. To a cornered Trojan prince pleading for his life, Achilles answered, "In days past . . . I had a mind to spare the Trojans. . . . But now there's not a chance—no man that heaven puts in my hands will get away from death. . . . You'll die in blood until I have avenged Patroklos."[23]

Mari Sandoz describes Crazy Horse's similar response to finding his friend Lone Bear dying on a battlefield: "As Crazy Horse lifted him, Lone Bear opened his eyes . . . and died in the arms of his friend, with Hump standing beside them, crying. But Crazy Horse did not cry for this man killed by the whites. . . . His heart was cold and black with an anger that could not be made good until many more of the white men died."[24]

My patient Steve, a Sea-bee in Viet Nam, admitted decades after the war that he volunteered for combat "because those bastards killed my cousin. I only went for revenge. I don't give a damn that we lost. I was a failure because I didn't kill anybody for my cousin."

Such hatred may lead to a killing wrath that loses all sense of boundaries and may result in atrocities. As Jonathan Shay demonstrates, Achilles was not just angry; he went berserk. And when the berserk state is reached, there may be no return.[25] Thus, decades after the war Lenny, a Vietnam War air force veteran, avoided Chinese restaurants and fled public spaces whenever he saw a person of Asian descent because, he said, "I can't tell them apart and if I got near I'd lose it and kill them."

On a veritable pinhead of time, in war our soul must make the choice, "kill or be killed." What are the ramifications? If our primitive urge to exact revenge overcomes our civilized feelings of restraint, we descend into the savage. If compassion overmasters our savage instincts, we are likely to be maimed or lose our life. Either way, there is no return to innocence. And if we are among the survivors, we protect ourselves by making the killing impersonal. The slain are enemies, expletives, body counts. We do our best to numb ourselves to the reality that they are human beings, whether or not we have been the agent of their deaths. Beth Marie Murphy, a war nurse on a hospital ship off Da Nang who has returned to Viet Nam with me several times, lamented, "There were so many deaths—our side, their side, especially their children. The helicopters just kept coming. While I was on the USS *Sanctuary*, my ship set a record—more than a thousand medivac landings in one month. Can you imagine how many wounded and dead there were? After a while, you can't remember faces or names, just blood and severed limbs. You just have to stop feeling."

These mass killings make modern war especially debilitating to the soul. The effect of a single act that would have felled a single antagonist in antiquity may destroy hundreds or even thousands of people today. Bill, who called himself "a mass murderer," described the first time he opened his aircraft's bay doors to drop bombs on European cities. He felt terrible resistance, nausea, sickness, headaches, despair. He couldn't do it, but his crew chief screamed at him, "Now! Now!" If he didn't, the mission would be a failure and it would be his fault. He finally pushed the button. Then he vomited. His physical action had been no greater than that of a Plains warrior shooting an arrow or an infantryman pulling a trigger. But this time buildings burned and hundreds died.

Techno-war also exponentially increases our sense of culpability. My patient Larry was an artillery captain in the Vietnam War who afterward served on American Eastern European nuclear weapons bases bordering the Soviet Union. He testified that his European service left him far guiltier and more traumatized than anything he experienced in battle. "In combat I faced off with other professional soldiers who were trying to kill me. But in Europe where everything was peaceful, I assisted in a conspiracy to blow up the world." Bill Karpowicz spent his air force service stateside inspecting "a B-52 with dark green bombs inside." His daily job was to crawl across the loaded nuclear bombs and check them and the plane's fuel lines for operational readiness. His inspections were conducted under the watch of an armed officer. He wrote about it afterwards as if it were still going on, "I'll get drunk tonight . . . and will stay that way for years, and will only realize twenty years or so later that I am conspiring with him to threaten the world." [26]

Larry and Bill both became alcoholics to anaesthetize themselves. But what if you don't stop feeling? What if you remember that the "others"—those who died—are people, too?

Either way is problematic. On the one hand, in order to heal and come home, survivors must learn to feel again. But on the other, awakening to the humanity of dead former enemies produces an anguish that in itself may become an impediment to healing. "They weren't human when I killed them," one combat veteran wailed during a therapy session. "But it's like they're returning from their graves. Now I see them as they were—not enemies, not things, just people. They weren't supposed to become human again!"

Edward Dahlstedt was a combat engineer in World War II. After the European victory he was on a troop ship traveling to the invasion of Japan. The atomic bombs were dropped while he was in mid-ocean. Loudspeakers announced the end of the war. While his shipmates celebrated, Dahlstedt first felt relief that his life had been spared and the war was over. His daughter Kate Dahlstedt wrote, "The ship came alive. Dance music in the mess hall. Laughter everywhere. My father wrote excited letters home . . . with love and dreams. He still didn't know what none of them knew: the price they had paid."

Dahlstedt continued on to Japan with the occupation forces and was in one of the first American ground units to roll through the ruins of Hiroshima. His daughter went on: "He didn't feel the shock waves then. They were imperceptible, distorted, clouded by the unreality of the victory. And when with mouth agape he saw the ravaged earth, the rubbled city, the people gone for miles, he still didn't know that he was changed forever. That there was no going home again. That no one would ever be home again."[27]

At eighty-one years of age, Ed Dahlstedt still asks, "I am grateful that I survived, but did I have that right if the price of my life was the deaths of so many others?"

In Viet Nam, soldiers evolved the phrase, "It don't mean nothin'," to tolerate the wholesale destruction surrounding them. To the soul caught up in the rules of slaughter, one dead or ten, a hundred or a thousand or a million "don't mean nothin'." When we arrive at "don't mean nothin'," we are in the realm of Stalin and Mephistopheles, saying, "This one is not the first—or the last; there will be others; their suffering does not matter." This is the danger confronting every one of us today.

This war is my war;

it is in my image and I deserve it. . . .

Thus, I am *this war.*

—JEAN-PAUL SARTRE,
Being and Nothingness

Part II

FROM
MYTH
TO
REALITY

Six

INSIDE PTSD:
IDENTITY AND SOUL WOUND

He tries to read, but the sentences don't hold together. He opens letters left lying on his desk for weeks and then tears them to shreds before completing them. He chain smokes. The light of the sun or a bulb burns his eyes. He doesn't wash. He doesn't fraternize. He doesn't clean his room, but he never leaves it, either. He can't stop trembling. He feels "his mind dislodge itself and teeter, like insecure luggage on an overhead rack." He squeezes his temples and holds on tightly. His friend, whose sister is majoring in psychology, delivers this word from home: "She says nobody gets a nervous breakdown from the war and all."[1]

This is J. D. Salinger's portrait, created out of his own experiences surviving some of World War II's worst battles, of a traumatized combat soldier in Europe shortly after the cessation of hostilities.

Strikingly similar is the description of a concentration camp survivor who came to me for treatment in 1997, shortly after arriving in this country. Ramiz, a Bosnian Muslim, was snatched from his home in Kiseljac and interred in Serbian camps for almost a year:

He chain smokes. He can't sleep, or, when he does, he has nightmares of camp experiences. He can't concentrate enough to read or write. He avoids his wife and family and has no friends. He hides in his apartment, which he cannot clean, during the day. He hides from the light. He spends hundreds of nighttime hours aimlessly walking the streets of the foreign city that hosts him, or sitting in front of the television watching programs he cannot understand, but quickly flicking off any pictures of violence. He is tortured by headaches for which he can find no relief. He rarely changes his clothes, and he keeps his hair cropped to the scalp as it was in the camps. He does not talk about his camp experiences. His wife and relatives say, "Nothing that can happen is terrible enough to make a person like this. He must be crazy."

From the trenches of World War I, Remarque wrote: "We are not youth any longer. We don't want to take the world by storm. . . . We fly from ourselves. From our life. We are eighteen and we had begun to love life and the world; and we had to shoot it to pieces." [2] Historian and social critic Paul Fussell said concerning World War II, "My boyish illusions . . . fell away all at once, and suddenly I knew that I was not and never would be in a world that was reasonable or just." [3] Kris, the mother of a marine serving in Iraq, reported that during leave between tours her son blurted, "Mom, I killed at least two people over there. You can't know what killing has made me. You don't know who I am now."

Veterans know that, having been to hell and back, they are different. We expect them to put war behind them and rejoin the ordinary flow of civilian life. But it is impossible for them to do so—and wrong of us to request it. Whenever Robert Reiter is asked when he left Viet Nam, he answers, "Last night. It will be that way till my soul leaves this old body." When the survivor cannot leave war's expectations, values, and losses behind, it becomes the eternal present. This frozen war consciousness is the condition we call post-traumatic stress disorder.

The affliction has had many names over the centuries, demonstrating that it is a condition accompanying not just modern wars but all wars. Its cluster of symptoms was first diagnosed as "nostalgia" among Swiss soldiers in 1678. German doctors at that time called the condition *Heimweh,* and the French called it *maladie du pays*; both mean homesickness. The Spanish called it *estar roto*, "to be broken." [4] Civil War Americans called it soldier's heart, irritable heart, or nostalgia. In World War I, it was called shell shock; in World War II and Korea, combat fatigue.

"Soldier's heart" indicates that the heart has been changed by war. "Nostalgia" and "homesickness" bespeak the soldier's anguished longing to escape from the combat zone and return home. *Estar roto* describes the psyche's condition after war—broken. Some World War II veterans have objected to the term "combat fatigue." In a novel based upon their wartime experiences, Sidney and Samuel Moss explain of a comrade evacuated for combat exhaustion, "It wasn't combat exhaustion. It was a horror that would inhabit the body forever. He would react to it whenever he heard the sound of a plane or the bang of a bursting bomb." [5] Others, such as Vietnam War veteran Bob Cagle, who has traveled with me back to Viet Nam twice, object to the expression "post-traumatic stress disorder":

> When I first heard the term PTSD, it sounded like one designed to describe what my wife experiences when she sees a spider and then calls me, at the top of her

lungs, to come and kill it. This is not a reasonable diagnosis for something so encompassing that it can and will engulf a person's life, ruin any chance for intimacy, keep horrid scenes in one's mind for thirty-six years (as in my case) or for life in the case of other poor souls. To be angry at the world, jump at the slightest sound or quick movement, and live within one's own mind because you know that no one would understand or try to help is to live in hell.

Another veteran says PTSD is "a name drained of both poetry and blame." He prefers "soldier's heart" because it is "a disorder of warriors, not men and women who were weak or cowardly but . . . who followed orders and who at a young age put their feelings aside and performed unimaginable tasks. . . . PTSD is a disorder of a good warrior."[6]

Society interprets and responds to trauma, including the trauma of war and its consequences, according to the views of the times. Since Freud, theories stressing early childhood development have shaped the thinking of the psychological community. Until recently with the advent of trauma studies, the dominant psychological model has been that our personalities are formed during our early years and do not change much in adulthood. Thus, the assumption has been that traumas experienced in adulthood do not have high impact. While serving in World War I, for instance, the young Remarque believed that older soldiers were more resistant to war trauma than the younger ones: "Our early life is cut off from the moment we came here. [But] all the older men are linked up with their previous life. . . . They have a background which is so strong that the war cannot obliterate it."[7]

However, personal accounts by veterans of all wars show that older soldiers can be just as traumatized as younger ones. In fact, while increased age at the time of trauma can mitigate the severity of its impact, older as well as younger survivors of wartime, from the Holocaust through the Iraq war, have reported devastating consequences to their psyches and their lives. For the psychological community to miss this fact and treat adult trauma instead as rooted in childhood can be excruciatingly frustrating to the client, as well as futile. Two decades ago Jack, a combat reconnaissance sergeant, declared that his therapists at the Veterans Administration "place too much emphasis on what happened in childhood . . . but steer me away from the war, as if its effects were only repeats of my childhood rather than problems in themselves. . . . I say, 'If you had seventy near-fatal car accidents in one year of your life between ages eighteen and nineteen, do you think that would mess you up all by itself? That's what it was like in Viet Nam.'"[8] It has taken survivors many years and much advocacy to gain recognition that violent trauma is severely damaging at any age. War and its personal aftermath are, as survivors have been telling us for millennia, something different from anything we know in civilian life.

Since September 11, and in the climate of the current war, the public and most professionals seem finally to accept PTSD as a genuine condition. We find increased public understanding and sympathy for the troops engaged in Iraq. To a greater extent than in previous conflicts, some mental health services now exist, including counseling for troops in the combat zone as well as debriefing upon return. Still, ample evidence shows that the war in Iraq is producing psychological casualties at an alarming rate, and the stopgap measures available will not halt the deluge of psychiatric casualties.[9] This high casualty rate is an inevitable cost of all modern war. Summarizing the findings from the field of combat psychiatry, Richard Gabriel writes, "In every war since World War I, more

American soldiers have become psychiatric casualties than were killed.... We have reached a point where almost everyone exposed to combat will, within a comparatively short period of time, be killed, wounded, or driven mad." [10]

The American Psychiatric Association first accepted post-traumatic stress disorder as a diagnosis in 1980. It was originally classified as a stress disorder because of the critical factor of a catastrophic stressor out of the individual's control that threatened severe harm or death and would evoke similar responses in anyone. PTSD remains classified as a stress and anxiety disorder even today. This classification leads to certain philosophies and forms of treatment that commonly alienate or fail survivors. We live, for example, in an era of biochemical interpretations and interventions for psychological problems. In this climate, many practitioners emphasize that trauma results in biochemical imbalances and impaired neurological and cerebral functioning.

Bioneurological functioning of the central and autonomic nervous systems does indeed change as a result of traumatic events. But these are only some of the physiological dimensions of what is in fact a holistic disorder. Treatment with medications alone does not and cannot transform PTSD; it can only control or alleviate some symptoms, and symptom control remains dependent upon the medication regimen. Many veterans will not cooperate with medication regimens—often as a form of protest against authority figures whom they experience as "bad officers," unconcerned with or not comprehending their suffering. Sometimes veterans display medication histories as though they were additional wounds or service ribbons. "I'm a walking chemistry experiment for some shrink's research project," one combat vet smirked as he unfurled a medication history many pages long. "Why doesn't he talk about my nightmares and memories and dead friends instead of asking how my meds are doing?"

We treat PTSD sufferers much as we do other patients. We wish to return them to mainstream functioning as civilians, consumers, producers, and wage earners as quickly as possible. We discourage disturbing stories or their pain from emerging. To control the symptoms we offer medications, teach the sufferer relaxation and stress reduction techniques, lecture and coach the survivor on war neurosis and proper behavior in public, and offer rapid-eye movement and other automatic therapies. We favor group therapy to achieve the belonging and support of like individuals, but we separate and isolate the groups from mainstream culture.

Isaac Bonilla, a Vietnam War veteran who recently died in his mid-fifties from the long-term effects of his wounds and exposure to Agent Orange, said that in the eighteen years he attended a hospital-based veterans therapy group, he and the other veterans were not allowed to tell their war stories even once because—they were instructed—it would upset them too much. "My therapists counseled me to avoid stress by not remembering," Isaac said, "but that only locked my memories in the prison inside my head." Combat zone nurse Beth Marie Murphy stated that a four-month-long intensive residential program for PTSD

helped me learn to manage my symptoms more effectively and validated my condition because I was finally given a refuge from the world with others like me. But the program squashed the horrors of war back down inside me because we veterans were only given a single afternoon session to discuss the war. How can you cover a year of horror in the war zone in one afternoon? I felt I was only given a glimpse of the trauma that I had pushed down for over twenty-five years and then given the skills to supposedly move on. But without uncovering the war I had buried I was not ready to move on.

As such accounts show, we do not provide the time or resources necessary for tending such deep and complex conditions as PTSD. We do not see the extreme damage done to survivors' characters. Veterans Affairs psychiatrist Jonathan Shay rightly refers to "the undoing of character" in combat trauma.[11] We do not help survivors rebuild dignity and rediscover inner peace. Certainly, in contrast to traditional cultures, our modern processes do not include sacred and communal dimensions of healing. Also, the recovery of each individual is no longer a priority to the larger social system because the system functions even with the loss of significant numbers of its adult population. Nor do we reserve special roles for our returnees; we want them to function the same as they did before. We do not recognize that they have been through a profound death-rebirth process and are significantly and permanently transformed.

From the 1950s until his death, Erik Erikson worked to expand psychoanalytic theory. Before the diagnosis of PTSD, Erikson described the damage done to patients he treated for "war neurosis" as an identity disturbance. He expanded the Freudian notion of early psychological growth stages into the epigenetic principle that demonstrates human development through the entire life cycle. According to Erikson, one of the most important achievements of development is a sound identity, formulated during adolescence and culminating at the ages at which we typically send young people off to war. He extended the significant sphere of influence on the psyche from one's parents to the entire society. And he demonstrated that our progress through later life stages is dependent on o development in previous stages.

"What impressed me most," Erikson wrote about veteran patients, "was the loss in these men of a sense of identity. They knew who they were; they had a personal identity. But it was as if, subjectively, their lives no longer hung together—and never would again. There was a central disturbance of . . . ego identity . . . the ability to experience oneself as something that has continuity and sameness, and to act accordingly."[12] Erikson's teachings seem to have had the most impact on our understanding of the struggles of adolescence and the concept of identity crisis. But his notion that a veteran must rebuild a coherent identity is important.

More recently, and since the advent of trauma studies, psychiatrist Judith Herman, a pioneer in understanding and offering strategies for recovery from violent trauma, has challenged narrow notions regarding PTSD. She says the current formulation of PTSD as a stress and anxiety disorder fails to accurately characterize the major symptoms caused by repeated and prolonged violence. She proposes an alternative analysis emphasizing these common and critical dimensions: multiple symptoms, somatization, dissociation, and severe or pathological changes in affect, relationships, and identity.[13] Peter Levine, as well, has recently extended our understanding of the scope of trauma by normalizing its symptoms, focusing on the ways the body internalizes trauma and can be healed from that somatization, and stressing the need for community involvement and safety in trauma healing.[14] These approaches argue that, rather than shrink PTSD into the narrow category of stress disorder, we need a complex, multi-leveled understanding of it that includes seeing it as a normative response to extraordinary conditions. They also demonstrate that we need strategies that address all its components: we need to include attention to the way the body carries trauma and to community and society as healing forces.

We can understand all symptoms and changes the survivor experiences as part of identity transformation. The common lament, "Why can't I be who I was before?" is one great source of grief and a plea from the survivor that we understand he is different now; he has not returned as the same person who left. The diagnosis of anxiety disorder wrongly assumes a pathological distortion that we can treat or medicate back into normalcy. This misunderstanding denies the ultimate nature of the transformation, causing survivors and their families to feel frustrated and alienated and demonstrating our culture's denial of war's impact. "Who am I now?" may be the most difficult and important question the survivor must finally answer. This is why, from the psychological perspective, it is so important to recognize PTSD as an identity disorder.

Moreover, such an understanding aligns PTSD with the archaic goal of war as a form of initiation. Modern warfare damages and destroys the youth and his character and threatens him with annihilation at the very time rites of passage are supposed to mature him in psychologically nurturing, socially useful, and spiritually enlightened ways. While the purpose of warfare today is primarily destructive, it still repeats the archetypal blueprint for initiation; it is still a rite of passage that takes participants from an immature to a new self, ushering them through a kind of death and rebirth. It may not provide us with a society of mature warriors, but it does leave us with a huge population of partially transformed survivors.

Veterans talk in both direct and symbolic ways about how an innocent went to war, what beliefs he held, what goals and dreams she had, what politics and values she upheld, what role models she followed, how he imagined his future. My uncle's story exemplifies the lifelong detriment to identity and its impact on an entire family that results from harsh experience. When my mother, Sharon, was fourteen, Stanley Sobel, her only sibling and an aspiring artist, departed for World War II. He left behind sensitive drawings and oil paintings of evening lights dancing on dusky rivers and cityscapes. He served as a medic at the Battle of the Bulge. For two months his unit was missing in action behind enemy lines. Upon notification, my grandmother's hair turned white almost overnight. She walked to her synagogue three times daily to pray for him. Stanley finally returned a broken man, hardly able to speak a coherent sentence. My grandmother died young only a dozen years later. Though my uncle became a professional, his relationships were disturbed throughout his life and he never again picked up his artist materials. The last time I saw him was at my grandfather's funeral. As we stood together before the coffin, he rattled so severely he looked like he might be seeing the war dead instead of a pine box. He disappeared soon after, and the family never heard from him again.

Post-traumatic stress disorder is a constellation of fixated experience, delayed growth, devastated character, interrupted initiation, and unsupported recovery. Many veterans who cannot get on with life are boy-men stuck in the psychic war zone, lost in an incomplete and horrific rite of passage. They remain in a state of shock because of what they have seen and are terrified for their lives. They struggle virtually alone, without a community to support their passage, without a mythic context into which to fit their personal story. Though they may seek guidance and solace from their religions, they generally lack the benefits of divine visitation or ritual support afforded warriors in traditional societies. Many of their symptoms—lack of impulse control, confused sexuality, drug and alcohol abuse, intimacy and employment problems, emotional explosiveness, mistrust of authority, alienation—characterize adolescence in our culture. Many veterans with PTSD are, psychically, shell-shocked teenagers unable to enter adulthood with its demands and rules. They have not figured out who they have become. They cannot shape their new self into an identity that can give them inner order, strength, and meaning and help them find a place in society and the cosmos.

We have seen that classifying and treating PTSD merely as a stress and an anxiety disorder fails to address its deeper dimensions. Moreover, while medication may rebalance biochemical functioning, it cannot heal the inner self. In the standard kind of treatment, the veteran feels pathologized and expected to "get on with life." He feels encouraged to measure his progress against normative civilian functioning rather than to do what is truly needed, which is to embrace the experience of inner death and seek a new identity and a spiritual rebirth. The common therapeutic model, that is, misses the point that PTSD is primarily a moral, spiritual, and aesthetic disorder—in effect, not a *psychological* but a *soul* disorder. All of its aspects concern dimensions of the soul, inasmuch as the soul is the part of us that responds to morality, spirituality, aesthetics, and intimacy. Such aspects can be healed only by strategies aimed at them directly in this context. For this reason, it is crucial that we expand our psychological focus to a more holistic view.

Almost all cultures and spiritual traditions of the world have had some concept of soul and the means for preserving its well-being. However, in our scientific and technological era, soul is not a popular concept. "Post-traumatic stress disorder" is our modern metaphor for the condition of soul sickness; the quasi-scientific name allows us to find a place for it among the psychological categories we use today to analyze the human experience.

In PTSD, our drive to preserve life and to persevere in our own existence; our self-awareness as autonomous and effective agents creating our destinies; our ability to think, reason, and understand; our will and motivation; our aesthetic sensibilities; our forms of intimacy, love, and sexuality; the functioning of our imaginations; and our capacity to function in society—all these characteristics are damaged, distorted, or transformed according to the realities of war. All are aspects of the soul.

Which aspects are wounded and how badly vary, of course, according to particular experience and the political climate of the war. And as Jungian analyst and World War II veteran John Gianinni stresses, different personality types will have different responses to traumatic stimuli; some personalities are not at all suited to the demands of combat. But whatever personality a soldier carries into battle, the nature of modern warfare is such that it will demonstrably misshape every function of the soul.

Some soul traits are more amenable to aid through standard resources than others. As we will later examine in detail, acts of reconciliation with the community and the government can help. For example, vets who feel dishonored often fight for disability benefits. These benefits serve as substitutes for the true recognition due warriors and at least demonstrate the assumption of some responsibility on the part of the country. Also, while not a panacea, the standard resource of medications may help alleviate debilitating pain and symptoms. And individual and group counseling may provide necessary guidance, support, and witness.

All these standard approaches can be good, but they frequently ignore certain dimensions of damage to the soul. Psychotherapists, for instance, are used to talking about intimacy, human relations, and will. But the way they discuss intimacy is usually more as a matter of child development and normative functioning than as a motivation of soul reshaped by war. Indeed, psychotherapists are trained not to talk much about spirituality or morality in the first place. But these are precisely the dimensions we must address in order to evolve strategies that facilitate identity reconstruction and soul restoration. Such strategies include healing from moral trauma, repairing the damage to aesthetic sensibilities, developing the capacity for healthy intimacy and sexuality, and the rehumanization of self and other. We can adapt some approaches from traditional cultures that have had a highly developed sense of spirituality for recovering lost parts of the soul and reformulating identity by following the warrior's rite of passage to completion.

The moral trauma calls for particular attention, since it is so severe in veterans, so neglected by the therapeutic community, and, under modern political and technological conditions, more endemic to the practice of warfare than ever before. During the Vietnam War, William Sloane Coffin, chaplain of Yale University, said, "The most profound experience of the self is the experience of the conscience, not the experience of private sensations or inner visions." [15] Modern war inevitably traumatizes this center of the self, the conscience.

Socrates taught that the soul is that which distinguishes good from evil; it is improved by choosing good and harmed by choosing evil. What are the consequences to the soul, then, if we must kill or destroy? Or if we do not believe in the cause for which we are fighting? Or, if in the midst of our action, we develop a different moral perspective? Consider this marine's testimony:

> I laid my gun across my legs and, while the Vietnamese family stared at me without daring to move, I stared out the door of their hut.

That doorway was like a picture frame on the world . . . like I was staring out through God's eyes. The men I fought with, the "good guys," yelled like idiots and pushed these little people around. I watched my buddies walk over to the hut right across from me . . . and torch it. I looked at the family cowering in fear by my side. I looked across the way at my friend, the good guy, and another terrified *mamasan* . . . the flames . . . destroy[ing] her home.

Something woke up in me. Good and evil. Honor and dishonor. Right and wrong. These had been automatic concepts . . . but at that moment . . . they were real, living things. You earned them by torturing yourself with questions until you really knew what was right and good and honorable, not because someone told you, but because you saw.

I watched my buddies burn another hut. . . . They weren't gooks, for God's sake! . . . They were a helpless mother and her terrified little children! After six months in the bush I saw them for the first time. . . . They weren't evil. They weren't the enemies. They weren't the bad guys. We were!

Everything was turned around. I wanted to raise my M-16 and blast away at these crazy marauding Americans who were wasting this helpless village. Now I had a soul, and I wanted to save it and these people by doing the right thing and defending them, even if it cost me my life.

I just walked off in a stupor while they . . . torched the hut. My hut with my family in it. Where I found my soul. Where I figured out the truth. I was in a daze for a long time. Then I went numb for the rest of my tour.

At the very moment I found my soul, at the very moment it woke up and I could see the truth for the

111

first time in my life, at that very second when I knew we were evil, it fled, I lost it.[16]

This marine is speaking not only of dislocation, stress, and loss. He is speaking of the moral ambiguity of a war in which he is the aggressor and is forced to confront his relationship to good and evil, right and wrong. He can no longer believe in the standards with which he was raised and trained. But he is unable to act on his new standards without killing his friends or losing his life. These conflicting forces plunge him into spiritual crisis at the very moment of his moral awakening. "How could I do right in this impossible situation?" he asks. "Ultimately, am I a good man or a bad?" His questions characterize the lifelong confusion, loss of motivation, and sense of not belonging that followed him for decades. It expresses the profound degree of dirtiness, stain, and inner tainting that throughout history has been associated with evil.

In Steven Speilberg's movie, *Saving Private Ryan*, the soldier Ryan, now an old man, asks his family as he mourns over the graves of those who saved him, "I was a good man, wasn't I?" This movie fiction holds a great truth. Concern with morality is pervasive among soldiers and veterans, is often uppermost in their minds, and can remain with them until death. During his tour of duty in Iraq, army chaplain Capt. Tim Wilson counseled eight to ten soldiers a week for "combat stress." He reports, "There are usually two things they are dealing with. Either being shot at and not wanting to get shot at again, or, after shooting someone, asking 'Did I commit murder?' or, 'Is God going to forgive me?' or, 'How am I going to be when I get home?'"[17] These GIs are dealing with ultimate matters: Will I live? Have I done good or evil? If I have done evil, then what am I?

Reid Mackey, a helicopter crew chief in Viet Nam, said, "All wars are over two words, *God* and *good*. The Creator is one and the same for us all, but we kill each other over our images of God. And all our wounds reduce to whether or not we were good. War is always terrible, but your lifetime of suffering is based on whether or not you know in your heart that you did good."

In order to kill, one must invert one's sense of good and evil. The impulse for destruction replaces the impulse for creativity. Robert Jay Lifton describes this shift through the eyes of a GI who participated in the My Lai massacre: "The predominant emotional tone here is all-encompassing absurdity and moral inversion. The absurdity has to do with being alien and profoundly lost, yet at the same time locked into a situation as meaningless and unreal as it is deadly. The moral inversion, eventuating in the sense of evil, has to do not only with the absolute reversal of ethical standards, but with its occurrence in absurdity, without inner justification, so that the killing is rendered naked." [18]

Endless stories demonstrate the spiritual poisoning that comes from such moral inversion among both soldiers and civilians during combat. Afterward, having betrayed their ethical codes when they had to, they cannot tolerate the betrayal. They feel trapped in moral dilemmas they cannot resolve in any acceptable way, and the impasse breaks the soul. This entrapment can occur even when the actor behaves in an extremely moral and self-sacrificing manner, as we see here:

A Jewish holocaust survivor told of having lived in a Nazi-occupied village. The German soldiers had created a large pen in the town square where they held their daily quota of Jews to be sent for extermination. Walking through the square, the man saw his ten-year-old son locked in the pen. The man knew it meant death for the boy. He begged the guard, one of his non-Jewish neighbors, to let the boy out. The guard said the Nazis would kill him if any Jews were missing, but he gave the father this option: The Nazis only wanted numbers; bring him another child and his son could go free. The father rushed to his rabbi for advice. Could he allow another boy to die in his son's place? After anguished soul-searching, he knew the answer was no. When he emerged from the meeting, he walked slowly through the square, staring at his son behind the barbed wire for what he knew was the last time.

Isaac Bonilla, the Vietnam War vet who eventually died of Agent Orange complications, was a Puerto Rican American who had been drafted. His unit included numerous Hispanic GIs but was commanded by white officers who could not speak Spanish. Since Isaac was bilingual, he had to translate orders to other Hispanic soldiers. Because the Hispanics were smaller than their white counterparts, and because, as in the dominant culture, they were considered expendable, they were often employed as "tunnel rats," being forced to drop into tunnels used by the Viet Cong to engage in hand-to-hand fighting underground. Isaac was supposed to pass the orders to enter the tunnels from his officer to his countrymen. He wanted to refuse but was told, "Give that order or you'll go into the tunnels yourself." When Isaac's friends begged him to let them off the hook, he answered in Spanish that it was not his order and that they had either to take their chances in the tunnel or to run away into the jungle. Once he did refuse to pass the order. His lieutenant put a pistol to his head and told him, "Deliver it or die." He delivered it.

During the 1994 Rwandan genocide, the dominant Hutus slaughtered eight hundred thousand Tutsis in ten days. Forty-seven-year-old Marcellin Kwibuka, a Hutu, was given this choice about his Tutsi wife: Kill her, or we will kill you and your family. He chose to kill her.[19]

All these stories are of good people caught in impossible dilemmas where someone had to die. The complexity of such choices can propel us far beyond the simple kill-or-be-killed situation inherent to soldiers in the combat zone. Like the Hutu husband, for instance, we may feel we made the lower choice—as he feels he did by killing his wife rather than being killed. Yet from another perspective, he sacrificed one rather than lose many—and took upon himself the burden of such a terrible decision for the rest of his life. Or, like Isaac Bonilla, we may, at the critical moment, forsake the moral edict "Thou shalt not kill" for the more primal urge toward survival, which says, "I must live—at any cost." Yet his friends would have been forced into the tunnel anyway, even if he had been dead. The hard thing was being the one who had to pass on the order. And like the Jewish father, we may find ourselves feeling that life is not worth living after our sense of morality is no longer intact. As he said, "To preserve my values, I cooperated with my son's murderers when I could have saved him. By doing right, I did wrong. I myself became my son's executioner." Yet in the horrible dilemma facing him, he made the supreme sacrifice of letting his own son die—the one who would have carried his legacy into the future—rather than inflict such an inconsolable loss onto anyone else.

Reflecting on war after a lifetime of participating in it, Robert J. McNamara concludes simply, "In order to do good, you may have to do evil."[20] Yet to our internal self-image, it does not matter that we had no choice; we are still haunted by the awareness that by killing we have committed the greatest wrong. The soul freezes on this moral crisis point. It says: I killed my own. Or, I killed whom I should not have killed and that is murder. I have become foul and cannot get clean again. "What you do, you become," as the saying goes. Even in old age, the Jewish father of the ten-year-old could never accept that he had made a proper, albeit tragic, moral choice.

Such impossible moral dilemmas are built into the nature of warfare. They become inevitable when wars involve massive killing or invasions for political/economic goals rather than for pure self-defense. And they push the soul to the breaking point. After crossing that point, it is most difficult for the individual ever to believe in his own goodness and worth again. As William Sloane Coffin observed, "There can be no victory if military victory spells moral defeat . . . sacrifice in and of itself confers no sanctity."[21]

Shortly after the Vietnam War, in 1981, Peter Marin published an essay called "Living in Moral Pain."[22] Many veterans still refer to that essay. Marin demonstrated that the moral pain of combat is a complex experience that extends far beyond anything civilians usually suffer, beyond the boundaries of psychological language and the scope of most treatment. Marin declared that veterans would not find peace or psychological well-being without "seeing through to the end . . . the moral journey they began in Viet Nam."[23]

Isaac Bonilla was in pain every minute of his postwar life—not just physical pain from his wounds, but also moral pain from his betrayal and loss of his Puerto Rican brothers. He was additionally in pain, as many minority group veterans are, from fighting "the white man's war."[24] He was usually medicated, but his soul's pain waited as if a booby trap was inside him, ready to explode again at any moment. Pain like his that is carried for life is not just an indication of too much stress, or of a psychological stressor being triggered. Rather, it is a marker of moral trauma. Wounds such as these cannot be healed or corrected with medications, stress reduction techniques, eye movement therapy, or other impersonal or value-neutral strategies. Therapy, as Marin said, must find some of its missing "gravity," participate in the veteran's moral journey, and include the world.[25]

As we see from our stories and these analyses, moral pain, with its incumbent harm to the soul, is a root cause of PTSD. If we do not address the moral issues, we cannot alleviate it, no matter how much therapy or how many medications we apply. Is it possible to serve in a war that is not immoral, that does not cause the soul severe inner conflict, and from which we may emerge clean? The novel and movie *Dances with Wolves* presents an alternative. John Dunbar, a white Union army soldier during the Civil War, becomes sick of killing and volunteers for lonely duty in the remote Indian territories. As the novel portrays, he eventually earns his place among the Comanche people and the name "Dances with Wolves." Dunbar supplies guns and a winning strategy for one battle between his adopted Comanche tribe and their traditional enemies the Pawnees. Afterward, as his grateful Comanche companions shout his name, he begins to see the fight and its victory in a new way: "This killing had not been done in the name of some dark political objective . . . [it was] not a battle for territory or riches or to make men free. This battle had no ego. It had been waged to protect the homes that stood only a few feet away. And to protect the wives and children and loved ones huddled inside. It had been fought to protect the food stores that would see them through the winter." [26]

At the end of the novel, Dances with Wolves retreats with his new Comanche bride and her tribe into the safety of the mountains, symbolizing the reconciliation of his inner conflict and newfound sense of inner peace. It is an eloquent statement to the effect that the only way a soldier or survivor's identity may emerge from warfare intact is if the purpose of the war "has no ego." A warrior is trained to surrender his ego, and his life, if necessary, for the greater group—whether it is his combat unit or his country. If, during or after battle, he adjudges that ego is what fueled the fight, moral trauma will inevitably result. To protect the soul, war cannot be waged for selfish ends. We cannot make death and destruction the weapons we wield for political or economic power or gain. The soul knows the difference. PTSD tries to tell us.

Seven

Eros and Aesthetics in Hell

War brings us into the most intense engagement with other human beings. It demands that we love some of our neighbors and destroy others. And it asks us to align ourselves—to love and hate thus—in the most uncompromising terms. Though in civilian life we might have disliked the man who is now our foxhole mate, in combat we love this soldier next to us more than life itself. We hate his counterpart across the battlefield more than the foul fiend; yet, as Thomas Hardy wrote, in civilian life he might have been someone we wished to sit down and have a drink with and get to know.[1]

Freud speculated that *eros* and *thanatos*, the drive toward union and the drive toward death, are twin aspects of the one life force. As he elucidated in *Beyond the Pleasure Principle*, published just after World War I, eros is the force that attracts, connects, and binds all beings. In opposition, thanatos is the death drive, the force that tries to separate and destroy what eros connects. Freud believed that these twin drives exist in an eternal duality. Eros drives us together, thanatos apart. Eros is at the core of love and sex; thanatos is at the core of suicide if turned against the self and of violence if turned against other people or nations.

The ancient Greeks expressed the same observation in their mythology. The god force that pulls all things together they called *Eros,* from which Freud borrowed the term, and the force that drives them apart they called *Eris.* While Eris is the goddess of strife and conflict, Eros is the god of love, the one who unifies and harmonizes. The Romans renamed him Cupid. Eros is the universal force of attraction that holds the planets and moons in their orbits. On the human level, it is the force we experience as desire, the sex drive, and love itself.

The Greeks wisely associated these minor god forces with two of their major gods. Eris is the sister of Ares, the god of war, whom the Romans called Mars. Eros is the son of the golden Aphrodite, the goddess of love and beauty, Venus to the Romans. Greek mythology expresses the overwhelming power that occurs when these two forces—war and love, belligerence and beauty—come together.

In a mythic twist of irony, Aphrodite was married to Hephaistos, god of crafts and the forge. The goddess of love could hardly be happy with this introverted and lame artisan god, the only imperfect one among the immortals. She secretly lay in her marriage bed with the savage Ares. One morning Ares and Aphrodite stayed in bed too long, and Helios, the sun god, whose light reveals all, spied them out and reported the affair. Hephaistos fashioned a golden chain that fell upon the lovers, binding them to one another in the midst of their tryst. Then he called the other gods to witness their shame. The gods laughed and the lovers fled. But their laughter was at Hephaistos. They, too, were overcome with desire. Some commented that they themselves would suffer shame to have the opportunity to lie with the shining Aphrodite.

This was not the only time Ares and Aphrodite slept together. In fact, she bore him three children, showing that love and war have an ongoing though illicit relationship that recurs again and again. Their affair demonstrates the primal urges of passion in the male and female principles. And the gods' declaration of their own desire demonstrates the irresistible power of passion when love and war meet. No other principle the various gods represent—reason, rulership, responsibility, community—would enable them to resist this temptation. Aphrodite and Ares together demonstrate the height of passion that occurs when love and beauty bed together with war.

Aphrodite embodies everything we know about tenderness, beauty, and feminine receptiveness, yet when coupled with Ares she takes on another aspect. She becomes enchanting in the expression of our lust for power—and in the relentlessness of that lust and its disregard for shame. So also, Ares, who on his own is sheer rage and rampage, when united with Aphrodite gains focus and becomes the strong, deliberate arm of war. Ares alone may be pure bloodlust, or, as Homer called him, "the god that delights in slaughter." With Aphrodite, he gains grace, beauty, and nobility. Pure slaughter repels the gods; they do not like Ares by himself. But they long to take his place with Aphrodite; they find the scene enthralling. Add "love of homeland" or "nobility of sacrifice" to Ares, and we have irresistible powers in combination.

Homer's *Iliad* wisely featured numerous appearances for Aphrodite in connection with the Trojan War, thus demonstrating the dominant element of passion in war making. Indeed, Aphrodite was instrumental in instigating the war between the Greeks and the Trojans. The conflict began when Alexandros, popularly known as Paris, chose to award Aphrodite instead of Hera or Athena a golden apple labeled "for the fairest." His choice empowered the most primitive and satisfying impulses over the more "civilized" choices of married relationship and responsible rulership. Upon receiving the apple, Aphrodite promised Paris as a prize the most beautiful woman on earth. She immediately led him to the palace of Helen's husband, King Menelaos of Sparta. Paris ran off with Helen, breaking the strict rules of guest-friendship that helped stitch together the ancient world. In their escape, we again view the power of passion to upset marriages, countries, and the established order of the world.

Paris's actions instigated ten years of overweening massacre as two great civilizations and their allies battered each other at the gates of Troy. But the fight was blamed on Helen, "the face that launched a thousand ships" and the object of Paris's lust. Thus are we warned that passion can drive us to set reason aside and risk the destruction of civilizations. Aphrodite represents our passion to have the most, the best, the fairest, the most intense, no matter how it offends custom or causes suffering. When we study the roots of war, we find this relentless dark side of eros at work. This has been true throughout history and is no less true today. Whether we name it revenge, oil, land, wealth, security, freedom, democracy, Communism, our way of life, or our God, we always war for a Helen.

And the price is always higher than we imagine. War transforms a combatant's relations to love and sex, and to beauty and order and form, in a way that comprises some of the most difficult dimensions of the survivor's inner world. These dimensions are soul-based, of our very essence. They work differently in the survivor. And as is true about other aspects, we can't force veterans to adjust back into mainstream civilian culture without addressing this fundamental difference. We must support the reshaping of identity in these terms, just as we do in others.

Revenge, for instance, is one expression of how war can transform love—in this case into passionate hatred. How fierce and personal, how reflexive and universal, how connected to lust is the desire for revenge! It is what drove Jack to enlist in the marines. He volunteered for Viet Nam, not just to uphold American ideals, but to avenge his best friend who had been killed there. Paul, another marine, left his unit and stomped off into the jungle on a personal killing rampage after he lost his best friend during a rocket attack. Still another marine, Howard, married a Vietnamese woman, his own Helen, "the kindest, most beautiful girl I ever knew." The Viet Cong killed her for collaborating with the enemy. Howard abandoned his unit and went marauding, not returning until he wore a string of blood-crusted ears. Yet these men were not sated, even after all their kills. They wanted the war to be personal, but no matter how they raged they could not find to destroy the one who had wronged them.

Moreover, part of their grief was due to their inability to defend their beloved. Jack had been stateside and Paul on another part of the base when their friends were killed. But both felt they had failed their best friends, and Howard believed he had failed his wife, all because they had been unable to protect those they loved.

Developing an abnormal sex drive is another example of how war can transform one's relation to love and passion. Ray, a medic, said, "I touched more dead bodies in one year than live ones in my entire lifetime." Though married before leaving for war, Ray returned to spend decades seducing every woman he could. When he did have sex with his wife, she said she felt like it was not with her; the desperation of Ray's sexuality made her feel frightened and dirty. Ray could say only that he was so deeply imprinted with death that he needed sex to feel the touch of life again.

Paul, too, was insatiable in bed. He returned from combat with a hunger for the restoration of life that only the intensity of erotic arousal could promise to fulfill. In his marriage, Paul insisted on having sex "at least three times a day—any way, anywhere, any time." When his wife could not perform at this demanding level, he found other women and lived a double life as a family man and secret Casanova. Finally, his wife felt shamed and used and could no longer tolerate being his "receptacle." The ex-marine divorced her to continue his exploits.

Women, as therapist and healer Deena Metzger writes, want but don't know how to take the war out of men. They often try by making love, but "it isn't enough."[2] Thus the lust awakened by war for bloodletting easily transfers to sexuality back at home. In its throes, only one's partner feels debased. The survivors often do not feel shame. Rather, they feel justified or as if they are acting of necessity. Either they have had too much thanatos—too much death—or Aphrodite possesses them in order to counterbalance it.

How do Ares and Aphrodite bed together on the field of battle? One army survivor confessed, "I wrestled men to death in hand-to-hand combat. That experience was far more intimate and erotic than love or sex can ever be." A marine vet of World War II and Korea struggled to explain the strange thrill he felt, and could never forgive himself for, when blasting his machine gun at Japanese soldiers as they fought over a Pacific island. Angry over Pearl Harbor, he had enlisted at seventeen. "I should have been learning to make love, but instead I was given the thrill of the kill. I've never been able to separate them since, and I've never felt clean."

Innumerable descriptions of wartime killing sound like acts of love or sex. A British paratrooper from the Falklands said that one attack "was the most exciting thing since getting my leg across." One American soldier compared the killings at My Lai to the guilt and satisfaction that accompany masturbation. An Israeli military psychologist described a machine gunner who, exhilarated by the squeezing of the trigger, the hammering of the gun, and the flight of the tracers, discovered a strange pleasure in combat—the primal aggression, the release, the orgasmic discharge.[3]

Bob Cagle vividly expresses the joining of Aphrodite and Ares in his poem "A Farewell Letter":

> A beautiful magnetism exists between us.
> A need to use. To be used. . . .
> I direct you and you react—
> Or is it the other way around?
> Sometimes, in the heat of the moment
> I lose control—all control.
> My hands, fingers and face moving
> Delicately, rapidly, sometimes slowly
> To the most sensitive parts
> With the purpose of hearing you yell. . . .
> Many times, in the dark of night,
> I have reached out for you
> And always find you next to me, ready and willing.[4]

To whom is the poem addressed? We know only in the last line, when Bob finally bids farewell to—"my rifle."

After the intimacy of the death struggle—finding your weapon so responsive or feeling your hands around another's throat or your knife plunging into a live body—a survivor may not be able to separate Ares and Aphrodite again, even long after the fighting has ceased. Thus a German World War II veteran reported, "As soon as I saw naked flesh [in the beginning of a sexual encounter], I braced myself for a torrent of entrails, remembering countless wartime scenes with smoking, stinking corpses pouring out their vitals."[5] Chuck, a CIA operative who carried out assassinations in Africa and Asia, reported that whenever he tried to make love with his wife, and often when just sleeping next to her, he was haunted by images of the mangled bodies of women and children he had helped kill. Staring into his wife's face, he commonly saw the round dark face of a young African woman he had murdered, her dead eyes staring back at him through his wife's eyes.

In these experiences, both on the battlefield and after, we find the power of eris and eros, strife and lust, blending into one. When conflict is fueled by lust, when sexual passion is aroused toward destroying, when we feel release, as Cagle wrote, "with each fire-spitting spasm," the urges combine with an energy and motivation that makes it difficult to separate them again.

Finally, and just as Ares and Aphrodite are clandestine lovers, coupling in secret, our lust for war leads us into duplicity. We hide it from ourselves to avoid the guilt we would feel were we openly to embrace war making. It takes the golden chain of Hephaistos—the craft of great art—to expose these powers' hidden complicity and disregard for the common moral restraints that make civilization possible. Held together by craft and beauty, love and war may appear to coexist without harm. All too often, though, such craft takes the form of manipulative rhetoric. When the arts portray war, when orators ennoble it with skillful and elevated discourse, we can be lulled into believing that war itself is not horrible beyond speaking. We can be seduced into feeling that it is beautiful, elevated, ennobling—or at least survivable. But unleashed to pursue their own devices, the raw powers that Aphrodite and Ares embody betray, confuse, and enrage where they should not. They do not evoke shame; they trample on loyalty and tradition and disregard the victims left in their wake. "Once we take war's heady narcotic," Chris Hedges says, "it creates an addiction that slowly lowers us to the moral depravity of all addicts."[6] Or, as Hillman puts it, we are enthralled in a "terrible love of war."

The positive dimensions of passion that surface during and after warfare are no less compelling. Think of the spontaneous sense of brotherhood that emerges. As a squad leader in Viet Nam, Jack felt so bonded with his men that, he said, "I remember how each one of them went down," referring to the fourteen in his unit who were killed during his tour of duty. "Sometimes they went down fighting, sometimes crying, sometimes in their sleep. Sometimes they went down trying to save their brothers." As his supreme example of brotherhood, Jack told this story:

"Ron and Mo were the first two I ever lost. Guys wanted to be in my squad 'cause I didn't want to lose anybody. I walked point myself rather than let them take that risk. I did whatever I had to do to keep us all alive. We didn't lose many. They thought I was their lucky charm.

"Ron and Mo were buddies. They helped each other through a lot of shit, always guarding each other's backs. Once we were dug in on a hill that seemed safe and quiet. We had to move out, so Ron went down the hill to check things out and we guarded him from above, getting ready to move. Suddenly, there was an explosion. Ron had tripped a booby trap. He went flying through the air, one leg torn off and his stump bleeding.

"We hit the dirt but no one fired. Ron was screaming in pain, bloodcurdling screams. I stood up, scanned the hill, and made a move like I was going to run down there. Another booby trap exploded. Ron was caught in the middle of a mine field. These were command detonated. They were watching us.

"Mo jumped up. 'I gotta get him,' he screamed.

"'No,' I ordered. 'It's mined. They're watching. He's bait.'

"'I don't care,' Mo yelled back. 'He's my friend.'

"Before anyone could stop him, Mo was tearing down that hill screaming, 'Ronny, Ronny, hold on! I'm comin'!'

"Mo got to Ron and laid down next to his screaming friend. It was so still, I could almost hear Mo whispering to him, soothing him. I ordered the other guys to cover them closely. But we were set up. I couldn't order them down the hill.

"Mo soothed Ron. His screams became sobs. Then Mo put down his gun, stood up, and hoisted Ron onto his back. Holding him by one arm and his remaining leg, he started to climb the hill.

"Then they opened up. Ron was getting it in the back. I could tell from the way Mo was shuddering. To protect him, Mo turned around to take the bullets himself. They both went down in an AK hailstorm.

"And that," Jack concluded, "is brotherhood." Perhaps as his unwitting expression of how deeply he felt it, too, he added, "Sometimes I think the only reason I'm still alive is to tell their stories."

The Civil War was renowned as a time when brothers fought on opposite sides by day and shared untold gentle moments of friendship and traded supplies by night. During the famous Christmas truce of December 1914, World War I enemies left their mud- and blood-soaked trenches to celebrate. British and German troops sang carols to each other, talked of home, exchanged gifts, competed in soccer, and helped one another recover their dead. At the close of the truce, their officers had to beat them back into their trenches to force them to fight again.

Consider also wartime romances as evidence of the intense intimacy engendered by warfare. This is a theme endlessly repeated in world literature and popular entertainment. Think, for example, of Hector and Andromache in the *Iliad*, David and Bathsheba in the Old Testament, Troilus and Cressida in Shakespeare, Rhett Butler and Scarlett O'Hara in Margaret Mitchell's *Gone with the Wind*, Robert Jordan and Marie in Ernest Hemingway's *For Whom the Bell Tolls*. Psychotherapist Penny Cupp described the loyalty and passion of lovers estranged by war everywhere in saying about her own separation from her military husband during the Vietnam War, "They Also Serve Who Only Stand and Wait."[7]

When war and love are juxtaposed, events become more compelling, sensual, and emotional. The slaughter seems more brutal because of the tenderness, and the tenderness more needed because of the slaughter. In war, Hillman explains: "Under the compression from which there is no escape, caught in the vice between duty on one side and death on the other, binding structures give way and the heart opens to a love never known before or to be known again. . . . To die for love—we say it, but soldiers do it."[8]

Aphrodite is the goddess, not only of love and sex, but also of beauty. Plato said that beauty is the food of the soul. Its importance to the soul's well-being cannot be overestimated; nor can the damaging effect of beauty's distortions engendered by the hideousness of war.

"I feel like I've lost my sense of grace about myself and the world," Walt said in one of our psychotherapy sessions. "I don't belong here anymore. I don't fit. I don't deserve God's love."

"That's a horrible condition," I answered. "How can you bear to go on day after day without grace?"

"I can't. It truly makes every day a living hell. My wife doesn't understand how I can feel this way. But it is why I sometimes numb myself with alcohol. It kills the pain."

"When was the first time you felt this loss?"

"It was during my first encounter with death in Viet Nam." Walt said." I see it all the time, even as I look at you." His eyes narrowed as he stared through time. "I'm sitting in a back-hoe, the same kind of construction vehicle we have here. My captain tells me to follow him. I drive my backhoe to a strange, barren slope. It's raw and muddy. Nothing's growing on it. It looks like it's been recently dug. The captain says it's a mass grave of Vietnamese we killed. He orders me to dig up the entire grave and move the bodies to another location.

"I don't want to obey his orders," Walt continued, "but if I refuse I could be court-martialed or worse. I'm a machine operator, but they could make me a grunt. I could be sent into the boonies to kill or be killed. What else can I do? I drive my hoe up to the slope. I bite into the earth and scoop it open. I move the earth from the top of the shallow grave. Then I clamp my heart closed and lower the hoe into the pile of bodies. The hoe is like a huge fist. I lift a steel fistful of Vietnamese bodies into the air and begin moving them. I feel sick as I watch the arms, feet, and heads dangle in the air. I fight not to puke. But I follow my orders and keep working.

"That moment when I saw the dead bodies dangling was when I felt myself fall. I felt my *soul* plummet, just like an angel thrown from paradise into hell. I deserved it. I was profaning myself, all of us, life itself by desecrating the dead. I was performing the penultimate sacrilegious act. And that was just the beginning. That whole war was sacrilegious. It tainted us all."

"Walt," I said, "So many vets have told me just how painful this feeling of being tainted is. Your soul feels banished from the divine presence. You feel cut off from the source of life itself, condemned to the dark place where there is no life."

"Exactly," Walt said. "In Nam we always said 'It don't mean nothin'. When you accept that as true, you betray the spirit and banish it from life."

"Is your spirit gone?"

"Not entirely, because I can still see beauty. Where there is beauty, there is grace. But Viet Nam was the place of no beauty. I'm not talking about the country or the Vietnamese people. They have a beautiful, spiritual heritage and culture. I'm talking about the Nam we created.

"From the day I arrived on my base, I did not see any beauty. Beauty is the manifestation of Spirit. It's the force that keeps the soul alive. Can you imagine not seeing a single speck of beauty for an entire year? Day by day I felt my soul withering away inside me. Day by day, I fell further away from grace. For an entire year, I lived in the American Viet Nam, the place of no beauty. That is the ultimate terror."

Walt and I sat in silence, sharing this vision not of Aphrodite in her splendor but of how we rape and abuse her, and of the world in her absence. Then Walt began to shudder and finally to sob.

"There's only one way forward," he said. "I have to relive the experience. I have to dig up those bodies again and this time feel it with my poor, battered heart wide open. No wonder I've had two heart attacks.

"God help me!" Walt cried, "Damn it!" He hit his fists against his thighs. "The long arm of that war just keeps reaching out over the decades, grabbing people by the neck and strangling them where they sit. O the horror! O the horror!"

The characters Kurtz and Marlow in Joseph Conrad's *Heart of Darkness* utter these same words, "the horror!" The novel, chronicling the effects of European colonialism in Africa, originally appeared in 1902, as if it were an oracle announcing the beginning of the twentieth century. Those same words expressed the end-of-the-world vision of the Vietnam War in the movie *Apocalypse Now*. Walt saw this vision and knew its name. And he knew the place created in its name—a place where the beast, the savage Ares in us—is allowed to kill without restraint. In doing what he will with Aphrodite, Ares awakens her dark and vengeful side; then she, too, can destroy the very traits we worship in her.

Yet in the midst of war's horror, shreds of beauty still remain. They are never completely obliterated, even on the battlefield. Preston Stern was imprisoned in Long Binh Jail for "quitting" the army after three months of combat duty in Viet Nam convinced him the war was immoral and obscene. Surrounded by war, with even his fellow American troops scorning him for his rebellion, he stared through the wire of his compound at *Nui Ba Den* (Lady Black Mountain) rising out of the emerald rice paddies far away. "That mountain steadied me," he explained. "It reminded me of strength and beauty and endurance when I could not find any in the destruction around me."

Sometimes the very intensity of war's destruction can open us to see profound meaning in the smallest detail. Xaralampas Patelos spoke with adoration about a stone that was slowly chipped away in front of his face by rifle fire during the Greek Civil War. "For a long time I watched every speck of dust that flew off that stone," he said. "It seemed to me the most beautiful rock on the planet. It saved my life."

It is in small epiphanies such as this one that Eros lives on the battlefield.

————————

We have inherited a curious footnote to the tale of Aphrodite's relationship to Ares, not recounted by Homer. One myth has it that Helen was not at Troy at all; rather, she took refuge in Egypt. In Euripides' play based on this tale, Helen declares, "I never went to Troy; it was a phantom." She confronts a veteran who claims to have seen her recaptured, saying, "Think. Could this be only an impression, caused by God?" This veteran, who had served loyally through all the suffering, awakens to the futility at the heart of war: Our ideals are lies and illusions; nonetheless, we chase them, mistaking them for reality. He cries, "You mean it was for a cloud, for nothing, that we did that work?" And Menelaos, reunited with his wife, the real Helen, cannot distinguish between truth and illusion, reality and fantasy, projection and living woman. He tries to choose what fits his interpretation of reality and justify the losses of long, hard war. Helen cries out to him, "And will you leave me for that empty shadow's arms?"[9]

In the modern era, having helped his battered, much-suffering, and ailing country survive World War II and the Greek Civil War, the poet George Seferis took up this same theme, a theme for all times and all wars:

> . . . so much suffering, so much life,
> went into the abyss
> all for an empty tunic, all for a Helen.[10]

Eight

RELATIONS WITH
THE MISSING AND THE DEAD

A commercial airliner lands at dusk in early snow at the local airport, carrying the body of a young soldier just killed in Iraq. Plane engines and snow plows rumble. A soldier in fatigues disappears into the cargo hold with a tightly folded flag and then emerges behind a flag-draped coffin. Six soldiers from a local armory escort the coffin past a small honor guard, a crowd of extended family members, and rows of rigidly saluting police officers. The casket is loaded into a black hearse and disappears into the fog, followed by a dozen police cars from surrounding towns. The procession arrives at the young man's home neighborhood. Its streets are lined with neighbors holding American flags. Some of them are weeping. Others, his old school friends, stare in shock or hold each other. The casket is delivered to the funeral home and into the arms of the silent, grieving family. Unsure what to do next, some people drift away, but others linger. His friends argue. Does his death signify that they should be for or against the war? One young man the dead soldier's age says, "Regardless of what your feelings are about the war, he was just doing his job."[1] It is December 7, the anniversary of the Japanese attack on Pearl Harbor, when across America a previous generation had been shocked by war come home as well. Pearl Harbor and September 11 stand out as similar traumatic attacks that belie American innocence. We have learned that we, too, are vulnerable.

Those living on American soil, safely distant from the war zones the United States has helped create, experience war primarily in its aftermath. For many, war's reality does not hit home until the cost of it becomes personal in the loss of a loved one or friend. At that point, how can we possibly frame such an overwhelming loss in a way that makes sense?

Every culture the world over has struggled with proper relations with the war dead and missing in action. Those who believe in the cause may derive solace from the thought that their loss has meaning. Others feel that lives were wasted. Leaders have poured forth endless public blessings over the dead. "So died these men," Perikles said over the Athenian dead in 431 BCE, "by courage, sense of duty, and a keen feeling of honor." Echoing him, Lincoln pronounced at Gettysburg: "These honored dead shall not have died in vain." In Viet Nam, monuments in military cemeteries proclaim, "The Motherland honors your sacrifice." And over the American soldiers killed in Iraq, George W. Bush orates, "Some have shown their devotion to our country in deaths that honored their whole lives, and we will always honor their names and their sacrifice."[2]

Throughout history, cultures around the world have created elaborate ceremonies to ritualize war death in an attempt to give meaning to the loss of lives. Some New Guinea tribes dressed the bodies of dead warriors in their regalia and carried them on thrones through the village, celebrating them as fallen heroes. In ancient Greece, the greatest honor a warrior could receive was to be laid to rest where he fell. The Greeks often erected a warrior's arms and memorial monuments on the site of his death. They held funeral games and feasts in a hero's honor. These could be so lengthy and elaborate that it took Homer an entire chapter in the *Iliad* to describe the games Achilles gave in honor of his fallen friend, Patroklos. That funeral included athletic competitions, oratory, blood sacrifices, and a huge, richly laden funeral pyre.

Plains warriors charged into battle shouting such slogans as, "It is a good day to die," or, "I am a Fox. I am supposed to die!" If a warrior found himself in a death struggle, he sought to meet his end with courage, nobility, and unflinching acceptance. Plains people had elaborate ceremonies for every aspect of the warrior's life—war and peace, victory and defeat, leaving the village and returning, and special dances for other occasions. Among the Lakota, sacred dances included the Scalp Dance and the Dance of the Dead.

The family of the dead soldier whose body arrived home on Pearl Harbor Day asked Robert Reiter, as County Veterans Service officer, to oversee the arrangements for their son's funeral. Reiter spent exhausting days orchestrating the large military-style death ritual. He says that for him as a combat vet, "It's not easy dealing with another war death. I've been through too many. Some people say I should be proud that the family reached out to me, but they have no idea what it does to my head."

Yet a warrior serves when called. "Like a good marine," Reiter says, "I took care of the sergeant." All the while he remembered his own best friend—also named Robert—who was killed in Viet Nam. Reiter cannot remember much of the incident but dreams of it regularly: the firefight they survived together; the helicopters extracting them; the flight to safety; and then a blinding explosion and his best friend dead beside him, horribly mangled in what was left of their chopper. "I pray to God that what I dream is not what happened," Reiter says, his voice choking and eyes sad. About his friend, he adds, "He is always with me." Even though Reiter has experienced numerous deaths of others in the service and since, his friend Robert's death has been the central loss of his life. In his memory, he now endlessly strives to ease the similar burden others must carry.

War is death. Veterans and survivors are saturated with it. They have stared down the barrel of a gun and viewed their own end. They have been covered with the remains of friends who have just died. They have been agents of death for countless others, many of whom were innocent. Robert Jay Lifton finds this "death immersion" to be one of the most debilitating factors in survivors, especially crippling when the survivor was involved in atrocities or in mass deaths, such as the Holocaust or the atomic blasts in Japan.[3]

The long-term impact is extensive. Survivors typically suffer nightmares that, like Reiter's, may recapitulate traumatic incidents. They may see themselves killing again, or friends and enemies dying again. They may have waking visions of dead friends, enemies, or both. They may also, in retrospect, feel moral anguish that the people they killed did not deserve to die. Often, as we have seen, they feel more intimacy with the dead than with the living, as if they themselves were already dead. From World War I, Siegfried Sassoon wrote, "Upon my brow / I wear a wreath of banished lives."[4] From Viet Nam, William Crapser wrote of "a continual falling of men obliterated in my eyes" and of the deaths of friends who "nurture themselves on me. . . . I am also that dead."[5]

Veterans may be suffused with a melancholy that makes them look to civilians as if they are permanent residents of funeral homes. They often feel as though there is a cemetery inside them; they feel an overweening responsibility to honor and not forget their lost dead. They can be tortured with remorse if they forget a name, a face, a story. Some war survivors search for decades to find the families of dead companions in order to honor their last moments or deliver their final messages. They see the dead in their sleep or beckoning to them from roadsides. They hear them calling in the mountains. They see dead children's faces behind the faces of smiling kids shopping for Christmas at the mall.

Chuck, a CIA agent on assassination teams in both Asia and Africa, participated in the massacre of an African village and the scattering of "evidence" to make it look like the actions of Communist insurgents. Now, awake and asleep, Chuck sees piles of murdered African civilians. "They won't let me rest. They're getting their revenge."

One of the Vietnamese employees at My Lai, now a memorial park and museum, is the niece and cousin of a family killed during the massacre. Though college educated and fluent in several languages, and though she spent time in large cities pursuing a profession, the woman returned to My Lai to serve as a tour guide. "I can feel my family's restless spirits crying out to me from the other world," she explained. "My doctor and husband tell me, 'Too much war. It is not good for you.' But it is my duty to tell the story of their last day for my entire life. It is the only way I can discover to give their death any purpose."

Shakespeare's Macbeth sees the ghost of Banquo, the friend he murdered; his Brutus sees the ghost of Caesar. These stories, along with that of Chuck and the tour guide, mirror the truth that nightmares, visions, intrusive memories, perpetual grief, and the eternal presence of the dead are some of the most common plagues of soldier's heart. An elderly veteran who committed atrocities during the Korean War retreated to a remote cottage in the Blue Ridge Mountains. There, every night, in disturbing visions and nightmares, he would watch "an old man and an old woman, indistinct faces, Asian faces, blurred by time but close at hand, accusing faces, faces of the dead."[6] One Vietnam War veteran would see countless dead from that war—enemy combatants, civilians, even his comrades—in his sleep, walking through the brush at the side of the road, beckoning to him through dripping windows.

It seems that survivors cannot find peace unless they *make* peace with the legions of dead with whom they may have any relationship—as relative, friend, comrade in arms, former enemy, or even as their killer. Relations with the missing and the dead, and with death itself, are at the core of the soul wound we call post-traumatic stress disorder.

What does it mean when afterimages of the dead return to haunt the living? Are the visions and nightmares due to a malfunctioning of the nervous system, or are they psychological or spiritual phenomena? By and large, the psychomedical field views them as symptoms to treat with medication. Medications, however, do not restore peaceful sleep because they do not heal relations with the dead. Traditional cultures the world over believe the dead are not entirely gone; rather, their souls have left their bodies to travel on in some spirit realm. This belief may correspond to the afterlife imagined by Judeo-Christian and Muslim people or to the cycles of reincarnation set forth in the Buddhist and Hindu religions. In any case, the common underlying belief is that the soul survives physical death and continues to exist in some dimension. Many traditions teach that when a person dies suddenly and violently, the soul is in shock from the separation. It may then linger in this world and need assistance before it can move on. Thus, from the psychospiritual perspective, visits from the dead in visions, nightmares, and intrusive thoughts are calls from the restless souls who have not found peace and are asking the living for help.

Sometimes the visitations are caused by guilt. Those who did not die often feel survivor's guilt; they endlessly ponder the question, Why did I live instead of them? Veterans often feel guilt for failing at revenge or retribution—for instance, if they could not kill their friend's killer. And they will especially suffer from guilt if they unjustly took lives or dishonored the remains of the dead. GIs can feel guilt even if they believed the killing was justified. In *The Naked and the Dead,* Norman Mailer described the discomfort of Catholic soldiers during World War II who were afraid they might die in battle before they could make confession and be purged of the killings they had done.[7] Much distress arises from the tension between combatant and civilian codes of religion, ethics, and conduct. But there is more.

We have heard testimony about the bond that develops between people under fire together. The lives of those who share the mud and danger and blood of warfare become intermingled. The power of this bond transcends all others, even the marriage and family bonds we forge in civilian life. The Plains Indians formalized this relationship through ritual and a code of ethics; two warriors who were best friends would be sworn to one another as "brother-friends." The duties of brother-friends to one another were to uphold the wish of one as "the law of the other" and to be "one in thought and action." Further, each was to "give preference to his brother over all mankind" and "give anything to, or do anything for, the other." And both would "pray and try to please the gods."[8]

Achilles and Patroklos were brother-friends. So were the Dioscuri of Greek mythology, Castor and Polydeuces, the two sons born to Leda, wife of King Tyndareus of Sparta. Polydeuces was fathered by Zeus, king of the gods, and so was immortal; Castor, fathered by the human king, was mortal. Always adventuring together, Castor and Polydeuces joined the quest for the Golden Fleece and rescued their sister Helen from abduction. Finally, on a cattle raid, Castor was killed. Inconsolable, Polydeuces begged Zeus, "Father, let me not outlive my dear brother." For Zeus to restore the dead to life would have been against the laws of the universe. But he did allow Polydeuces to share his immortality with Castor; both spent their days living alternately in Olympus as gods and under the earth as shades.

This myth expresses the profound sense of connection that forms between warriors and brother-friends in war. Surviving hell together, endless grief when separated, a vision of the common end, the wish always to share the embrace of a brother—these sentiments describe in broad strokes the supreme bond that makes brother-friends of men at arms and replaces all other relationships as the most primary. Men in combat today call each other "bro." Brothers-in-arms—or sisters-in-arms—become like two souls having one identity. If one dies, the other, as Robert Reiter puts it, "is always with me." The survivor carries the consciousness and burden of the lost friend, living for two and sharing half of his remaining life, even as Polydeuces shared half his immortality.

Traditional peoples teach that we the living are responsible for the souls of the dead. The great Lakota warrior and medicine man Crazy Horse summed up the importance of one's relationship with one's own people who have passed on: "My home is where my dead lay buried." Native Americans teach that this responsibility extends especially to those whose lives we take in combat. "When you kill an enemy warrior, you become responsible for his soul," said contemporary Lakota elder General Grant. If warriors properly propitiate the souls of their dead, including their enemies, then the powers of those souls can enter and aid the survivor. But if those souls are not propitiated, they become trapped and can turn against and harm the survivor. Thus, without proper attendance to the souls of the dead, the souls of both the deceased and the living are at risk.

Like our veterans, Odysseus was a survivor of a prolonged and brutal war. He was lost and could not complete his homeward journey without first descending to the Underworld and meeting the restless souls of dead comrades. The shades of the dead gathered and pressed on him with their eternal anguish.[9] The first command Odysseus received in the Underworld was from his unburied companion, Elpenor, who died during a drunken accident and whose unburied body had been left behind on Circe's Island. Elpenor's shade instructed his captain to return to his death site and give his body proper burial. In the same way, spiritually, veterans cannot continue their homeward trek and take up civilian life again until they first feel that they have adequately honored their dead.

These traditional stories and beliefs offer us a psychospiritual viewpoint from which to understand the recurring nightmares and intrusive waking visions of the dead that are among the most common and troublesome symptoms of PTSD. Perhaps it is not just a traumatic memory that plagues the survivor. James Hillman argues that dreams are paths to the Underworld through which what has become invisible can become visible to us.[10] Perhaps PTSD visions and nightmares are the wounded soul's attempt to offer the survivor a chance to reconcile with the dead, a gateway to his or her own Underworld through which restless lost souls can return to the living, call attention to their deadly actions, cry to them for proper grieving, and demand that they make new and truthful meaning from their deaths.

The United States had over 4,400 missing in World War I, almost 79,000 in World War II, and over 8,000 in Korea. In comparison, the 2,000 still missing in action from the Vietnam War, while still the source of profound heartache, is a relatively small number for such a brutal war. But the Vietnamese record over 250,000 missing in action from that same war, which they call the "American War." With its massive bombings, napalm, white phosphorous, Agent Orange, and other modern weaponry, such staggering numbers are inevitable.

In Vietnamese Buddhist belief, a soul lingers near its family for a century after death, guiding and helping family members for four generations. But the soul cannot then move on to the spirit world if the body has not been given proper burial rites, preferably in its *que houng*, its ancestral home. Today, with over a quarter million missing, many Vietnamese country people report that theirs is a country of lost souls trapped in the limbo between the physical and spiritual planes, unable to continue their karmic journeys. The Vietnamese have made great efforts to recover as many of their missing—as well as ours—as possible. For decades after the war, their search teams operated in remote places. To this day their television stations carry daily broadcasts from families seeking lost relatives or their remains. In *The Sorrow of War,* his fictionalized account of a Northern soldier's life in Viet Nam during and after the war, Vietnamese author Bao Ninh describes Kien, the head of an MIA team and the team's encounter with one of these unreleased souls:

His entire life was gathering corpses. He was preoccupied with this sole duty. . . . He used to describe his work as though it were a sacred oath, and ask others to swear their dedication. . . .

His group had found a half-buried coffin. It had popped up like a termite hill on a riverbank. . . . Inside the coffin was a thick plastic bag, similar to the ones Americans used for their dead, but this one was clear plastic. The soldier seemed to be still breathing, as though in deep sleep. . . . His handsome, youthful face had a serious air and his body appeared to be still warm.

Then before their eyes the plastic bag discolored, whitening as though suddenly filled with smoke. The bag glowed and something seemed to escape from it, causing the bag to deflate. When the smoke cleared, only a yellowish ash remained.

Kien and his platoon were astounded and fell to their knees around it, raising their hands to heaven praying for a safe flight for the departed soul.[11]

Bao Ninh's story also describes hearing or seeing these lost souls crying in anguish, begging for help to be released from limbo and move on:

Sometimes the dead manifested themselves as sounds rather than shadows. Others in the MIA team . . . said they'd heard the dead playing musical instruments and singing. They said . . . deep inside the ancient forest, the ageless trees whispered along with a song that merged into harmony with an ethereal guitar, singing, *O victorious years and months, O endless suffering and pain.*[12]

Other survivors have reported similar encounters. Among Greek inmates of Nazi concentration camps, during and after liberation, forced laborers reported, "I see the dead in the pit loading stones on their backs." Others reported that "ghosts went around at night. The sick heard laments from the dead."[13]

In the folk beliefs of peoples against whom we wage war, we may discover that we damage, not only their people, military, culture, and political systems, but their very souls and the spiritual lives of their communities. For example, we may justify incursions into another people's cemeteries as a military necessity. But Native Americans, Muslims, and Buddhists perceive such an act as a profound travesty or desecration. Religious frenzy against our attacks is sometimes the spiritual zeal of a people to protect beloved souls from destruction by our weaponry and ignorance.

The Vietnamese call their wandering souls *co hon*. They know that many dead will never be recovered, but their souls must be helped to cross over to the spirit world and continue their cycles of incarnation. Once a family accepts that their missing loved one is dead and will not be found, they build a *ma gio*, a windy tomb. A windy tomb is an empty tomb built just like others and set in the family burial plot for the soul whose body is missing. In Viet Nam the fifteenth day of the seventh month is a national holiday, the Day of Wandering Souls, on which families tend their windy tombs, praying for their own and all lost souls, setting out food for them, helping them find their ways through the cycles of reincarnation. Southern air force veteran Tran Dinh Song explains:

My uncle was VC. His son was in the southern army. Father and son fought against each other for north or south, just like in your Civil War. My uncle was buried alive when an American tank crushed his tunnel. My cousin was buried in a mass grave. My family searched for many years but could never find them. We finally built windy tombs for my relatives so that father and son could rest together again in peace. Our entire family gathers together to visit the tombs, bring them rice porridge and cookies, and talk to their souls every year.

As foreign as these customs may sound, they could nevertheless hold something of great usefulness to us. All of them acknowledge the palpable reality of the soul in ways our own culture as a whole does not. As the experience of many disturbed veterans shows, we ignore this reality at our peril.

Given the technological brutality of modern war, the pragmatic perspective is that we would naturally have a significant number of people missing in action. Is it possible that America's long-standing national anguish over this issue and other war losses unites us with our former enemies? Is it possible that we Americans sense, as traditional cultures teach, that the souls of the missing and the violently slain are not at peace, and that they cannot be at peace until we recover their bodies, names, and stories and propitiate their souls? Our anguish corresponds with ancient religious as well as contemporary beliefs that rituals, sacrifices, and offerings are necessary to aid the souls of the dead. In ancient Greece, too, souls were trapped on earth if not given proper funerals. In Sophocles' tragedy, *Antigone*, against the rule of the state and at the cost of her life Antigone buried her brother after he had been killed in a rebellion. The prophet Teiresias lectured the king against punishing her and refusing the enemy dead proper burial:

You have . . . bitterly dishonored
a living soul by lodging her in the grave;
while one that belonged indeed to the underworld
gods you have kept on this earth without due share
of rites of burial, of due funeral offerings,
a corpse unhallowed. . . .[14]

And in modern Korea, we hear: "Restless spirits abide . . .
in a landscape not found on any map. In old Buddhist lore
it's a place called 'Nine Springs,' *Kuchun* in Korean. The souls
of those who died unjust deaths wander there in search of
peace, crying for the injustice, the *han*, to be set aright."[15]

Vietnam War vet Bob Cagle had been haunted for thirty-six
years by nightmares of a fourteen-year-old Viet Cong soldier
he had killed in a nighttime firefight. He sometimes saw the
boy dead, sometimes walking toward him as a ghost, or well
and playing, or the boy's family searching for him. He relived
the firefight in the terrifying jungle night over and over again,
as he tells us in his poem "Here and There":

I had a dream, again tonight.
God was there and I was here.
My voice cried out to him,
Vexed with terror.
He was there. . . .
Praying for peace inside and out.
Trying to feel His presence,
A need for cleansing.
He was there.
Standing over dead VC
Counting holes.

Oh, how the lead pierced,
Slowly turning red . . . Dead and dead.
He was there.
I'm still here.[16]

Upon his first return journey to Viet Nam in 2001, Bob plunged into a disturbed trance by the sound of AK-47s firing on a target range at Cu Chi. Then, as our bus rolled through long green stretches of rice fields, he saw ghosts of dozens of war dead, Americans and Vietnamese, slogging through flooded paddies toward him. Finally emerging from among them, he saw the boy he killed. When we disembarked at a Cao Dai temple, Bob started to cry. That moment, when he was flooded with old and enduring grief and pain, was the first since the war that he had felt his own soul returning to him. By filling with pain, he could begin to refill with soul.

We had much more work to do to repair Bob's connections to his dead—the lives he lost and the lives he took—as we will see later. Here, what is important to note is that it was when he accepted the haunting presence of the dead as real visits by lost souls that he began to find a sacred philosophy that could guide his own soul in its recovery. Like Odysseus, he could then return from the battlefields and far shores of death. The stories of both men—the real and the mythic—hold a crucial truth for many of our suffering veterans and survivors today.

Nine

THE SOUL OF THE NATION

P lato taught in *The Republic* that the qualities in each of us will be evident in our state and that what is harmonious and healthy in any nation will be true of its citizenry. Conversely, what is destructive in a nation will be similarly expressed by its people. War in this way affects everyone and everything. It not only disorders our individual psyches, it also rearranges our collective guideposts and cracks our social containers. Our senses of unity, morality, values, roles and responsibilities, and codes of conduct are all distorted according to its dictates, along with our allocation of resources. By encouraging the expression of the instinctual, bestial, and cruel dimensions of a people, war evokes the cultural shadow, revealing both the best and the worst in a society and in its citizens as well.

We have seen that the normative functioning of individuals with PTSD is disordered because they have been *re*ordered according to war's terrible necessities and then abandoned in the transformation. If citizens mirror the condition of the society itself, what, then, do the prevalence of PTSD and our response to it say about our nation? One clue is the countless broken warriors littering our landscape.

I walk through Times Square in New York City. A scruffy man sits against a building. His dirty gray beard and curls fall in tangles from under his stained camouflage hat. A cardboard sign leans against his knees. A torn paper cup is his beggar's bowl. I sit by his side and read his hand-lettered travelogue aloud to invite conversation: "Dak To? An Khe? Kontoum?" The man describes them to me. His battles, firefights, and dates all check out. His is not one of the invented histories. "I haven't had a home since I left my Central Highlands hooch," he says, pointing to his sign, wistful for the days when he knew where he belonged and who was on his side.

As a guest on a Veterans Day radio talk show, I speak about the prevalence of homelessness and PTSD among Vietnam War veterans, about the unrelieved moral pain many carry to their graves. Ben, a World War II vet, calls in. Though sobbing, he forces himself to speak. "What about us?" he howls over the airwaves. "What about me? It wasn't better in World War II. Just because history calls it 'the good war,' don't believe it. It always hurts to kill. I want some peace before I die. Please, someone out there help me."

A few days later, I drive into the Catskill Mountains to a crossroads hamlet. I turn up a back road until I find a ramshackle motel that rents rooms for near-vagrants and wastrels. Ben invites me into his tiny room. It is jammed full of books, ragged clothes, pots and pans, World War II memorabilia. He pours me a glass of orange juice and we toast. "Thank you for coming," he says in a voice burdened with sorrow. "I can't believe you came to see me after what I said on the radio. Usually people run the other way when I talk like that." His eyes water. "I tried working. I tried marriage. But everything I touched was ruined. It all began with World War II. That war taught me that I'm a killer. Since then, places like this miserable room have been my only home. Is there any chance for me to find peace and forgiveness before I die?"

Homelessness is not just an individual pathology, not merely the failure of the single person to cope with the demands of adulthood. Estimates are that, a decade ago, 271,000 of our country's 26.4 million veterans were homeless on any given night, 55–60 percent of whom served during the Vietnam War era.[1]

We can say that the hundreds of thousands of those veterans have been psychospiritual casualties of war.

War can also alter the life course and render "homeless" those who choose to protest it rather than fight. Bud Mahoney is a lawyer who worked in the antiwar movement during the sixties. He passionately believed in American devotion to justice and in its system of checks and balances to keep power from running amok. Rather than seeking affluence through a law practice, he gave decades of legal service to political and social justice causes. He never owned a home or the other accoutrements of American success. Now in his sixties, Bud's face droops with exhaustion and disillusionment. "It's no accident," he says wistfully, "that I haven't had a place to call home since Nixon was elected. I've lived on the road ever since."

Our culture heard the pain of Vietnam War veterans from the time they first returned from Southeast Asia. Alienation, nightmares, flashbacks, violent behavior, drug and alcohol abuse, intimacy and employment problems, throwing medals at the Pentagon, refusing to vote or pay taxes—all began before the war was even over. *Home from the War*, Robert Jay Lifton's seminal psychohistorical work exposing veterans' suffering, appeared as the bombs were still falling. The massive protests and demonstrations staged at home indicated not just veterans' pain but overwhelming generational anguish and doubt. No matter what one's opinion about the correctness of the war, not to have adequately addressed our veterans' pain has amounted to denial on a national scale. Jon Haker, a tank corps veteran, said, "The main lesson I learned in Viet Nam is that Denial is the name of the all-American disease."

We see reports of similar pain and the denial of it emerging from the troops in the present Iraq War. Eileen Mathena, a career navy officer just back from war zone service says,

> I didn't come away unscathed, as few do, and am visiting the VA on a regular basis to resolve some issues: a back injury, nodules on all the joints of both hands, more insomnia and PTSD from harassment from a stalker disguised as a trusty commander, and guilt for having left everyone behind, including my best friend.... Many others follow me with injuries to lungs. Three of my fellow sailors are on their way home right now, but those who are most valuable to the unit are being made to stay.... I avoid the news from my unit because each day it gets worse. A really nice guy suffered a breakdown.... He has only been in the reserve a few years, and his wife and children weren't handling the separation well. The worrying and lack of empathy from the command—and their not getting him the help he needed—sent him over the edge.

What are we denying about our war making? We deny our own complex human nature, including our capacities for greed, evil, and doing harm, clinging instead to the belief in our own innocence and goodness. We deny the true destructive nature of modern warfare in order to cling to its mythic foundations. And we deny that war changes its participants forever, promoting instead the belief that PTSD can be repaired and that vets and survivors can resume an ordinary civilian identity.

War in its traditional role as a rite of passage may have taught participants that existence is short and fragile, that its challenges must be met with courage, and that lives truly depend upon one another. As a mythic arena, war can teach that every life is a story that matters and must be redeemed through witness, restitution, and service. We can learn that we are servants of both creation and destruction and so must act with wisdom, restraint, and compassion. These lessons, however, are difficult to embrace even under the most generous conditions. They are rendered virtually invisible by the denial in American culture and the common interpretation of PTSD.

America claims innocence and goodness as fundamental traits. We believe that our young men and women should be able to go to war, get the job done, and return home blameless and well. That is how the quintessential American hero, John Wayne, portrayed the experience of warfare to generations. Many Vietnam War veterans referred to him as a guiding image: "I was seduced by World War II and John Wayne movies."[2]

Popular culture helps condition our innocence. In our modern information age and technological society, the media replaces elders as the transmitter of myths of war and warriorhood. I had the following conversation with a twenty-four-year-old man:

"I'd be just like the hero of Tom Cruise's movie *Top Gun*," he declared. "I can handle it—war, combat, anything to get the job done."

"Even killing?" I asked.

"Anything! Killing is just a job. It wouldn't bother me!"

"And being wounded or killed yourself?"

"Ain't gonna happen! Just give me a cool weapon like Cruise had. That would protect me," he declared.

Movie-conditioned innocence occurs even in the combat zone. On his new base camp one night shortly after his arrival in Viet Nam, Preston Stern watched Yul Brynner in *The Magnificent Seven* shoot down evil banditos. Even though Preston was against the war, he declared at the time, "Now I know why I'm here and what our government wants me to do."

Ironically, John Wayne himself successfully avoided conscription during World War II and never served in or experienced war. Yet through public performances of how he, and we, wished war to be, he established himself as the model for American GIs. In contrast, actor Jimmy Stewart, who did serve, said, "When I got back from the war in 1945, I refused to make war pictures." [3]

American servicemen home from World War II were portrayed as returning with no pain. The supposed minority of psychological casualties was hidden in the back wards of veterans' hospitals. One of my parents' childhood friends returned home after completing twenty-five combat missions in Flying Fortresses over Europe. He died in a motorcycle accident within a week. "Everyone suspected suicide," my mother said, "but in those days we didn't talk about it." Millions of people—indeed, our entire society—seemed happy that the great adventure was over. America was proud of its participation in the world-wide battle against evil and moved on to the good life as defined by consumerism.

Yet loss of innocence is inevitable — even in "good wars." It is a necessary component of initiation and identity transformation. The end of innocence can be enlightening or damaging, depending on the context. War is unquestionably devastating to identity transformation if it destroys one's ability to participate in the culture's mystique of goodness and its forward propulsion at war's end. Once you know the truth, you can no longer believe in the fiction.

One World War II participant confessed: "We had become accustomed to horror; it was the character of our lives now; and the railing against [it] seemed to us as futile as railing against the nature of things. . . . But [for one who] would never put up with it . . . there was that in him which would ever regard the war and the civilization from which it arose as a stupendous abomination."[4]

Writer and social critic Paul Fussell, who survived World War II combat, experienced war as evil and confessed to displacement both upon going off to war and returning. He reported about his return, "I was being hauled bodily into a world where the idea of evil would be unthinkable." America was a civilization that "lacked . . . a sense of evil and of infinite human complexity. . . . [It was] mired . . . [in] optimism."[5]

As bad as World War II combat was, participation in it had, and still retains, an aura of heroism. It was a necessary war for a good cause. We popularly refer to veterans and other era survivors, after Tom Brokaw's book, as "the greatest generation."

The Vietnam War experience, by comparison, stripped away the American presumption of innocence for countless American military personnel and citizens. Frank Houde, an air force squadron commander, realized, "We were the bad guys," as he watched us napalm virginal mountains along the Laotian border. Walt realized the same as he exhumed and relocated bodies of enemy dead. Forward artillery observer Conrad Silke saw in a Zen-like flash, during a skirmish with Viet Cong soldiers who had thrown themselves against his emplacement, that "these people we called enemies were human beings, too." After the firefight, he stooped over the body of a Viet Cong man he had just killed. He took out the dead man's wallet and contemplated the tiny black and white photos of his young wife and children awaiting his return. Conrad cried, "That moment defined my life. Right then and there, I realized that these gooks I had been taught to hate and fear were the good guys and I was the bad guy. Why? They had something they were willing to die for. They were willing to sacrifice their lives to protect their country, homes, and those they loved. All I cared about was getting home in one piece, even if I had to kill them to do it."

Steve Trimm, who resisted the war and was in exile in Canada, testifies to a devastating loss of innocence that began with Viet Nam but has become a chronic grief:

> I include the Iraq War among my "war experiences," and every other war since the close of hostilities in Viet Nam. I was such an innocent; I really believed Viet Nam would give war a bad name. . . . A heavy heart is the heaviest burden to carry. Millions died during the Depression. They never saw the barren days get better. Millions died before World War II ended. They died in despair, not believing the darkness would pass. I never imagined I might die during such a bleak period, but now I know it's possible. It feels like my heart will be heavy from now 'til the end of my days.

As a culture, we claim innocence, as though we Americans are immune to the unavoidable truths war teaches about pain and suffering. While we accuse Muslim extremists of fundamentalist terror in the name of their God, we believe and behave as if we ourselves are doing God's work when we destroy other peoples. But they feel the same. "God destroy their houses!" an Iraqi woman shrieked in front of the wreck of her home Americans had destroyed.[6] While we use advanced weaponry against civilians as well as soldiers, we condemn others for fighting back with their own primitive methods.

Europeans took North America from its original inhabitants by violence and terror. As people do in every culture, they operated out of a complex and inherited mythology. The conquerors believed they were chosen by God to create a new Eden in a new world; its resources were theirs for the taking because of their "superiority."

George Santayana notably said, "Those who do not remember the past are condemned to repeat it." But to escape history demands more than study. The psychoanalyst Theodore Reik observes that repetition compulsion—the unconscious and obsessive drive to repeat our traumas—operates in nations as well as individuals. As the United States, we have been repeating our birth drama of violent conquest under the shield of God ever since we first founded this nation on new-world soil. We claim that our conquest of others—whole societies, their land, their political systems—is our manifest destiny and "for their own good."

All our modern wars have been conducted within this mythological framework. In the war against Hitler, our civilization embraced the moral duty to stop Fascism. The point is not that it was wrong to stop Hitler. Rather, it is that we don't know how to imagine solutions outside the paradigm of war. Gandhi wrote about nonviolent resistance to Hitler, for instance, yet those who objected to violence as a political solution during World War II were treated as criminals and imprisoned.[7]

Later, we believed we were right in using our military to fight the spread of Communism. We justify small wars (El Salvador, Panama, Grenada, Lebanon), undercover subterfuge and assassinations (Chile, Cambodia, Angola, Sudan, Nigeria, Zambia), and political actions that punish and cause suffering (the boycotts of Nicaragua, Cuba, and Iraq) with the same mythic arguments. It is the same with the war against terrorism today. We are always the good guys, while evil is outside us in other people and their systems.

Not the reports of atrocities in Viet Nam or Iraq; not the stalemates, inconclusiveness, losses, or shifting political tides following modern wars; not the pain, anger, and dysfunctionality of returning veterans have taught us to examine our culpability. Many soldiers' most devastating lesson is the discovery that we are *not*, after all, the good cavalry led by John Wayne to save the helpless settlers from savages; nor are we the blessed crusaders slaying the turbaned barbarians from Evil Empires. Instead, what soldiers often discover is that those we are trying to save see *us* as the savage invaders, needing to be stopped by their own painful, heroic sacrifices. When women and children are willing to die to stop us, and we cannot distinguish between enemies and civilians because an entire population resists us, then our soldiers' belief in our goodness cracks—and so does their spirit.

Anna, a young U.S. marine, grew up with a fascination for guns and for playing war. After basic training, she proudly demonstrated her proficiency with machine guns to her family. Then Anna was shipped to Iraq, where her job was to collect dead and wounded children. What was worse, she herself had to aim her beloved gun at children, because they were aiming their guns at her. Home at the end of her tour of duty, Anna didn't want to play war anymore. She despised the guns she had loved. She stood in line with other returned soldiers and fought with officials to receive more than a few hours of therapy for her depression. Then the Marines extended her commitment beyond her completed four-year term. She tried to join the Coast Guard to avoid returning to the war zone, but was told she was already trained for duty in Iraq; the Marines couldn't spare her. As she was being redeployed, Anna said farewell to her family, declaring she had a feeling she wouldn't survive this second tour. Perhaps she didn't want to.

Another returnee from Iraq, the sailor Eileen Mathena, reports that her front line friends referred to their officers as the "Morale Suppression Team." She and Anna speak for all American soldiers who have reached a breaking point of despair, revealing in microcosm the widespread moral deterioration of the army, the nation, and the cause.

Recall, also, the marine who found and lost his soul while watching his comrades burn village huts and fought the urge to turn his gun on his squad. About turning a gun against one's own troops, Norman Mailer observed in World War II: "The time soldiers start doing that is when an army is about to be defeated."[8]

It is possible to resist dehumanization of the enemy even in the midst of what appears to be a life-threatening situation. Howard was on a mission with his squad in territory heavily infiltrated with Viet Cong. They had been out for four days searching villages but had found neither enemy suspects nor arms or supply caches. Now they were on their way back to their base camp.

They came to their last tiny village. Howard and his men questioned and searched the villagers with their M-16s at the ready. Once again they found nothing suspicious and left relieved.

Only a few kilometers were left before they would be back at their rendezvous point where evacuation choppers would pick them up. They were coming back together, alive and unwounded. The troops relaxed as they filed through the jungle, letting their weapons dangle loosely at their sides.

The squad filed into a small sunny clearing. Suddenly, a squad of Viet Cong in their black pajama uniforms broke through the tree line opposite them. They, too, had thought they were alone and carried their weapons in a loose, casual way.

The two squads froze. Men from each side pointed their guns. Nobody fired. Howard stared into the eyes of men he had been seeking to kill. Small, intense, dark eyes stared back at him. A few inches at a time, Howard and his squad stepped toward the enemy. Only yards apart, he saw that they, too, were young and nervous. His fist tightened around his weapon.

Then one of Howard's companions raised his gun, pointing its muzzle not at the enemy but up in the air, toward the trees. In response, a Viet Cong did the same. A second grunt raised his gun. A second VC raised his, then a third. Howard slowly tilted his gun up, raising both arms until his gun and free hand were both in the air.

A few enemy soldiers smiled and nodded. Then the rest of his squad and the entire enemy squad did the same. Slowly, without turning their backs, the squads traded positions. The trails were now open for Howard's squad to return to their base and for the Viet Cong to continue their trek. The squads walked to the edges of the clearing and disappeared from each other's views.

During such events, the hatred and fear that blinds a soldier dissipates. The other becomes human again, no longer a thing or an enemy. The soldier joins him in their common humanity and in the process restores his own integrity. Although such restoration can occur during warfare, it rarely does. Usually, it must happen during healing.

The cloud of despair and the moral stain that settled over America after the Vietnam War has remained with us ever since, like a national soul sickness of which the tens of thousands of anguished veterans were the most apparent symptoms. Yet America still clung to its self-image of innocence and goodness. The first President Bush and his military leaders staged the Gulf War in part to overcome the stigma of our performance in Southeast Asia. The senior George Bush confided in his diaries and declared in public that he wanted a decisive outcome finally to "kick in totally the Vietnam syndrome."[9]

The public belief was that our national sickness of soul stemmed not from moral culpability but from losing the war. But now we have the mysterious Gulf War syndrome, by 1995 afflicting more than thirty thousand of the over six hundred thousand soldiers sent to the Gulf[10] and recognized by the Veterans Administration in 25 to 30 percent of vets.[11]

This syndrome ushers in another generation of veterans suffering a gestalt of body and soul sickness nobody can explain. Our strategy of reclaiming our innocence through another "good war" did not work, and our veterans again carry the stain. As one combat veteran blurted to me, "All the Gulf War proved was that we Americans don't like to lose."

Enemy territory is dubbed "Indian Country" in Iraq today, just as it was in Viet Nam. We can think of these wars as the frontier myth displaced to far lands among people as different from us as were Native Americans to the colonial settlers' European ancestors. Think of them as reenactments to a frenzied extreme, with "Kiowa Warrior" helicopters in place of cavalry horses and machine guns and with grenade launchers in place of sabers. This is how Americans fight when we have not integrated the wounds of our historical past but instead create yet another undifferentiated mythic arena in which "the only good Indian is a dead Indian."

John Wayne may have inspired the generation that fought in Viet Nam, but he never behaved in the movies the way we did in that war. An honest examination of our behavior demonstrates how the shadow—the dark, denied, unacceptable or sinister dimensions of our national character—may emerge during warfare.

In Viet Nam, "waste" was the code word soldiers used to indicate killing. To waste was to kill an enemy, whether combatant, civilian, or livestock. Soon to waste was to destroy a hut, a village, a rice paddy or jungle. In Viet Nam, we attempted to waste an entire people. Many people in the Muslim world today believe we are attempting a similar genocide against them.

"Waste them" referred not only to the Vietnamese. American minorities and the poor and rural populations filled our troops in numbers far beyond their proportions. The war occurred concurrently with the Civil Rights movement and heated up along with racial unrest at home. The military has always been one of the few ladders up and out of poverty and hopelessness. But during the Vietnam War, the way out was through absurdity and fire—which is never a way out. And when too much protest brought the injustices of the draft to light, it was answered with a lottery. Long after our leaders believed the war could not be won and much of the population declared it should not be, we still "wasted" our children.

"Waste them" also applied to the treatment of returning veterans. Being spit upon at airports instead of celebrated in homecoming parades were the surface signs.[12]

For decades, Agent Orange complaints were ridiculed.[13] Even as Agent Orange diseases and disabilities appear among the grandchildren of exposed U.S. veterans and Vietnamese, they are still underresearched, underfunded, and denied, and their cases are thrown out of court to this day. At VA hospitals, veterans complain about being dispensed drugs like candy and confined in body coffins during flashbacks. By the late 1980s, over sixty thousand veterans had committed suicide since returning from Viet Nam, more than were killed during the entire war;[14] by 1998, the number had topped one hundred thousand.[15]

The black wall of names that is the Vietnam Memorial in Washington would have to triple in length to accommodate these numbers.

Another example of our national shadow appears in "friendly fire"—the phenomenon of our soldiers killing their own. During the Gulf War, friendly fire was responsible for at least one-quarter (veterans say perhaps as many as half) of all coalition casualties.[16] Moreover, friendly fire deaths underscore persistent problems of modern war. David J. Morris, a marine veteran of the Gulf War, calls such deaths fratricide.

Stories of surviving friendly fire have been reported in every war since World War II. I worked with a spotter pilot almost shot down by our side and with a Gulf War veteran trapped in Khafji between opposing armies while both tried to destroy him because he was in the way of their fight. I counseled a marine who on orders assassinated an American colonel for black-marketeering and a grunt who helped shoot down his commanding officer's helicopter. Earlier, we heard of Isaac, who felt guilty of fratricide because he had been forced to order his Hispanic comrades to death in the Viet Cong tunnels. Here is another story:

Even though Preston Stern was against the war in Viet Nam, he volunteered for combat duty in order "to witness the defining event of my generation." During one patrol, his infantry squad bivouacked in a large shell crater, trusting that its high sides would protect them.

Preston volunteered for first watch. He climbed outside the crater and leaned against its earthen rim, facing the jungle. Suddenly, shells exploded overhead and from behind. Shrapnel flew over his head. One shell had fallen directly atop his sleeping squad.

Preston charged into the crater, now filled with cries, groans, curses, and silence. He radioed for help, patched up and carried his comrades to safety, and went searching for his sergeant, who was also his best friend. He found him lying still, a single shrapnel hole oozing red blood over his heart.

Not until the next morning did Preston realize that the shell that had wasted his comrades was one of our own, a long-distance bombardment that accidentally fell short. As he reported the incident to his commanders, the artillery officer in charge of the barrage joined the conference, shrugged, and said, "It don't mean nothin'." Preston "quit" and served five months in Long Binh Jail, and then another month in the field, before being shipped home.

All such events occurred in war zones during military operations, and their casualties were classified as combat deaths. Survivors felt outraged and mistrustful because they had become the targets of their own side. The cause is partly in the tremendous power of modern weaponry, which makes no distinction between one side and the other. Peter Minucci, on the destroyer USS *Rowan*, lived and worked in fear of who and what our big guns were actually destroying as they lobbed huge shells at targets many miles away.

But technology alone does not account for all friendly fire. Assassinating dangerous officers or causing the deaths of comrades are some of the inevitable distortions of character that can occur in any of us when immersed in unrelentingly brutal conditions. When the rule is "kill or be killed," we cannot emerge unscathed.

A third example of the release of our national shadow in war is, of course, atrocities. We must expose atrocities as soon as possible to curb troops from giving free rein to their primal impulses. The My Lai massacre in Viet Nam did not come to public attention until a full year had passed. Groundbreaking journalism revealed the No Gun Ri massacre during the Korean War only half a century after it occurred. Perhaps we can derive some small hope in that only months had passed before the disclosure of sadism by American troops against the Iraqi prisoners at Abu Ghraib. Most of the offenders in these modern massacres have been ordinary people, not sadists or psychopaths. What, we must ask, can drive people to such acts?

Robert Jay Lifton has coined the phrase, "atrocity-producing situation." When fear, threat, violence, loss, proximity to death, moral confusion, alienation, disbelief, immersion in horror, power and control over others, and sheer exhaustion coincide long enough—and when the enemy has been sufficiently dehumanized—we are in an atrocity-producing situation. Moreover, former vice president Al Gore observed that when we create a culture of immorality, abuse, and mistrust, we also create conditions in which usually decent people may descend into atrocity.[17]

Long ago, Sophocles demonstrated another atrocity-producing condition in his play *Ajax:* One of the great Greek warriors at Troy, Ajax was slighted before his army by not being awarded the dead hero Achilles' armor. In response, he went on a killing rampage. Thus Sophocles showed that honor can restrain even the fiercest of fighters from descending into the savage. When, to the contrary, honor is compromised, atrocities can result.

Torturing prisoners renders another human being an "it" of the lowest degree. The proud display of torture at Abu

Ghraib before comrades and in pictures demonstrates the complete breakdown of the GIs' moral integrity. If it is soul that enables us to distinguish our moral principles, we might say that the GIs who perpetrated the abuse at Abu Ghraib had become nearly soulless.

Only extraordinary people can resist the gravitational pull of an atrocity-producing situation. The single GI wounded at My Lai shot himself in the foot so that he could not participate in the slaughter. Other GIs had the character to report the My Lai and Iraqi atrocities. But many people succumb, acting out ugly dimensions of our human and cultural shadows. When nations behave as colonial powers, demeaning occupied people, atrocity is "not surprising . . . unexceptional," the inevitable extension of colonialism.[18] It was perpetrated by the Dutch in Indonesia, the Belgians in the Congo, the Japanese and Germans before and during World War II, the French in Indochina and Algeria, the Russians in Afghanistan, and the Americans against Native Americans and in Korea, Viet Nam, and now Iraq. Ironically, when soldiers do not believe that the killing they are asked to do is justified or that its cause is morally incontrovertible, atrocity is a likely result. "What you do, you become." Wars produce atrocity because soldiers steeped in horror will finally become that horror.

American leaders denied, justified, and rationalized the torture of the Iraqi prisoners, marginalizing and blaming individuals. Some expressed concern, not with the unjust suffering of the victims, but with our image before the world. President Bush claimed that these actions "do not represent the America that I know," and Donald Rumsfeld labeled them as "fundamentally un-American," something our people would not do. But our people *did* do them. Such rhetorical ploys demonize the ordinary servicemen and women who performed the deeds in order to shift blame away from the context in which they occurred and from any higher officials in charge.

In short, it is not true that the prison abuse was inconsistent with American values. Rather, it revealed our disguised colonialism, perhaps our soldiers' disillusionment about their participation in it, and certainly the numbing of their own higher moral functions. Many, perhaps all, of the perpetrators and victims will suffer for the rest of their lives.

These three consequences of modern war—wasting, friendly fire, and atrocities — exemplify aspects of the American shadow that can dominate during warfare. While we continue to insist before our citizenry and the world that we are good and innocent, dangerous aspects of our cultural psyche break through and are inevitably expressed through our soldiers. Wasting represents the extreme dimensions of consumerism and dehumanization; friendly fire, how far we will go to achieve our goals; and atrocities, how sadistic our soldiers can become in the morally confused environment we create in asking them to kill without clearly just cause.

Our veterans' terror is real. They come home stumbling out of hell. But we don't see them as they have become. Instead, we offer them beer and turkey dinners, debriefing and an occasional parade, and a return to routine jobs and weekends in the shopping malls. Because we as a nation are trapped in a consciousness that cannot acknowledge abject suffering, especially if we have caused or contributed to it, we do not see the reality of war. Meanwhile, survivors feel trapped in that apocalyptic reality and rarely try to explain it to people who will not understand.

The severity and extent to which veterans suffer with post-traumatic stress disorder is in direct response to our culture's blindness about war's true cost. PTSD is the expression of the anguish, dislocation, and rage of the self as it attempts to cope with its loss of innocence, reformulate a new personal identity and cultural role, and awaken from massive denial. Veterans with PTSD are people whose belief systems have been shattered. They no longer believe their nation and its values and actions are inherently good. These survivors often feel outcast because they no longer share the country's mythology. "I'm not an American," says Scott, a helicopter gunner who has never voted, paid taxes, or obtained a driver's license in the thirty-seven years since he returned from war. "I'm a citizen of the underground."

Overwhelming incidences of substance addiction plague our nation. Domestic violence and abuse are rampant. Marriages and families are rife with intimacy problems, and divorce occurs at an astronomical rate. Our society's criminality is excessive; we have the second largest rate of imprisonment of any developed country. We experience unstable employment patterns and high rates of unemployment. People by the millions suffer nightmares and sleep disorders. In the privacy of the home, in the workplace, and on our streets and roads, we encounter sudden fits of violence, rage, and dangerous acting out. Rape, incest, harassment, stalking, and other forms of sexual abuse are endemic. Our suicide rate is high. Many people from childhood to their senior years have conflicts with authority. We witness untrustworthiness and duplicity, including lying and graft, among public and private officials. We are bombarded with reports of betrayals and disloyalty on every social level. Our citizenry exhibits unprecedented levels of anxiety, depression, and stress-induced illnesses. All of these factors signify epidemic proportions of that cluster of symptoms we now call post-traumatic stress disorder.

Philosophers, sociologists, anthropologists, archaeologists, political scientists, and psychologists have taught us the importance of culture and society in shaping the individual. Recall Plato's teaching that the same qualities in each of us will be mirrored in the state. If he is correct, then PTSD may not be just of individuals. What if it is not merely and primarily a personal disorder? What if, instead, it is a *national* disorder that the individual carries? What if PTSD perpetuates the circumstance of lost souls imprisoned in their private terror while allowing the rest of us along with our leaders to perpetuate the public fantasy of our own innocence? We speak of the soul of a nation. Is PTSD our country's soul sickness?

Ten

WARRIOR OR SOLDIER, HERO OR WASTE?

Sam, an Iraq War veteran in his mid-twenties, awaited redeployment for a second combat tour. He wanted to return for three reasons: "Bragging rights, adventure, and to do some good." By bragging rights, Sam meant, "When people complain about struggling to pay their bills, I can laugh and say, 'Yeah, while I struggled to stay alive.' I've got the civilians beat," he observed. "But lots of guys are into their second tours; they're ahead of me." About adventure, he said, "I work for a funeral home. Nobody wants to hear about that. But war stories are something to tell!" And about doing good, "I don't want just to prove my stuff in the fight. I want to leave something behind, like helping rebuild people's schools— something to be proud of, something they'll appreciate."

This soldier wanted modern versions of counting coup, the right to wear "eagle feathers," and recognition as a brave warrior. He sought the same traits of character development, tribal membership, and universal meaning that men have always sought through war—excitement as an antidote to life's tedium, honor and meaning earned through moral behavior, and the experience of doing things beyond oneself. In short, Sam wanted initiation and transformation.

But does war work this way now? Bernard Herbert served as a marine in World War II. He enlisted in 1940, before the United States was attacked. Herbert survived a difficult depression-era childhood and was attracted to the Marine Corps for its discipline and promise of adventure. Early on, the marine was enthusiastic about service. One of the first short stories he wrote, about surviving a hurricane, seemed to embrace the newfound strength and pride he felt that he hoped would help him face adversity. It seemed as if he were maturing from character-forming experiences.

But then Bernard was on the front lines of the brutal island-to-island combat against the Japanese in the Pacific theatre of the war. He spent the rest of his life working like a marine as a street cop, in emotional turmoil at home, and squeezing the late hours to pursue his secret vocation as a writer. He stopped writing after publishing half a dozen stories—war and police adventures, conflicts over being Jewish, encounters with anti-Semitism, the struggle to live with integrity.

Bernard Herbert died in his mid-fifties. He left three children behind, including a son in his early teens. His character was a cauldron of explosiveness and frustration mixed with heroism and the ability to battle adversity. Did he experience initiation and transformation? Yes and no. It is an old story that repeats to this day.

War, as we have seen, has traditionally been a rite of passage through which an adolescent would be transformed into an adult. He would develop his character, face death, and learn how fragile life is. His culture would help heal and shape him into a mature warrior who, having been tested and proven, would take his place in society. Even now, we still yearn for the initiatory process war once offered. The long shadows cast by suicide bombings and the horrors of the modern battlefield have not extinguished our spiritual hunger for righteous service.

The marketing strategies used to attract young people into the military appeal to this yearning, as does our socio-political atmosphere, saturated as it is with the fear that an evil other lurks just out of sight, seeking to destroy us. Television and billboard advertising; nationwide military, historical, and cultural performances; and school visits by recruiters all display images of gallant warriors in colorful dress uniforms, carrying gleaming swords and utilizing the most advanced technology. In a direct appeal to our hunger for heroism, recruitment ads and video games portray these modern warriors as literally slaying medieval dragons and dragon-like machines. The American armed forces attempt to attract young people by offering them a path to fulfilling the mythic ideal of the warrior, the cultural hero whose service is blessed by the Divine and who makes the strife-ridden cosmos safe for his people. And our youth respond.

Whether it is Parris Island or a terrorist training compound, the goal of a boot camp is to prepare the uninitiated for war. To create a soldier, the mold of civilian identity must be broken. Training must overcome acculturation and restore the individual's access to the primitive bundle of instinctual impulses that can destroy without hesitation. Ideally, soldiers learn to discipline these impulses strictly, so that they are used only under orders and with particular direction—not wildly lashing out at everyone in sight, but making moral distinctions between friend and foe, combatant and civilian. The savage must be carefully controlled.

The combat that follows this training then provides the novices with an experience from which there is no return. The initiate is forged, through immersion in fire and blood, danger and threat, comradeship and fear, into something else.

Military personnel in noncombatant support services—and in modern wars there must be millions—also go through an initiatory change from civilian into soldier. But they participate at a lower level of engagement. Noncombatants do not earn the same "bragging rights" as combatants do; they are veterans without coup. Spared from facing the ultimate, they tend to devalue their service as inferior or unworthy. Yet they, too, have undergone the transformational process into the military. Even though theirs is a lesser degree of transformation, they, too, are veterans.

"The warrior is an instinctual energy form," says Robert Moore, "and it is here to stay."[1] As we have seen, the pattern and manifestation of war, warriors, and warfare are so universal that they must be a part of human inheritance. There is an archetypal warrior nascent in psyche and culture that always awaits awakening.

Think of Genghis Kahn, Alexander the Great, Shaka Zulu, Crazy Horse, General Patton. Each of these men was a flesh-and-blood embodiment of the universal warrior story. Each of their lives was such a complete replication that it stands forth as a myth.

Through the millennia, great people and small have played out the warrior story in their own lives. Together, these individual stories and our foundational myths about heroes point to an archetypal ideal that each of us, man and woman alike, is called to emulate. It unfolds through biological and cultural inheritance, education, experience, and effort.

But being an ideal, even in exemplary lives it develops only imperfectly. It usually does not dominate for the whole of life but is integrated as one important component of the greater personality.

Robert Moore calls the archetypes "basic building blocks of the psyche." He identifies four periods that both men and women pass through during archetypal development. In each period, one archetype dominates and needs maturing before leading into the next. The archetypes are the warrior, magician, lover, and king. The order of development for males is warrior-magician-lover-king. The order for females is lover-magician-warrior-queen. In both genders, those aspects of the psyche that most contribute to warriorhood control a particular period of development. Young men are prone to unfold the warrior archetype during late adolescence and as part of their transition into adulthood. It is no wonder that those who don't have military experience—though they may feel lucky, blessed, or clever for having avoided it—may also feel incomplete. Women are controlled by the lover archetype in that early stage, orienting them toward mating and motherhood. It is usually after the mothering years that the warrior awakens in the women's pattern.

What, then, are the characteristics of the warrior? The ideal warrior is assertive, active, and energized. He or she is clear-minded, strategic, and alert. A warrior uses both body and mind in harmony and cooperation. A warrior is disciplined. A warrior assesses both his own resources and skills and those arrayed against him. A warrior is a servant of civilization and its future, guiding, protecting, and passing on information and wisdom. A warrior is devoted to causes he judges to be more important and greater than himself or any personal relationships or gain. Having confronted death, a warrior knows how precious and fragile life is and does not abuse or profane it.

Each of these traits has shadow dimensions as well, which can emerge when the warrior is imbalanced, immature, inadequately trained, or traumatized. Shadow traits may include aggression, vengefulness, or cruelty. Instead of exercising discipline and control, the warrior may show wildness, emotional explosiveness, and impulsivity. He may be hypersexual and compulsive. At his shadowy worst, the warrior becomes masochistic or sadistic. We tend to associate soldiers with many of these traits because they are commonly unleashed during warfare. But they do not embody the ideal warrior of health, balance, and virtue; they embody only the berserk warrior.

The warrior archetype needs specific conditions to be realized successfully. Initiates need to experience a complete process from training through proving. The process begins early in the ways children inculcate warrior stories from their families and culture and play games replicating them. Later, through formal and informal means, elders guide young people in developing the skills and awareness of warriorhood. Initiates are tested in numerous ways. Their ultimate test traditionally comes in battle. If they survive, the test must be repeated as long as they are required or able to serve. Through that survival and successful service, they prove themselves worthy of being deemed one of their culture's warriors.

The proper training of a warrior must be not just the physical and intellectual dimensions of military performance but also the values and traditions of warriorhood. This education must be achieved in an environment that fosters dignity and honor. In addition, guidance must be highly personal. The initiate must feel that his or her survival matters to concerned elders and that the transformation he or she is undergoing is critical to the culture's preservation.

A warrior knows what he is fighting to preserve. Like a bull buffalo flanking his herd to protect it from predators, a warrior knows he is essential to his people's survival. He knows he belongs. He receives honor and blessing from his community for the service he willingly provides, and he in turn blesses his community with his devotion and willingness to sacrifice his life, if necessary, for its well-being.

Moreover, warriorhood must be directed toward transcendent goals. It must be based upon universal principles and connected to divine and honorable powers and purposes. Sitting Bull sang:

> Young men, help me, do help me!
> I love my country so;
> That is why I am fighting.[2]

Sitting Bull and his warriors, or other bands from innumerable traditional cultures, were never plagued with self-doubt about the value of their mission, as many of our soldiers are today. In order to do battle with a whole heart, the danger and threat to one's home must be real, and the people must experience it as immediate and about to threaten their existence as a whole. They and their warriors must be in unity. Their cause and need to fight must be absolute—in the sense that there is really nothing else they can do to preserve their food, families, and culture. When, to the contrary, wars are based on false pretenses, a moral vacuum results. As Martin Luther King Jr. observed, troops then experience "not simply the brutalizing process that goes on in any war," but also "cynicism to the process of death, for our troops must know after a short time that none of the things we are fighting for are really involved."[3]

Testing and proving are stained when the required acts of destruction are aimed at innocent people. Larry, an artillery officer who survived hand-to-hand combat, said he felt great respect toward enemy combatants he had slain, and no guilt. He *was* tortured, however, by the knowledge that, under his command, artillery had destroyed innocent villages. The soul knows the difference between firing upon armed combatants who are firing at you and firing upon unarmed civilians and their homes. As terrible as the kill-or-be-killed situation is, when someone is trying to kill you, your violent response is in part self-defensive and so perhaps honorable and less traumatizing. Larry was an officer who had schooled himself in the history and mythology of warriorhood. He believed that a fair fight was defined as armed combatants facing each other, and that even if a cause was suspect, fairness and equality between warriors wiped away much culpability. In contrast, when huge armies are arrayed for conquest, imposed social or political changes, attrition, or terror, then killing can become random and transform into murder.[4]

Ideally, the testing and proving of a warrior is limited in its destructiveness. Rites of passage often present the possibility of death, and in some cultures they are not considered complete until the initiate takes another life. But not *numbers* of lives, and never slaughter or the destruction of an entire people. Threats and losses must not be arbitrary, impersonal, or overwhelming.

For the warrior's experience to be transformative, it must also be indicative of personal valor. But in contrast to the time when personal courage and strength made all the difference, in modern combat the best soldiers are often injured or killed. Behaving according to archaic principles of warriorhood in the face of high-speed weapons technology makes warriors more vulnerable instead of more heroic. Once a man who raced across a battlefield might become a hero by successfully dodging spears or arrows. Today, the same act would likely get him slaughtered in a storm of fire. And when skill, intelligence, and nobility do not count, then nothing is proven by survival. I have worked with veterans who rejected their Purple Hearts because the cause for which they received it was morally suspect. I have worked with others who rejected it because their injuries came about through randomness or accident and so the honor felt unearned. On the modern battlefield, "The cowards are wounded as readily as the brave. Shell fragments don't care about the current moral status of the men they penetrate."[5]

Warriors are meant to play major roles in the lives of their communities, providing help in times of need and restraining rather than encouraging violence. They need guidance from others who have been through similar experiences, and they need to pass their values, wisdom, and experiences on to younger initiates. Ideally, during all phases of service, warriors interact with their people rather than remain separate from them. This is not the case in modern society. After soldiers are utilized for political and military purposes, they are called veterans. Other than receiving certain assistance, benefits, and occasional public ceremony, they are expected to return to civilian life and function accordingly. "Warrior" is not even a recognized social class; and a veteran, especially one with disabilities, appears to many as a failure in terms of normal civilian identity. In training and combat, soldiers are taught to release primal destructive impulses when threatened or ordered. Later, under stress, they are prone to resort to their old training. Veterans sometimes easily explode, attack, and strike out; what was normal during warfare becomes criminal or dysfunctional in peacetime. Veterans receive little help or compassion for these challenges

181

and have no socially useful roles into which to channel these tendencies.[6]

Parades and mass thanksgiving rituals are not enough to welcome a warrior class home. Warriors need elaborate rituals cleansing them of pain and stain. They need to express their stories and related feelings. They need to transfer responsibility for their violent actions to the society in whose name they acted. Whenever the warrior class is denied such ritual cleansing and storytelling, the war stays "locked in our heads," as many vets testify. The truth about war and the noble or pained experiences of our warriors then do not become part of our culture's mythic history. If, instead, we substitute the offerings of politicians and the media, if the veterans are blamed for their actions rather than viewed as a society's representatives, then they carry the moral and spiritual stain of their destructive actions alone, with crippling consequences.

Though young people in the military may hunger to become warriors, in most cases they become soldiers instead. Warrior and soldier are different roles, different archetypes. The role of soldier may be the modern remnant of the warrior archetype, in that it is mass produced, wired with technology, and given no honest sense of transcendent purpose or lifelong usefulness. Today's initiates do not have the two years of military training that ancient Athens required of its youth before entering danger. And they certainly do not have the lifetime of preparation required by such warrior cultures as the Native American or ancient Spartan, or the specialized training in body, mind, spirit, and art required of spiritual warrior classes such as the samurai. Rather, today's recruits are trained quickly and efficiently to behave as part of a mass machine of destruction. Their purpose is to serve as a functional part of this machine and to survive if they can. Compared with the individualized headdresses, shields, war paint, and spiritual totems of traditional warriors, the uniforms worn by soldiers today are usually just that—*uniform* so that individuals are hardly distinguishable from the group. The depersonalization makes it easier to behave as a mass unit, easier to kill, and easier to order or lose your subordinates to killing.

Nor are soldiers able to fulfill the role of honorable, returned warrior when they leave service. For instance, Doug was a military policeman who survived the Tet offensive. "My government spent over $50,000 and many months to train me for Viet Nam," he commented, "but not a penny or a day to help me come home. How was I supposed to act civilized after being trained to beat and brutalize and then use that training against other Americans? After having watched my buddies get blown away? It takes a lot more time, effort, and money to recover from that than it does to turn a man into a beast who can behave like I did. That's why I never had kids. I can't trust myself."

As Vietnam War intelligence officer Ed Murphy, who has since been a tireless veterans' advocate and worked to reconcile the two former enemies, declares simply, "*Warrior* and *veteran* are not synonymous." Unexpressed moral and spiritual conflicts as well as physical handicaps ensuing from the battlefield can all render veterans "disabled." Shame and guilt accumulate in place of nobility, dignity, and pride. Dishonor itself can engender disability. Too often our veterans hide from the *polis* rather than appear before it as first citizens. They often feel rage toward our government rather than loyalty, trust, and devotion. They have lost their innocence but have not replaced it with wisdom; nor are they regarded as elders. They may cling to patriotic or religious platitudes for support rather than experience the loss of meaning that haunts them. And if they have the courage to face this loss, they confront a terrifying and painful social, moral, and ontological chasm.

In the context of modern warfare, the mythic warrior identity is betrayed. It is replaced with the anonymous soldier, the disabled veteran, or the military bureaucrat who walks the halls of the Pentagon. The person who once dreamed of warriorhood, of serving as cultural hero, discovers that he or she is, after all, only "the God-damned infantry"—or worse, "waste."

We now have legions of veterans, both anonymous and disabled. We have legions of uninitiated men who feel "something missing." We have mistrustful men and women abandoning the operations of our society and feeling alienated from the state. Countless youth ache for guidance and initiation from elders, but few elders are mature and devoted enough to provide it. The ways we make war and the ways we fail to initiate our youth before, during, and upon return from service are significant contributors to this condition.

We need mature men and women who can help stitch together those dimensions of the commonweal that are unraveling. We need wise and strong guides who are devoted to the coming generations, to the good beyond themselves, and to giving all they can to nurture the people in their sphere and the best values of civilization.

One way to create mature elders is to restore the warrior archetype in its fullness and wisdom. We can do this by changing the ways we rear, teach, and train young men, and now women, in their conception of the warrior. We can do it by completing the warrior's education and initiation before and during service. And we can do it by restoring a complete initiation of the soul and healing efforts for our homecoming veterans. We can learn from an amalgamation of traditional wisdom and practices coupled with the insights of modern depth psychology and the social sciences. Traditional wisdom can teach us about the ideal warrior, that role in culture, and the longing we feel for that identity. Modern psychology can teach us how to integrate warrior traditions into our conceptions of self and society and help us update traditional practices to useable contemporary theories and practices. Long ago, Lao Tzu taught, "Stay with the ancient. Move with the present." This is the proper remedy regarding warriorhood by which we can heal our veterans and complete what is missing in our psyches and our civilization.

Let my spear lie idle for spiders to weave

   their web around it.

May I live in peace in white old age.

May I sing with garlands around my white head,

Having hung up my shield on the pillared house

   of the goddess.

May I unfold the voice of books,

   which the wise honor.

—EURIPIDES,
Erechtheus

Part III

THE
LONG
ROAD
HOME

Eleven

THE SOUL'S
HOMEWARD JOURNEY

Bill Ridley is a tall, broad African-American combat veteran from rural Georgia. He wears his hair plaited in neat parallel rows. "African warrior's braids," he explains.

It is the second morning back in Viet Nam for a group of veterans and civilians I am leading on a reconciliation journey. We are eating breakfast in our hotel in Ho Chi Minh City, the old Saigon. Bill bursts into the restaurant, throws his arms open wide, and shouts, "I did it!"

We look up from our plates of sliced mango and dragon fruit and our bowls of steaming *pho*—Vietnamese noodle soup.

"I slept a full night. Six uninterrupted hours. It's the longest I've slept in thirty-five years. And I didn't have a single nightmare. This hasn't happened since the war."

During the Vietnam War, Bill was an army ranger patrolling the Central Highlands and coastal plains. He was in the battle that destroyed much of the old imperial city of Hue. His patrol also reconnoitered the hamlet of My Lai, where the villagers welcomed him and his comrades and fed them rice. His squad reported a safe, friendly village to their superiors. Three days later, Lt. Calley led the massacre there.

Because of late flight connections, Bill had arrived in Ho Chi Minh City after the rest of our group. He found himself alone in a large crowd of Asian travelers. For months, I had helped him prepare for this return to the country where he had fought. He knew that customs officers would be wearing the same uniforms the North Vietnamese Army regulars wore during the war. He understood that this was 2002 rather than 1967. Nevertheless, he trembled when a guard singled him out from the crowd and called him forward. "I knew they'd been waitin' for me all these years," he said. "It was time to get my comeuppance."

He stepped through the crowd and stood before the officer. He looked for weapons but didn't see any. His mind flashed through scenes of imprisonment, torture, execution.

"How long has it been since you've been here?" the guard asked.

I'm tall and black in a sea of Asian faces, Bill thought. It's obvious. They know. "Thirty-five years," he gulped.

"In that case," the man smiled, "you have a lot of catching up to do. Let me be the first to welcome you back. You are our honored guest." Then the Vietnamese officer escorted the dazed American veteran through passport control and out to the street.

I met Bill outside the airport. This incident was our first topic of conversation. "I've been afraid for months," Bill said during the taxi ride to our hotel. "You told me I'd be welcomed back, but with the war in my head, I couldn't believe it. Now I see that the Vietnamese are friendly and welcoming and that the fear I have is about things that live only inside me. I'm going to have to sort out this confusing new information."

At our hotel, I sat up listening to Bill's stories until the wee hours. Finally, he encouraged me to go to bed: "Doc, I was in Recon. I don't sleep. I always have one eye open and catnap the other for an hour at a time. I trained myself to it in the bush. But you've got to lead our group. Get some rest. I'll be okay."

The next day, we visited the old Presidential Palace. Bill stood before the Russian T-54 tank famous for busting through the palace gates on April 30, 1975, bringing the long war to an end. Bill remembered fighting these tanks. "My commander insisted the Vietnamese didn't have any tanks until they rolled through our wire and sent us running," he said. This day I took his picture as he leaned on the "metal dragon," smiling and relaxed.

Our second night "in country," Bill went to his room early. The next morning he boomed his news.

"The VA hospital has given me dozens of different pills in every combination for sleep, nightmares, nerves, stress, depression, and every damned PTSD symptom you can name," he expounded at our breakfast table. "Tell me why none of it ever worked. Then tell me why it only took two nights back in this country to get my first full night's rest in thirty-five years!"

Bill slept peacefully and without a single nightmare every night of the three weeks we were in Viet Nam. By the middle of our journey, he was having good dreams. "Haven't had one since childhood," he said. "Since the war I've been so frightened of nightmares I never let myself sleep long enough to dream. Now the dreams are sweet. Now I can sleep."

Bill's return to Viet Nam occurred in 2002. He has slept peacefully and well since. Many of his other PTSD symptoms have disappeared as well. Bill is calmer and far less anxious, angry, and reactive. He gets along better with his family members and in his community. He has become more active in veterans issues and works hard to help other traumatized veterans. He strongly recommends that they, too, take their search for healing out of our hospitals and return to Viet Nam. Returning to the country one fought against is not necessarily a miracle cure, nor does everyone who returns experience the immediate relief Bill did. Yet this story and many others like it demonstrate that radical, successful, and long-lasting healing is possible.

When we understand PTSD as an identity disorder and a soul wound, we can begin to understand the ways to heal it. A veteran or survivor with PTSD can heal if he or she embraces the mythic dimensions of the war experience truly to develop the identity of spiritual warrior. A survivor must never profane war itself by denying its painful truths and terrible losses. Rather, a survivor who becomes a warrior accepts that he must serve these truths for the rest of his life. As Joseph Campbell's work teaches and I have written elsewhere, "Healing is the leap out of suffering and into myth."[1]

At first glance, we may assume that mythic terminology and concepts are antiquated in today's world. Yet the study of archetypes in traditional and modern cultures demonstrates that the mythic realm is real and active in us; and, as we have seen, the power of myth in war is very present. It is in the language and imagery the military uses to attract new recruits. It is what calls us to seek warriorhood, no matter how incompatible with the realities of modern war that role may be. Warriorhood as a psychospiritual identity and a social status, along with the rituals, ceremonies, values, and traditions associated with it, uniquely offers the means for a soldier's healthy return home after the war is over. Even in the modern world, survivors can walk the warrior's path.

We know that Homer, composing in the seventh century BCE, understood the importance of this return, in that he devotes his second epic, the *Odyssey*, entirely to Odysseus's ten-year homeward journey after the Trojan War. Though the *Odyssey* is literature, it provides, as Jonathan Shay demonstrates, a map for the human stories we find replicated in world traditions and real life.[2] During the war, Odysseus had lived for a decade in "a place of no beauty." Like modern veterans, he emerged from that experience stunned and lost. In order to find his way home, reconcile with his wife and son, and ultimately return to his throne, Odysseus had to become more than a soldier, more than the "master mariner and strategist" he had been in the *Iliad*. His homeward journey, which lasted another full decade, was rife with confusion, anguish, ordeals, loneliness, promiscuity, mistakes, harmful pride, and grief over lost companions. He was seduced and waylaid by goddesses and beasts, even as veterans are today by their sexuality and other primal energies. He struggled against belligerent creatures and enemies, sea storms, and whirlpools. He needed divine aid and expert interventions. Ultimately, Odysseus was told he could only find his way home by receiving instructions from Tiresias, the blind prophet who lives in the Underworld. Called Hades in Greek mythology, the Underworld is the shadowy realm where the insubstantial shades of the dead dwell forever.

Bill Ridley, as we have heard, experienced his own Odyssey in thirty-five years of ordeals. He had repeated difficulties with intimacy, community, and employment. He was in perpetual grief over lost comrades. He struggled against inner belligerence and experienced the outside world as full of threats. And he needed expert help and interventions to take his healing journey abroad and successfully bring it home. Bill's return to Southeast Asia was his own descent to the Underworld, in the sense that Viet Nam was where he had lost and taken lives during the war. The Vietnamese had remained enemies in his imagination until his unexpected welcome by the officer wearing the same uniform Bill had fought against. The officer's smile marked the beginning of Bill's return to a state of inner peace.

Almost no one wants to suffer. Veterans commonly use their defenses, some of them learned in war, to avoid feeling the pain of their condition. Their emotional volatility commonly overwhelms the facilitators who would help them, which may explain in part why many strategies counsel avoidance of painful memories. Yet war is such a profound immersion in death that revisiting it in memory is essential for the survivor to recover in heart and mind. Indeed, spiritual and mythic traditions teach that the path to healing must include this second descent to the Underworld. But this time, rather than in a life-threatening confrontation, the veteran can make the descent imaginally—that is, as an act of the imagination— and supported in community. Thus protected, the heart can feel what was forbidden to feel in the war zone and return to life again.

This imaginal return is a key factor in addressing PTSD appropriately as an identity disorder. In contrast to stress reduction strategies that counsel avoidance of disturbing memories, the healing cleansing of veterans can only occur when we relive memories and their accompanying feelings so that they may be expressed and relieved. Shrapnel must make its way to the surface and be removed; similarly, traumatic events need catharsis and witness.

Years after the combat is over, our souls may still wander in the horror of the war zone. It is critical for survivors to become aware that they are stuck there and that this state is "sane," as grunts said in the bush. To bring about healing, the condition must be embraced and ritualized, as traditional cultures teach. Once survivors see themselves as metaphorically being in the Underworld, they can realize that it is possible to return from it. Hence, they might be willing to make the effort and endure the pain it takes to complete the journey. Psychotherapy and other healing techniques must teach and model these dimensions. Training survivors to avoid stressors or to use medications to mask symptoms works in the opposite direction, leaving the mines buried in the soul rather than removing and defusing them.

Saying "yes" to the necessary second, imaginal descent is often the most difficult step a survivor must take. But it is an act that restores the essential affirmation of the soul: I Am! It affirms what the veteran experienced in the war—not that it was good or right, but that it was, and therefore is part of this person's honored history. With this resolve, and if the guide or therapist is open to making the journey with the survivor, the veteran may be willing to descend a second time. Then the imaginal descent becomes a personal odyssey into the Underworld in search of one's lost soul.

Through active imagination techniques in psychotherapy, Ray, a former medic, spent most of two years returning to the Underworld and revisiting the dead and wounded with whom he had worked in his firebase emergency room. Ray had been one of two emergency room attendants on a heavily fortified firebase. He had spent his combat tour on the night shift, treating the wounded or accident victims who came for emergency help, bagging the bodies that died under treatment or were brought back from patrols. Thus he said, as we have heard earlier, "I've seen more bodies, more death, than I have life."

Our therapy sessions were shaped by Ray's forgotten memories that emerged during or between sessions. When we began, Ray remembered only one of his patients, a nineteen-year-old named Tucker. Then he remembered a dead second lieutenant whose poncho liner Ray had slept on to prove he was brave and not superstitious. The memory of one death led to another. Early in his service, a major was brought in whose spleen had been shot out by a rocket. While others treated the man, Ray held his hand, reassuring him as the man babbled about his family in the States. Ray watched the man slowly turn purple, then gray. "I had never watched a man die before," Ray groaned. "Now I feel like I carry the man's soul."

"What is that soul saying to you?" I asked.

"It is saying, 'Be a soldier.'" Ray felt that he had betrayed the major's trust in his last moments of life. "I lied to him," Ray moaned. "I knew he was dying but I told him he would be all right instead of helping him face his death. Then, while the others stuffed him in a body bag, I just mopped up the bloody mess instead of honoring him."

Our therapy was an exhumation, Ray's descent into the Underworld where he met with more of the dead than he thought he could tolerate. Each face had to be brought to consciousness, grieved, and laid to rest. One by one, we staged encounters with each suffering soul. We sought to discover what each one wanted from him. We talked to them until Ray could release them.

In Joseph Conrad's *Heart of Darkness*, the character Marlow does not turn away from exposure to murderous horror but says instead, "I was fascinated. It was as though a veil had been rent." During his wartime emergency room duty, Ray looked again and again with each wounded and dying patient, sometimes six or more times a night, through that veil. This nightly occurrence fascinated him to the point of obsession.

One night outside the surgery room, Ray was talking with two other orderlies. Next to them was a stretcher with a body on it, zipped into a body bag. To prove himself before his buddies, Ray playfully zipped and unzipped the bag, looking again and again into the dead man's face. The other men turned away in disgust. They knew the lower half of the corpse had been blown apart. But Ray only unzipped the bag part way, being careful not to expose the wound. He felt shame for his disrespect. But he also felt one with the dead and sorrow for the part of himself that was lost and dying. He routinely had to clean bodies, tag them around the neck or their big toes, and load them into bags. Sometimes he had to stuff limbs forcefully that were already stiff with rigor mortis.

I guided Ray in a dialogue with the man in the body bag he had zipped and unzipped. He called him Bag Man. "I felt guilty for what I did to Bag Man," Ray said after writing out the dialogue. "But he spoke to me with wisdom and compassion. Bag Man told me that Viet Nam was my youth and that I lost my youth there. He gave me permission to leave the war behind. He told me I could let it become my past, a period in my life that was over, instead of my perpetual present. "'You did your duty,' Bag Man said to me. 'Go on and live.'"

After a year of performing imaginal exhumations, Ray finally began to feel, for the first time, that he had the right to live a full life. His form of reconciliation with the dead was to make it his duty to carry forward their words, names, and memories. Not able to escape what he had seen, he accepted the responsibility to bear witness to it.

Before therapy, Ray had fruitlessly sought to live a civilian's life, "as normal as the rest of America." After therapy, his denial was gone; his military service was no longer something to be hidden. His secrets were cleansed, and he was no longer obsessed with them. Ray had, like Odysseus, traveled backwards and downwards. By returning to the war in his imagination, he had emerged with a new identity.

When a survivor undertakes a healing journey of this type, PTSD can evaporate. Traumatic wounds shrink as the soul grows big enough to carry them. The survivor gives his or her experiences meaning by serving as witness and servant of restoration. What was once a wound that dominated life and yet could not be spoken becomes instead—a story.

For the survivor's soul to heal, he or she must revisit the experience of war in a way that tells the truth and frees the heart from bondage to the past. The formula for successful return can be called an imaginal initiation into warriorhood. This is a demanding process that requires several steps. Even as war and violence are disowned, the original call to service must be reaffirmed, and the universal pattern of the warrior that has been damaged must be restored. Along the way, the veteran studies the history and meaning of warriorhood, practices its traditions, and evaluates his past experiences in this light. He faces those people, places, and memories he most fears. He stares his demons in the face without resorting to violence. He does service that redresses the wounds he caused. He reshapes his identity in ways that include both the mythic dimensions and the difficult realities of his experience. The new identity that emerges constitutes a rebirth. He eventually achieves an initiation through both inner change and outer deed and ritual.

Achieving inner warriorhood is a mark of a fully developed personality. "Good warriors," Robert Moore summarizes, "have full command of their resources, their gifts, and their abilities, and they can mobilize them, organize them, channel them, and direct them in the service of transpersonal commitments toward transpersonal goals." A true warrior demonstrates "mature deployment of forces and resources in a significant struggle" and "represents mature ego function."[3] Warriorhood is not an outer role but an inner spiritual achievement.

Said differently, attaining warrior status is a matter of character. The development of a mature warrior entails the restoration of moral fiber that Jonathan Shay demonstrates is undone in combat. With such restoration, the healed veteran embodies high qualities of decency, honesty, kindness, compassion, and cooperation along with strength, courage, clear-mindedness, and vision. Ironic as it may seem, these qualities can be born, or reborn, out of the conflagration of war and developed in direct relation to the wisdom the survivor has garnered through his sojourn in the Underworld.

While traditional cultures and mythology the world over teach us the way of life and service that is a warrior's path, the specific term "warpath" is a Native American concept. In the indigenous tradition of North America, being on the warpath does not just mean going to war. It means walking the path of a spiritual warrior at all times—in war and peace, on the battlefield, and in the village. Thus the warrior's path is essentially a way of life, and it always includes the teaching and practice of the journey home.

Close study of myths and rituals traditional peoples used to facilitate this journey reveal four essential steps: purification and cleansing, storytelling, restitution in the family and the nation; and initiation as a warrior. Let us next consider each of the steps and how we might apply them in contemporary settings for helping survivors return from the modern battlefield.

Twelve

PURIFICATION AND CLEANSING

On a reconciliation trip to Viet Nam, our group of veterans and civilians visits the Central Highlands, arriving in the busy city of Pleiku, inhabited by part Viet and part indigenous mountain peoples collectively known as the Montagnard people. Until American forces constructed a huge military base nearby, Pleiku was only a dusty crossroads. Now we wander its market, which teems with vendors of fruits, vegetables, animals of all kinds, and Montagnard weavings and baskets.

Bill Keyes, a former marine engineer whose duty had been to clear dirt roads of live mines, dresses in garish Hawaiian tourist garb. "Last time I walked this market, I feared every step I took. I never knew who might toss a grenade or shoot at me from behind the melons." Bill strokes his yellow-flowered shirt. "I want to be sure there are no mistakes. I'm a tourist now!"

We drive out of town, watching for landmarks, road signs, anything that looks familiar as we search for the vets' former bases. Lynn is now a family woman with children and grandchildren all affected by the Agent Orange she was exposed to here. During the war, she was an operating room nurse at an emergency combat medical unit in the hills outside this town. We find the site of her former outpost up a dirt road and behind some ramshackle houses and stores. Among them stands a small medical clinic. Lynn walks the uneven ground where her unit stood, then poses under the clinic sign, hands held high as she points to herself and the current facility.

We wend our ways up other dirt roads behind Pleiku past huts and gardens, water buffalo, pigs, chickens. Soon we arrive at the green plain stretching to nearby Dragon Mountain. The green mountain erupts from the flatlands like the torso of its namesake. War planners built lookout posts and landing pads on its summit and constructed the area's largest military base at its feet. We stand in the dirt and grass that were once the churned mud of a bustling base.

Some in our party remain near with Hai, our local guide who is the son of a South Vietnamese army veteran, to hear the history of this area. But vets wander off, alone or in pairs. Jack, a military chaplain, and Lynn both spent time here. They point and remember.

Carl creeps toward Dragon Mountain, searching the ground, the summit, the sky. He stoops and picks something out of the grass. At about the same time, I pick up a small white ceramic disk attached to a short green rod. I look toward Carl. He stumbles to a bush and grabs onto a branch with one hand. He bends over. His other hand holds his stomach and he wretches. I rush over to him. I arrive at his side along with Beth Marie and Jim, two other veterans.

Carl vomits up the noodles and vegetables that were in his breakfast of *pho* a few hours earlier. At the same time, this usually soft-spoken religious man pours forth a string of obscenities. Beth Marie, Jim, and I surround him, placing supporting hands on his shoulders and back.

Carl's stomach churns again. Curses fly faster. He looks at us and says, "This isn't me."

His roommate Jim says, "Yes it is. You've been cursing in your sleep the entire trip."

Carl says, "I never curse."

"Never?" I ask.

Carl spits up more soup, and then says, "Not since I was a grunt in the bush."

"Maybe you are again," I say. "Maybe this is what's been locked inside you since the war."

"Thirty-six years?" Carl asks. Then between coughs, he laughs and cries. "It's true. I've been carrying this sickness for thirty-six years." We all hold him until his stomach and heart are empty. Later, I ask what set off the fit. Carl opens his hand to show us what he picked up in the grass. It is a disk and rod identical to the one I found. "It's an old mine pressure plate. Step on this and you're dead. I used to bury these around my base in the jungle."

"It triggered you today," I say. "What was it like when you first set them?"

"Just like today," Carl says. "But then I couldn't scream or curse or vomit. I wanted to. I felt sick to my stomach. But I forced myself to hold it all in and stay silent, or I'd give away our positions and maybe get my buddies killed."

Jim says, "That's what you sound like in your sleep—a grunt in a firefight."

"Congratulations!" I say. "Your body and mind are finally releasing the nauseating feelings you had in jungle combat but didn't dare let out at the time."

"Yeah," Carl laughs. "I can't believe I've carried it for so long. But it's out now. I feel clean inside. I haven't felt this clean since the war. I feel great!"

As Carl's story suggests, it's often not until the war frenzy has dissipated that its participants can reflect on what they have done. Then, whether or not they actually killed, veterans often feel sick, dirty, or sinful for having participated in the taking of life. Another veteran, George, was an Italian-American and a devout Catholic who had fought in the Allied invasion of Italy during World War II. I conferred with his hospice team during his terminal illness. Though a participant in "the good war," he felt sinful even on his death bed. He was unforgivable, he said, and his sin made worse because he had raised a weapon against his own ancestral people. Reviewing his life in preparation for death, he declared that even though he went to war against Fascism, ultimately the cause did not justify his actions, and he feared eternity in hell. "God didn't want me to do it, but my government put a gun in my hands and ordered me to kill." In six decades of life after war, George never found cleansing. He believed that he would never achieve absolution and that God would turn from him in judgment.

We spend our childhoods being educated to behave with civilized restraint. Then war reawakens the primitive in us, and the conditions of battle necessitate it. We simply cannot take another's life without this reversion to the primitive, which leaves us feeling different and sullied. To feel qualified to return to society again, the first step we must take is to purify and cleanse.

Cleansing and purification of body and soul often occur through a thorough catharsis. The body needs to release the adrenalin rush it still feels and disown the addiction to that rush it developed during war. It must be radically slowed down, literally brought back to earth. It needs to empty of the sickness it felt during combat and may still carry. The heart also has to release the anguish it could not experience during combat, even as Carl spontaneously did at Dragon Mountain.

Veterans often live in perpetual fear. Typically, they sit in corner seats so they can survey the world in front of them. They are hypervigilant and startle easily because they remain, as Art said, "on red alert." Purification also entails cleansing this fear. Bill Keyes danced through the Pleiku market as a way of proving to himself that there was nothing to be afraid of. Bill Ridley's welcome by a Vietnamese officer in the Tan Son Nuit airport showed him, as if in a moment of enlightenment, that the war was truly over. His mind and heart were washed clean of fear, and within two nights his body responded such that he could sleep and dream peacefully.

Cleansing and purification need to penetrate the soldier's moral and spiritual dimensions as well. Veterans often feel anathema. They sense themselves cursed by those they fought and sometimes by those at home, and they fear the curse of divinity. Purification lifts the curse.

One of the most significant ways we can cleanse is by giving meaning to our experiences. We sometimes ask of life's hardships, and we often hear survivors cry out, "Why did this happen to me?" James Hillman turns "why" on its head with a mythic perspective that asks, instead, "What does the problem want *from* us?"[1] The word for "why" in Greek is *yiati*, which literally means "for what." We cannot know why something happened to us and not to someone else. But we *can* lift our feelings of being cursed and of having done wrong by giving meaning to the purpose for which we served or by working to alleviate the suffering of others after having experienced it ourselves.

The Biblical story of Job tells of a great spiritual quest that arose out of the worst trauma. After losing everything but life itself, Job lay on the dung heap crying out to God. Veterans and war survivors are often much like Job, asking questions with every breath that few of us may ever suffer with such intensity: Is there a God? If so, how could God let this happen? Is there any meaning to life? To suffering? To striving against evil? Are suffering and evil part of God's plan for us? If so, do I want to go on living in such a universe? It was right and necessary that Job relentlessly struggled with such questions until he received a vision that provided an answer.

Veterans must do likewise, and their guides must facilitate their search. This imperative necessarily plunges psychotherapy and other healing modalities into the realm of a spiritual journey. Shortly after the Vietnam War, Peter Marin declared that its veterans live in "moral pain" and deemed such a journey essential for veterans to heal, lest therapy prove "morally insufficient."[2]

Victor Frankl affirmed the necessity of this struggle for meaning and purpose in his seminal work developed out of his experiences in Nazi concentration camps.[3] While in the camps, Frankl did not deny or avoid the conditions in which he was trapped. Rather, he sought meaning there, developing his character in such a way that even his camp experiences were soul shaping. He practiced soul making as a slave laborer in Auschwitz. His lesson for survivors is this: We cannot change the horror to which we are condemned. But we can, to a large degree, respond even to the worst circumstance with transcendent meaning and loving responsibility. War provides instinctual, unconscious, and collective meaning; their collective power is nearly irresistible. In order to survive and transcend it we must provide even greater moral and spiritual meaning to counterbalance these more primitive forces. But how can we make meaning? How cleanse the soul?

World spiritual traditions provide strategies on which we can draw through various forms of repentance, realignment, and cleansing. Catholicism offers confession. Judaism offers the Ten Days of Repentance. The Native American tradition offers the purification lodge. Shamanic traditions offer journeys to the spirit worlds where we can encounter the dead. Buddhists embrace the wheel of karma in order to transform one's legacy after hurtful actions. We can extract principles from all these traditions to support the survivor on his or her moral journey home.

The wisdom of the Jewish High Holy Days provided the breakthrough in the therapy of one veteran whose life was stuck in a rut of loneliness and uselessness. For twenty years after returning from Viet Nam, Don Pfister had not held a job or been able to sustain a loving relationship.

Don's job in Viet Nam was base casualty-control coordinator. Never in combat himself, he wrote to the families of those killed in action and shipped home the belongings of dead young men he had never met. While in Viet Nam, he took a vow to those men, promising he would never take up a normal life or seek success until he had done something important to end war and give their sacrifices meaning. He spent the next two decades living the life of a reclusive poet and spiritual seeker, offering volunteer services to prisoners and children, writing antiwar poetry, and organizing rallies.

"You haven't been able to go on with your life because you gave yourself in a vow," I said during one of our meetings. "Vows are utterly binding. When a good man gives his word, he follows that word or fears he will lose his soul."

Don nodded and sobbed. We had arrived at his grief not only for the dead young soldiers but over his own lost life. As Ray had done, Don, too, clung to the tomb, but through his moral imperative in contrast to Ray's death imprint.

"That's why there are Biblical injunctions against vowing," I continued. "Vows are heavy, constricting, awesome burdens to bear."

"God forgive me," Don said, "but I can't carry the burden of my vow any longer. I can't stop war all by myself, and we're not going to stop it in our lifetimes."

"No," I said. "You can't and I can't, no matter how much we want to." I paused while Don's sobbing quieted, then asked, "Do you want to be released from this vow?"

"I feel as if I have to apologize to the dead for this, but I'm not dead," Don sighed. "Yes, I want to be released. But since vows are binding, is release possible?"

"In Judaism," I said, "the prayer that begins Yom Kippur, the Day of Atonement, is called Kol Nidre. It is exactly what we are talking about. It is an annulment of vows."

"How can we annul a vow?"

"When we realize it is beyond our ability to keep. Judaism lets us cancel vows we made to God that we cannot fulfill."

"But I made my vow to the dead as well."

"When we make vows to others, we may be released with the consent of those people. Do you want to ask the dead to release you?"

Don nodded.

"Close your eyes," I said. "Breathe deeply. Let yourself see the Memorial in Washington. Stand before all those names. See your face reflected off the Wall, superimposed on all the names of the men whose deaths you helped administer. Look into their lives and your own face. Tell the dead your dilemma. Tell them you can't fulfill your vow by yourself. Tell them it's too heavy. Ask them what to do."

Don sat with his eyes closed. Tears ran down his cheeks. Soon he nodded. "They tell me to live," he said. "Go on. Have a life that is useful and full of service and goodness. But let go of the vow. Don't make yourself one of us. Don't be another casualty of the war."

Don opened his eyes, wiped them, and smiled. "What now, Doc?"

"You release your vow, ask God to release you, and live."

By utilizing Judaism's ritual of atonement as a model, this non-Jewish veteran was able to become free from his bondage to the past and lift a curse he had placed upon himself by taking an impossible vow. Don's healing included forgiving himself for being too human to save his comrades, stop war, or achieve his vows; forgiving others for harm done to us; asking forgiveness for our foibles; and asking for divine compassion and release.

All these dimensions of forgiveness are necessary if the war-wounded soul is to move forward on the path home to inner peace. During the High Holidays, Judaism teaches that prayer, repentance, and acts of righteousness and charity can gain us forgiveness. The key concept of repentance is *Teshuvah*, which means "return." Like Jonah we have fled, like Odysseus become lost, like Job felt banished from God's presence. The pollution we accumulate through participation in war interrupts our connection to the Divine. The soul may achieve a return to divine presence through any religious or spiritual tradition; it is a simple yet profound prescription for healing and moral realignment. On the road to return, we cleanse, purify, rejoin the world community and the flow of life, and attain forgiveness.

Unlike our contemporary culture that attempts to conduct life as usual even while we are waging a war overseas, tribal people realized that an entire society is afflicted by war and must participate in its warriors' healing. In traditional cultures, purification was the first order of business for bringing a warrior home. The Papago people, for example, held a sixteen-day purification ceremony for young warriors when they returned from their first experiences of taking life. During this ceremony they were tended only by older warriors, so that they had the benefit of their elders' experience to facilitate their transition back into civilian life. This is not to say that warriors in traditional cultures did not have what we now call PTSD. But the rituals around the condition did help to minimize its effects and lead to recovery. The condition was treated as a communal rather than an individual problem, and those who suffered from it were not pathologized. In a report on Native American Vietnam era veterans, Steven Silver points out some of the benefits for tribal people even today:

> Their ritual explicitly embraces and approves the killer's psychic numbing and prescribes a way for dealing with it. The fear of intimacy, of touching and being touched, that is common in battle survivors and that, in the twentieth century, is labeled a sickness . . . is accepted and even enforced in tribal warfare as an appropriate response to the experience of inflicting death in battle. . . . The successful warrior usually is isolated from everyone except older killers and specifically is forbidden to touch or feed himself, to experience sexual intimacy, to touch the ground. . . . In effect, the numbing is externalized and formalized in a series of taboos; it is prescribed as a chosen response.[4]

When veterans are led thusly by experienced guides, they do not become psychically frozen as the isolated survivor so often does in our own society.

Native American cultures were supreme at healing warriors as well at rearing them. Their methods of using the medicine wheel, seeking spirit guides, undergoing vision quests, and participating in sweat lodges are good and effective ways, but not the only ones, for achieving radical cleansing and purification. In our modern psychological era, experiential psychotherapy techniques such as those practiced in gestalt therapy, bioenergetics, and psychodrama may engender a strong degree of catharsis, purification, and healing. Some creative art forms—writing, dramatics, visual arts—encourage catharsis as well. Other new therapies, such as rebirthing, or old therapies, such as yoga and acupuncture, also help achieve catharsis and purification. Dr. Stephanie Mines, who specializes in healing trauma from both violence and sexual abuse, catalogues thirty forms of interventions using energetics, body-oriented strategies, and other alternative therapeutic methods for healing trauma and explains the contributions of each.[5] Crucial is that the choice of a strategy be matched to the survivor's need and worldview in order to achieve the full range of physical, psychological, moral, and spiritual cleansing. It is best done through ritual in the context of a supportive community.

One of the most powerful ritual practices of purification is the Native American sweat lodge. Its Lakota name is *inipi*, which has various meanings. It is called the place of the spirits because, in the inipi, we leave secular space behind and drop the ordinary barriers that stand between us and the spirit world. In the inipi, we may have visions and be entered by spirits, or, if you prefer, awaken archetypal energies and images.

The inipi is also called the purification lodge. Its heat is so intense that it cleanses and purifies us body and soul. In the inipi, a person cannot tell a lie. We are purified by standing before the Divine in truth. And yet another name for the inipi is the stone lodge, or the stone people's lodge. In Native American teachings, everything—rocks, air, water, and the earth itself as well as all plants and animals—is alive. When heated, the stones in the lodge awaken and give their lives for us so that we can purify.

The sweat lodge is both a place and a ceremony. Everything is done in a reverential manner, carefully designed to restore balance and order as the primary ingredients of health. When we follow the order of the ritual, the physical, emotional, mental, and spiritual cleansing is quite intense. In contrast, veterans in our modern society stress the extreme degree to which they feel dirty, sinful, impure, and immoral, and they can carry this sense of being soiled for the rest of their lives. Our culture has no means to help veterans purify from their combat experiences before reentering civilian culture. They take the energies and emotions of war directly back into ordinary life with neither cleansing nor transition. This state of affairs is confusing and dangerous both to returning vets and to the community welcoming them home. Sometimes, as evidenced by the higher than normal homicide and suicide rates among vets, it proves to be deadly.

Lack of purification also helps explain why alcohol abuse is common among veterans. Alcohol temporarily anesthetizes the impure feelings and energies that veterans carry. But being a depressant and a potentially addictive substance, alcohol is not a purification agent and cannot provide the true physical, moral, and spiritual cleansing needed.

Especially orchestrated for veterans, the sweat lodge can be a powerful tool for purification in several respects:

To begin with, the inipi is a safe place; entering it is symbolic of entering Mother Earth's womb. It is a place where we are held and embraced and can feel protected. And because of the inipi's status as a place of change, it can provide veterans with a much-needed symbolic transition from the combat zone back to a world at peace. The inipi can serve as a tunnel of return, transporting vets from the interior war zone they still dwell in through the inner and spirit realms and then back into our common world cleansed.

The inipi is also a place that, literally as well as figuratively, melts away the defenses that the soldier by necessity had to develop during combat. In the intense heat, and with other participants as witnesses all around, the prayers are sincere. A person cannot help but be open, honest, and vulnerable. Psychic numbness eases so that true feelings can be reactivated. Since veterans' numbness is chronic and severe, such measures that counteract closure and defensiveness can be especially effective.

Further, the inipi is a communal experience. Everybody is a brother or sister in the lodge and each just as vulnerable as the other. We turn everything over to the Divine, in whose eyes we are all equal and whose plans for our lives we cannot see. No person or experience is judged or shunned. It is important for vets to feel like equal members of a circle of vulnerable and open people. In the inipi, anything they say is respected. They can feel accepted in ways they need and may not have experienced.

Finally, the inipi is sacred space. After we have dropped our defenses through ritual and sensed them melt away through steam and heat, we may connect with energies of nature or spirit we cannot ordinarily experience. We seek these connections in a sincere and reverential manner. Veterans feel that they have lost their souls, their grace, and their relationship with divinity. Telling them otherwise does no good. They need to experience a connection for themselves.

They need to feel their souls alive inside their bodies. Through the inipi, they may have visions or energetic infusions that can help reawaken their souls and bring them home. Through such a radical ritual, they can begin to feel an order and a purpose and compassion in the universe that includes them.

Inviting a veteran to participate in an intensive ritual such as the inipi is not a casual step. Rather, we must be confident that a vet is ready to purify and to risk radical opening. The ego must be sufficiently strong to handle an experience of defense loss. He or she has to have sufficient belief in some sense of divinity in order to surrender in trust and safety. The vet has to have a strong enough connection to nature in order to trust the energetic experiences he receives and to perceive himself as being supported by powers much larger than the society he scorns. It is no coincidence that existentialism—the philosophy that teaches that we ourselves create the meaning of our existences in an essentially godless and meaningless universe—arose out of the experience of World War II. In combat, soldiers frequently lose any sense of divine purpose, presence, or guidance in life. Afterward, veterans cannot risk traveling in spiritual realms if they do not have faith that a divine being is there ready to receive them.

For some vets, the sweat lodge or other radical rituals of purification can be powerfully and deeply cleansing. In the heat and darkness of the inipi, veterans readily cry as they grieve lost friends or revisit lost and unwanted memories. They may call out the names of dead companions or have memories of combat so intense that they seem to be occurring again. They scream battle cries and shout "No!" or "Kill!" or "Get away!" as they had done in firefights. They sob as they see themselves kill again or see someone they loved die again.

One veteran, Tony, said, "The heat of the lodge burned the skin on my hands and arms until I felt myself holding my

M-16 again. I was blazing away in the midst of a firefight. My gun was heating up and burning me, just like in the war. I feared for my life and saw enemy soldiers dying around me again." After several long minutes of this sensation, Tony opened his eyes, saw he was safe in the inipi, and broke into tears. He sobbed through the rest of the ceremony. When we emerged and he told us his story, he glowed with peace, warmth, and relief.

He had achieved a catharsis, a purgation. He had not merely remembered a war story and retold it. Rather, he had drawn its living energies and emotions up from where they had been hidden in his body and mind. He had reexperienced the war as if it were happening in the present moment. Like Carl at Dragon Mountain, this veteran had finally felt the original feelings he had repressed for decades. He had finally relieved himself of the need to stay blocked against them. He had overcome psychic numbness and reclaimed his body, heart, and soul.

Whether or not vets enter an inipi, any form of therapy or healing they pursue must allow opportunities for catharsis of this intensity. Veterans' flashbacks are not simply symptoms of derangement. They are the psyche's spontaneous attempts, in the absence of purification rituals, to achieve catharsis and heal itself.

Flashbacks sometimes occur spontaneously in therapy. They are not indications of mistaken therapy. Rather, such flashbacks indicate the psyche's attempt to heal at the core level. When properly contained and guided in the therapeutic setting, they can be safe and effective. Moreover, we can tap into this healing modality by deliberately inducing flashbacks in controlled settings, as either traditional therapy or the inipi can provide. The key is to evoke and support catharsis in a safe environment with trusted companions.

Twelve

When veterans emerge from the dark inipi into the light and look around at the rocks, trees, and mountains with fresh eyes, they feel unburdened and relieved, just as Tony did. Similarly, when Ray completed his imaginal exhumations, Carl emptied through vomiting, and Don utilized the ritual of atonement, the thousand-yard stare disappeared from their eyes. They began to see the world and the people around them again. They felt as if they were good and necessary and supported beings on the planet once more. When this happens, the world is restored to its proper order again, and it is good.

Thirteen

THE HEALING POWER
OF STORYTELLING

According to author and healer Deena Metzger, a story is a "map for the soul." It is "a living thing. A divine gift."[1] When we tell our own stories and listen to those of others, we come in touch with all three: life, divinity, and soul. Telling our story is a way of preserving our individual history and at the same time defining our place in the larger flow of events. It reveals patterns and meaning that we might otherwise miss as we go about the mundane activities of living; it invites us to see the universe working through us. Storytelling also knits the community together. It records or recreates the collective history and transforms actor and listeners alike into communal witnesses.

The second step in bringing the warrior home, after being cleansed and purified, dressed in fresh clothing, and brought to sit at the communal fire, is the telling of his or her story. In traditional cultures, returning warriors told their stories at length to their families, to each other, to their warrior societies, and to the entire tribe. In Plains Indian cultures, for example, having stories to tell of one's own risk taking and courage was a requirement for manhood. Contemporary culture calls this "bragging rights." It is a secular version of the coup stories by which tribal men affirmed their prowess and carried forward the history of their people through tales of their personal contributions to it. We might conceive of it as "story rights."

Considered from the mythic point of view, our lives are individualized versions of universal stories. As Metzger points out, we begin with the individual stories but weave and interweave them until we embrace the collective story and find each participant's place in history. Story, she explains,

> is an essential structure of mind and an active principle, a living narrative structure.... 'What happened'...
> is the least of its functions. Story gathers and integrates the elements of event and imagination.... When it opens, meaning emerges in a flow or explosion of light and understanding.... Perhaps, ultimately, we are each a story... resonant with larger stories that form a universal grid.... September 11 was such a point in time.
> ... The larger story became one story... a global story.[2]

Like a hologram, one person's story extends into others to reveal the larger story of what happened to us all and what meaning we might discover in it. A personal war story is always about everyone who participated in the war, as well as their family members, their friends, and their communities. War stories are about the earth and the damage done to it. They are about the nations who wage war and the histories and politics, beliefs, and values that lead up to them. And they are about the wounds and deaths that result and how they shape the future of everyone and every place involved.

People in traditional cultures often accompanied the stories with some form of artistic expression. War narratives were often danced or dramatized before the tribe, serving as a form of psychodrama that brought home the energies of war and gave them healing or aesthetic functions in peace. This was the original purpose of the war dance. Warriors might paint significant battle scenes on weapons, tools, or walls. Among the Samurai, a man could not receive his sword unless he had also mastered a fine art form, such as painting or composing haiku. Also, these warriors used Japanese Noh dance and theatre as forms of expressive discharge and transformation. Artistry balanced the passions of war, providing an outlet for creative expression and giving aging warriors a peaceful occupation. In Celtic society, poets, who did not fight, would march off with the warriors in order to witness battle. Afterward, they would commemorate the events in poetry. All such creative activities helped transform war stories from violence into art and from personal story into tribal myth.

The story of participation in the wars of one's tribe is so important that it may serve, for good or ill, as the defining event of a life. Aeschylus, for instance, one of ancient Greece's greatest playwrights, asked to be remembered, not for his artistic contributions that we still honor, but only for his military service, which he considered to be his greatest contribution to his culture. Inscribed thusly is the monument to Aeschylus the Athenian,

Euphorian's son, who died in the wheatlands of Gela.
The grove of Marathon with its glories
Can speak of his valor in battle.
The long-haired Persian remembers and can speak of it, too.[3]

The stories we leave behind can even become the purpose for which we experience the sufferings of war; dying with honor has been a major motivation in shaping men's wartime behavior for millennia. Cassandra was a prophetess and the sister of the Trojan hero, Hector. After Hector's death at Achilles' hands, she consoled their mother Hekabe:

> This is the truth: he died, the best, a hero.
> Because the Greeks came he died thus.
> Had they stayed home, we never would have known him.
> This truth stands firm: the wise will fly from war.
> But if war comes, to die well is to win
> The victor's crown.
> The only shame is not to die like that.[4]

Thousands of years later, Preston Stern's community and the veteran comrades he left behind remembered him for the moral courage he demonstrated in quitting the war, no matter what the personal consequences. To his surprise and healing, before his death veterans told Preston he was more courageous than they who had stayed to fight. The epitaph inscribed on his gravestone reads:

> Pause, friend, by this green bed
> Where one lies well loved
> By wife, children, family, friends,
> Who braved the Yellow Land we made
> To rain with fire and pain.
> He returned to sing
> And plow our purple home with truth.
> Salute him here and say of him
> He chose not to kill but to love.

It is important not only that the veteran tells his story but that he experiences it as being heard. Today, we tend not to think of people as living in tribes. But we all need a sense of belonging to a tightly knit community in which we have significant relations that matter to and help uphold us all. Having one's story validated is a critical step in the transformation of identity into warriorhood and mature adult status. The public platform is necessary for the story to get passed on and become part of the community's collective wisdom and mythic history.

Notoriously, however, few of our veterans seek a public platform; nor are they offered one. Veterans most often withhold their stories, not only because of the pain evoked in telling them but also because they fear that, in our culture of denial, we won't properly receive them. And without telling their stories, veterans cannot truly become warriors. Instead, they become stuck in the role of scapegoat, carriers of the tribal shadow. If we are to redress this situation, we have a profound responsibility to be a supportive audience for those who went to war in our name.

Psychotherapy can meet this need to some degree. It helps to tell one person your story, and that one witness may become a bridge to others. Group therapy, as well, can be a useful setting for telling stories in that it can serve as a family or small tribe. Veterans' groups, moreover, are helpful to the extent that members feel they are with people who understand what they have been through. These groups reproduce some of the qualities of traditional tribal warrior societies, providing the brother- and sisterhood of those who, by virtue of similar experiences, "get it." Groups can also be a source of advocacy and much-needed assistance for floundering survivors. At the same time, in being closed, groups unwittingly reinforce the alienation of veterans from the rest of society.

Storytelling at its most effective must go beyond the therapeutic setting and an exclusively veteran audience to take
place before members of the general populace.

These days, it is usually the media that serves this public
function of storytelling. Many veterans felt relief when certain
movies, such as *Saving Private Ryan* and *Platoon*, first
appeared. These films, in contrast to the John Wayne-style
movies idealizing patriotic service, brought before the American "tribe" stories that veterans adjudge to be close to the
truth. Media-carried stories, however, do not have the same
healing impact as personal storytelling. It cannot be overem-
phasized that, in order to heal, survivors need to gather and
share in living community.

Like everything else, storytelling has its shadow. War
affects our physical, emotional, and spiritual dimensions with
an intensity that produces the strongest "high" the soldier
will ever experience. Afterward, veterans often become
addicted to taking life-threatening risks in other settings.
As one combat vet said, "I wasn't addicted to the killing but
to the high." Fights, drunken binges, automobile racing, and
compulsive sex are a few means by which veterans attempt
to replicate the high produced by war. Storytelling can
become another way. To the extent that veterans use it to
get a rush, the storytelling becomes compulsive and so
counter-productive to healing. As Robert Jay Lifton observes,
compulsive war storytelling can become a means for veterans to hide from rather than access feelings. And our culture,
which craves various forms of getting high, exacerbates the
problem by encouraging stories that glorify war in order to
gain a vicarious thrill. Thus the compulsive storytelling rein-
forces our strange cultural ambivalence about war—we can
get high on war stories while shunning war's reality and failing its victims.

To counteract this thrill-seeking and become healing, veterans' stories need to be told in a way that transfers the moral weight of the event from the individual to the community. Survivors need facilitators who, in addition to representing the tribal audience, encourage diving deep into the story. Otherwise, a survivor might endlessly repeat the details of an event but not experience the release of related emotions, the accurate reordering of history, or the making of meaning—all of which are essential in the recovery from PTSD.

PTSD and the story of what caused it always concern more than just the survivor. Until properly addressed, it reverberates through our relationships and down the generations harming everyone it touches, as it did, for instance, in the life of Carole Evans.

Carole is the daughter of a traumatized World War II veteran. After high school, she married a young Vietnam War combat vet who was alcoholic and abusive. She became pregnant by him but, perhaps due to stress and abuse, lost the baby. She tried and failed to help her young husband heal. After they divorced, she lived with a Polish survivor of Nazi labor camps for twenty years. Repeating the pattern in Carole's life, he, too, was alcoholic and abusive. "I thought his soul was strong and beautiful because he didn't show any pain," she said. "I thought my own soul was weak and petty because I hurt so badly that it was difficult to function. Through therapy, I realized that my pain, fear, and sorrow were signs that my soul was alive and kicking, while the souls of all these men, my men, were lost, damaged or dead."

Like others touched by war and its aftermath, Carole needed for her story to be witnessed and her pain acknowledged as a proper response to her losses. At the outset, she had believed it was merely her own dysfunction that had led to a series of disappointing relationships with male survivors.

But reframing her story in the light of the full scope of her family background allowed Carole to transform her identity. She began to see herself, too, as a survivor. And she found new pride in being a survivor in several war-ravaged families who through her love of veterans had participated in history. She now marches with veterans and counts herself among the millions of women who are spouses and children of war's victims.

Reconciliation retreats are one of the most effective tools for addressing the healing needs of both veterans and nonveterans. Such retreats incorporate the individual, group, aesthetic, and spiritual dimensions of healing, while relying on the healing power of story.

Fourteen men arrived for a long weekend at a remote retreat in the Berkshire Mountains of western Massachusetts. We had a kitchen, a meeting room with a wood stove, cold outdoor showers, and a camping area.

Among the men were Conrad, Pat, and Phil, all members of my combat veterans group. Together we were studying the warrior's path, and they were seeking to move through the steps of return. Frank Houde joined us. He was a career air force pilot who had risen to the rank of colonel before retiring. Two era vets also signed up. Era vets are people who served during the war but were never in combat; they have "in-between" identities with unique sets of issues and challenges. One of the era vets, Al, had been stationed stateside awaiting deployment to Viet Nam when he had a nervous breakdown and was discharged. The other, Rich, had been a lieutenant in the army stationed safely in England during the war. The rest of the group was made up of seven non-veterans, all of whom were anxious to examine the effects of the war years on their evolving manhood and to reconcile with veterans.

It was a cold, dreary September day when we arrived on top of the mountain. We spent the first few hours gathering enough wood to stoke the stove for our three days together. Men alone on a mountain bond quickly when the choice is either to stay warm or to freeze together.

With the wood piled high, the men were anxious to do a sweat lodge to initiate our retreat. We went to the inipi site, gathered wood and stones, and built a fire. I called out our need for a talking stick—the decorated, ceremonial stick that traditional people passed around a council circle. Its use has been a custom found in numerous cultures around the world and dates back several thousand years. When a man held the talking stick, he was honor-bound to speak his truth, and everyone else was honor-bound to put aside all personal concerns and listen. Pat immediately went in search of a stick, and he and a few other men decorated it with ferns, leaves, bark, and feathers. For the rest of the encampment, Pat was our keeper of the stick.

We sat in a circle and passed the talking stick. While the stones heated, each man spoke about what he wanted from the weekend. Each man in his own way declared that he felt the lack of an indefinable strength and confidence. Each felt he was in part still a boy. Each felt, whether in Viet Nam, in service elsewhere, or as a civilian, that he had been failed during his adolescent years. The men felt uninitiated and had gathered here to seek initiation and to help others find it as well.

This first sweat became a brotherhood lodge. In the steam and darkness, fourteen men sat in a circle and prayed for understanding and compassion from the others. They prayed for courage to face the pain, loneliness, anger, and emptiness that they carried from the war years, and to be given guidance in purging those feelings and replacing them with new ones that could energize their lives and help them mature. Then we emerged from the sweat, crawling on all fours through the mud, and huddled around the fire to dry. In the deep night, we returned to camp for a late meal.

The next morning, the sky stretched like a gray cloak across our mountaintop. A chilly wind blew, carrying cold raindrops that stung our skin. Rapidly, the rain grew thicker, and the men huddled into their coats. At midmorning we went into the meeting room, a three-sided log room with a small wood stove near the open end. We built a fire in the stove and sat in a semicircle around it, facing our one common flame in the center.

I began the session with an introductory story from the samurai tradition teaching us to embrace others beyond our fear and hatred. Then I held the talking stick out toward the men. "There will be no judgments, rejections, criticisms, or condemnations here. You do not have to speak, but each man who does speak will be honored and respected. Now who would like to begin?"

First one man, then the next, stepped forward and took the seat by the stove. With the talking stick in his hand, each searched for the memories and feelings that wanted to emerge. Then, one by one, everyone present told his story of growing up during the war.

The first to grab the stick had been Pat. "I ain't waiting any more," he said. "You brought me all the fuck the way from Viet Nam to this mountain. Now I'm gonna get it all out."

After Pat told his "in-country" story, Conrad and Phil told theirs: about life as grunts, surviving fire fights, and brotherhood found and lost. Phil told about his loneliness and fear as a spotter pilot—the lone crew of a small, unarmed, low-flying scout plane—and his search for the brotherhood he never had. Each vet told about his struggles to find respect and manhood and to heal his PTSD since returning home.

Frank took the stick. He cradled it for a long time. Then he began by insisting that he had been a career air force man, not a Vietnam War vet. During the war he was first stationed in Japan and later was in charge of a squadron of reconnaissance aircraft that patrolled the skies over all of Southeast Asia. His planes flew very high and were not often in danger. But they helped locate enemy troops and bases. Frank saw numerous attacks he had helped stage. He watched as the beautiful Vietnamese mountains, all that lush greenery, turned into fire and smoke. "I remember flying into the sunset once," he said. "At first, the sun was a great red ball perched on a verdant mountaintop. But, as I watched, our jets blasted that mountain. God help anyone who was on it. I kept flying my course, directly into this huge, steady column of smoke that rose so high and thick it blackened out the sun and the entire mountain below us. I flew that course again for several days afterward. It was still black, still burning."

A colonel with the Strategic Air Command, Frank had been summoned to headquarters in Japan and offered higher staff positions if he kept performing in good fashion. "I could have been a general commanding SAC," he said. "I would have been had I not gone to Viet Nam. For years, I was a just a cog in a huge military machine. I was good at what I did and did it without questioning. But when I saw what we did to the Vietnamese countryside, I couldn't go on. I retired from the military as soon as possible."

Al, one of the era vets, took the stick. His story was simple. He had unloaded body bags at Fort Dix while waiting to be shipped to Viet Nam. He was an only child of older parents and had already lost friends in the war. He couldn't take the fear of leaving his parents childless. He began to have nightmares, headaches, and panic attacks. When the attacks finally rendered him helpless, the army discharged him. He still had the same symptoms at the time of our retreat.

"That body bag detail was horrible!" Pat told Al. "It was enough to make you crazy. In Viet Nam, I was given graves registration as punishment for being bad but not bad enough for the brig. I loaded those bags for you in a big hanger in Da Nang. Bodies were stacked like cord wood. We had to wear gas masks against the stench. 'Get the fuck away from this, no matter what you have to do,' I said to myself. I couldn't get the stink out of my nostrils."

"I'm angry at all of you," said Rich, the second era vet, when he took the stick. He had gone through college on ROTC, was commissioned as a second lieutenant, and sat out the war in England. "It never would have bothered me if the rest of you hadn't suffered," he said. "The service was a party for me. It made college easy. I had nothing to complain about until I heard what it did to you. Now as I listen to you, I feel guilty and inadequate. At the time, I felt as if I was left out of history the easy way. Now it isn't easy."

Then each nonveteran took a turn. Jim, with long gray hair tied in a pony tail behind his head, had been a Catholic priest in Boston. He was vehemently against the war and thought the church was the natural place from which to oppose it. He spent most of his time fighting to get the church to stand against the war. By the time the war ended, he was so disillusioned he resigned the priesthood.

As Jim remembered the war years, he cried. He looked directly at the vets, saying, "I wanted so badly to bring you each home in one piece. I tried. I did all I could. But I was just a young priest. I couldn't do enough. Please forgive me."

"Forgive *you*?" Pat asked.

"Yes," Jim said. "Forgive me for not stopping the war and bringing you home safely."

"Father!" Pat cried out. "Forgive us. You're the man I want to protect. You're the man of the future. If being a warrior has any purpose whatsoever, it's to protect the gentle evolved souls like yours so that you can guide us into a future that makes sense. Father, we were the ones who killed. Please forgive *us*."

Jim and Pat looked at each other for a long time, then stood and hugged. They parted and Jim dried his eyes. The ex-antiwar priest took the former Marine recon squad leader by the shoulders, smiled, and said, "Thank you."

Pat hung his head before the man he still honored as a priest. "Thank you, Father," he said.

Larry had been drafted and was being considered for Officer's Candidate School. He was interviewed by a board of three officers who were impressed with his qualifications and ready to admit him. "I'll be happy to be an officer in the army," he told them respectfully, "and I'll strive to serve my country well. But I want to make it very clear that, while I'm not against military service, I am completely against the Vietnam War; if I agree to this appointment, it has to be with the stipulation that I won't go to Viet Nam."

A major, the highest-ranking officer present, leaned across the table and stared Larry in the eyes. "Do you know you're talking insubordination, Boy?" he asked.

"I'm not being insubordinate, Sir," Larry said. "I'm just being honest. I want to serve my country in an honest and honorable way."

"That is not the attitude of a United States Army officer, Boy," the major said. "We don't like your attitude."

The young man bristled. He looked the major in the eyes and said, "Well, I don't like your attitude, either."

The officers dismissed him and classified him unfit for military service.

Another man, one who had faked a 4-F, said, "I never felt guilty about not going to Viet Nam, but I felt guilty about getting out so easily and heartbroken that the rest of you were going through such hell." Yet another man abhorred the war with such intensity that he left the country for several years and considered never returning. Viet Nam, for him, symbolized everything that was wrong with America. He still felt brokenhearted and homeless in America and as a result had never settled into a profession or a home.

Then another nonvet, Harry, told his story—of being frightened and confused during his antiwar efforts, of being at Woodstock trying to sing the troops home, of being chased at bayonet point at the First Moratorium Against the War in Washington, D.C. He said he was searching for his warriorhood, too, based on his own history.

"There's a part of my story I'd forgotten until listening to you," Frank suddenly said to Harry. "During that Moratorium you attended, I was on leave, at home in Massachusetts. I was getting ready to return to Ft. Bragg when my seventy-year-old mother got a call from a friend, saying, 'Let's go to the peace march.' My mother said yes. As I drove to Bragg I passed busloads of people going to D.C. I thought, I'll get to Bragg and they'll call me to help take the 82nd Airborne to D.C.

"I was right. My unit was mobilized to help break up the demonstration. I was ordered to it immediately. As a pilot, I ferried troops from Bragg to D.C. and briefed my passengers of sixty troops with jeeps and water hoses. I said to them, 'My old mother is one of the demonstrators. Be careful with those things.'

"Later my unit rushed through the streets of Washington, blowing tear gas and chasing demonstrators wherever we could find them. Many of the troops you encountered were under my orders."

Frank paused and looked closely at Harry. "Those GIs who stopped you on the street," he said, "could have been my men. The one who threatened you with his bayonet could have been my man. It could have been at my orders. It could even have been me. I'm sorry. I didn't know what I was doing. Please forgive me."

Harry looked into Frank's misty blue eyes. Later, he said he had never expected to be asked to hug someone who might have once threatened his life. But he saw that both of them had been frightened and confused. Both had done what they believed was right. Harry said that a huge ache in his heart let go at that moment. Men representing our government had hurt and scared him. But Frank was stepping forward as a brother and a friend. Among the warriors of the Plains tribes, highest honor was given to an enemy who stepped forward without fear and addressed his adversary as "friend." Harry and Frank were no longer adversaries. The bayonet was finally lowered. They hugged.

After each man completed his story, others asked questions to clarify what he had done and how it had affected his adult years. Each vet, in-country and era, said he had never told a nonveteran his story before. Each nonveteran said he had never before focused on that part of his life and how it had affected his adult years. By the time the stories and responses were finished, it was long after midnight. We had been talking and listening for sixteen hours. No one had left for a meal; no one had broken the circle. We had started the day as separate entities of a shattered history. Now one man called out, "We're a team."

"We're a team, a squad. We're all in this together," another said.

"It's all of our stories," another said. "It isn't you against me or who was better or worse or right or wrong. We were all lost."

"All confused."

"All fucked over."

"We're a team."

"Hey, we're cool! We aren't sissies because we didn't go to war or didn't like the war we went to. We're tough. An A-Team!"

Several men yelled together, "Fuckin' A!" Everyone laughed and slapped hands. Then at 2:30 A.M. on a cold, damp night, the new team gathered in the kitchen for an impromptu dinner.

Our last day was cloudy but dry. I told the men that, having told our stories, we would now have another sweat to plummet into the grief we still carried from the war, in order to pull our feelings up and release them from our bodies and hearts.

Again we made the fire. Again we heated the stones and sat in a circle. But this time, the team was going to sweat and purge and cleanse—combat vets and protestors, era vets and 4-Fs all together—helping each other through the buried pain not just of one man but of our entire generation.

Fourteen men squeezed into the shadows of the lodge. The ground was cool and clammy, but would soon be warm. Rocks were carried in for the first round. Soon we were in the dark with the glowing stones.

In accordance with the tradition of numerous Native American tribes, our first round of prayers was to the east—the place representing awareness and new beginnings. The men gave thanks and prayed that this be the beginning of deep healing for themselves, the generation, and the country. We brought in more hot stones for the next round, which was to the south—the place of passion and heart, of childhood and innocence, of the eternal feminine energies that burst forth in summer bloom.

One by one, each man prayed, taking a very long time. Then they told stories again, this time looking into the center of the circle. This time, their buried feelings were coming up with each story.

Chris, a nonveteran, talked about his stepfather, who was in the occupying forces in Japan after World War II. He had engaged in black marketeering and committed atrocities in Tokyo. This stepfather had been alcoholic, difficult to talk to, unnecessarily harsh. He had had nightmares, headaches, and explosive rages. Now Chris understood for the first time that his stepfather, too, was a veteran who had poisoned Chris's childhood because he suffered from PTSD. Chris sobbed for the stepfather who was still tortured and for the hurt little boy he himself had been.

Again and again, rocking and sobbing, Pat called out the name of his best friend Hutter, who had been killed by rocket fire. "This is Dante's Inferno," he cried through his tears. "This is as close to hell as I want to get."

Conrad saw himself back in Viet Nam, his base being overrun. He begged the enemy soldiers to go back, crying, "I don't want to kill you. Go home."

Frank said, "I've always said only that I was a career military man. I've never admitted this before, but now I realize I must: I am a Vietnam veteran. I helped fight that war. I helped those bombers find their targets. I helped destroy that country. I didn't want to be, but I am. I am a Vietnam vet." Then he, too, began sobbing.

In the heat and steam, men leaned over, lying on their backs, flopping over one another. As each man spoke, his chest heaved. Men who had already spoken cried at each new story. By the time we had completed the round to the south, everyone was faint, and several men had to leave. Someone pointed out that we had been in the lodge all day; the sun was beginning to sink below the mountains.

We had entered something like a group trance. Each story had piled on the other and brought buried grief flooding to the surface. Every man was drained. There was no time, energy, or need for further catharsis. I led the men who still had some strength in brief final prayers. Then we returned to camp to say goodbye.

I apologized to Pat, Conrad, Phil, and Frank. I had wanted to do an initiation ceremony to complete their transformation. "Don't worry," Pat laughed. "After that lodge, I know I've been initiated."

The "team" did not want to disperse. These men were now brothers, old friends. They had received each other' s broken youths, honored each other's struggles and choices, respected each other's differences, and balmed each other's wounds. Fourteen men, who had arrived having never told their stories to men who were different, left feeling newly a part of a team, a generation, a history, and a shared story.

Fourteen

RESTITUTION IN THE FAMILY AND THE NATION

O
n April 18, 2005, Patriot's Day, 137 additional veterans were posthumously honored at the seventh annual In Memory Day at the Vietnam Memorial in Washington, D.C. Since this ceremony's inception, more than 1,500 vets who died as a result of wounds, emotional difficulties, or toxic exposures have been recognized and, while not inscribed on the Wall, entered on the In Memory Honor Roll.

Preston Stern's name was included this year, a decade after his death from Agent Orange-related illness. His mother, Enid, was at the ceremony. "My personal feelings about the ceremony were ambivalent," she said. "Practically our whole family had been against the war, and so I felt some bitterness about the idea that this militarily-oriented occasion could be 'healing.' But I was glad that those young Americans who came home damaged physically and emotionally were finally being given the recognition they deserved."

As Enid's words imply, the moral responsibility for a war must ultimately fall not upon the common soldiers who fought it but upon the nation and its leaders who created it. Hence, we arrive at the third step in healing the warrior, which concerns the role played by society. The social group must not only witness the stories of its warriors; it must also accept responsibility for their deeds during war and their condition afterward.

Shakespeare dramatized the moral needs of common soldiers through two men who argue with Henry V the night before the battle of Agincourt. Says Bates, "If his [the king's] cause be wrong, our obedience to the king wipes the crime of it out of us." Says Williams, "But if the cause be not good, the king himself hath a heavy reckoning to make. . . . Now if these men do not die well, it will be a black matter for the king that led them to it, who to disobey were against all proportion of subjection."[1]

Shakespeare's men asked from their king what our veterans today still ask from our leaders. Inevitably, veterans will assign responsibility for war to our government, presidents, congress, and generals. This is no mere psychological defense; nor is it just an individual's refusal to accept fate or accountability—as indeed, one of our nation's old enemies understood. Ho Chi Minh, during the Vietnam War, told his people neither to hate nor to blame ordinary American GIs for their participation in the invasion of his country. Hold the leaders responsible, he counseled; fight the GIs, but remember that they are victims, also.

Our leadership's refusal to accept responsibility for our wars helps explain the rage and mistrust veterans and their families often feel toward authority. The young man or woman, after all, went to war in the nation's name. Except in rare instances, a soldier did not kill because he was criminal or insane or possessed by selfish motives. To the contrary, and while striving under the most adverse conditions, he killed because his nation ordered him to do so in its service. Ultimately, he killed because, otherwise, he and his companions would be killed themselves. The nation and its leaders defined the enemy, provided moral and ideological reasons to go to war, trained the soldier for it, and put him in the kill-or-be-killed situation. In Plains cultures, "a war leader was held responsible for the casualties of his command." His people expected him to carry that difficult responsibility and judged him adversely if he did not.[2] So should it be today.

Our society must accept the responsibility for its war making. To the returning veteran, our leaders and people must say, "You did this in our name and because you were subject to our orders. We lift the burden of your actions from you and take it onto our shoulders. We are responsible for you, for what you did, and for the consequences."

Without this transfer of responsibility, the veteran becomes the nation's scapegoat and carries its secret grief and guilt for all of us. Psychologically and socially, veterans often crawl into the dark corners of our culture and collapse under the crippling effect of carrying the moral and spiritual burdens of an entire nation alone. The "black matter for the king" remains upon the grunts. This state of affairs helps explain the degree to which veterans become ill with their feelings. Given our nation's denial of responsibility and disowning of suffering, the only socially acceptable role left for them to collapse into is that of "disabled veteran." It is this abandonment of them, as much as the war experience, that causes PTSD .[3]

Once the collective assumes responsibility for the war, the veteran's PTSD symptoms begin to disappear. The vet can stand with dignity, for even if the war was immoral or ill-advised, even if we did not win, he or she is still our honorable warrior returned from a war fought in our service. It is imperative for the health of our veterans that they experience other ordinary Americans and our leadership as walking with them and accepting accountability for our wars.

As is the case with storytelling, the transfer of responsibility from the individual to the group can occur in part through psychotherapy. A therapist can guide a veteran in finding appropriate audiences for his stories—family members in and out of the therapy setting, friends, community groups, schools. In traditional therapy, the prevalent view is that healing can best occur if the therapist remains emotionally detached from the client's life and material. In working with vets, though, the opposite is true: If the therapist maintains detachment, the story remains solely the burden of the patient. Therapy becomes effective only when the therapist can affirm that he is personally engaged with the veteran's story and accepts the need to help carry the collective responsibility. Dr. John Rhead spoke to me of his own transformation as a result of his psychotherapeutic work with veterans:

> Working with vets has been the antidote for the illusions with which I grew up. I did not question the moral certitude of John Wayne and company as they defeated the evil Germans and Japanese until I witnessed the profound spiritual wounding of my peers by their experiences in Viet Nam. They went to war under the misconception that they were risking only death or dismemberment. Knowing as we do now the larger risks of psychological and spiritual torments makes me forever grateful that I was spared this fate. I strive to channel this gratitude into bearing compassionate witness to those who were not so spared. These feelings also call me to participate in, and sometimes initiate,

healing ceremonies at the Wall. These ceremonies are as much for my healing as for the veterans'.

Therapists need to be more open and self-disclosing with veterans than with almost any other group of clients. Since "war brings forth the man," veterans will test their therapists by war's standards. Veterans must know what their therapists did during war and how they feel about it and veterans, now. Essentially, as Dr. Rhead indicates, the therapist must become part of the veteran's warrior society. And, as Rhead affirms, we must all be willing to be transformed by the experiences of our warriors.

Some nonveterans are readily able to affirm this collective responsibility. Dick Hughes, for instance, was a conscientious objector who went to Viet Nam during the war to avoid the draft and protest our actions. He worked with street children and orphans in Da Nang and remains a proveteran activist today, crusading on behalf of families with Agent Orange diseases in both the United States and Viet Nam.

But for other civilians, sharing responsibility is *not* easy to do, and it touches the alienation they may feel as well. During one journey to Viet Nam, a professor who had been an antiwar activist for years shouted, "I did everything I could to stop this war and the harm we still see. Don't ask me to accept responsibility! It was the *government's* war, not *ours!*" As his rage illustrates, it is not enough to provide witness for our veterans alone. Rather, as a nation, we must embrace the history of everyone affected by our war making, including those who refused to participate. They may be as deeply wounded by their histories as veterans are by combat PTSD. But resisters' stories do not appear in a country's official history. How, then, do we find the opportunities to honor their experiences?

Steve Trimm was a draft resister who went into exile in Canada. For decades after he returned to the United States, he suffered severe alienation, feeling even more alone than the vets with whom he most identified because his story was excluded from public consideration. Finally, he searched for the means to tell and honor the stories of people like himself. He reports:

> The Vietnam War was such a strange and potent event that it damaged even those who opposed it. Many of those who refused to go to war were sent to prison, where not a few were abused and tortured. Others who resisted were turned into fugitives or driven into exile. Even conscientious objectors were scorned by society and rejected by their families. One way or another, all who resisted the war were made to suffer and to sacrifice—years of their lives, portions of their minds. As much as any soldier, they were the war's victims. And heroes. And they, too, deserved to be remembered.
>
> I had been a member of the Resistance. I knew our country needed to remember my comrades and me and to think about what we had gone through and stood for. In 1990, I paid for the casting of a small bronze plaque that read, simply, "Honoring Those Who Refused to Fight in Vietnam."
>
> It took a while to find a home for that little plaque. One institution refused to display it because its sentiment was not broad enough. That institution thought the message ought to read, "Honoring Those Who Refuse to Participate in War." Another institution rejected the plaque because its message was *too* broad. This institution thought the message ought to read, "Honoring Those Who for Reasons of Conscience Refused to Fight in Viet Nam."

At last, in 1992, the Washington Square United Methodist Church in New York City offered to display the plaque just inside its front doors. That October, we held a dedication ceremony. During the war's darkest years, this church had granted sanctuary to resisters—who nevertheless had been arrested by the FBI and dragged off to prison. In April 1993, my thirteen-year-old daughter, Arielle, and I were in New York City for the Mets' opening-day game at Shea. We had visited the World Trade Center which, just a few weeks before, had been bombed by terrorists, and now we were in Washington Square.

It was time to show Arielle what had become of the plaque. She had seen it at my apartment and even snapped photos of me holding it. But at age eleven or twelve, there was no way she could understand what the plaque represented. Even at thirteen, she couldn't fully comprehend it.

But she saw the plaque on the church wall, and I knew she would remember where it was. In my mind's eye, I could see her as an adult, mature and worldly wise at last, bringing her kids to that church. And I could see her, a person of kindness and good heart, pointing to the plaque and saying to her children. "Let me tell you about your grandfather and what he did—and refused to do—during a war."

Traditional cultures performed rituals that lifted responsibility off their warriors and transferred it to the people as a whole. Part of the purification process sometimes included this transfer of the stain of bloodguilt. Ultimately, both civilians and leaders would acknowledge that they, and not their warriors, were the ones accountable. During reconciliation retreats, I stage such rituals. First the veterans tell their stories, and then the civilians speak of their own losses of loved ones, hope, and trust due to wars. We become a united community. Finally, we place our veterans in the center of our circle. Each civilian addresses them, speaking of our collective responsibility for what the veterans did during the war and have suffered since and of our willingness to join them as life-long witnesses.

Such rituals can occur in other settings as well. The 2005 Vietnam War Memorial ceremony was one such event. At the Wall, Preston Stern's mother, Enid, felt troubled again at the misuse of his and other veterans' deaths for patriotic ends. But Preston's twenty-year-old son, Gabriel, who was only ten when his father died, was at the ceremony as well. As he tells it, his perspective was somewhat different:

On April 18, 2005, my dad's name was accepted as a part of the Vietnam Memorial Wall. I hadn't thought much of it before that day; I recognized the gesture as a tribute to my father, but saw its purpose mainly as a means for my mom to tell the world what an extraordinary man her husband had been. I always eagerly share my father's story with a sense of pride. I was willing to help with the process of getting him on the Wall, but still, I thought, we were doing this mostly for my mom.

When the day came for Dad's induction, a large group of family members attended. My mother had made a book for the occasion that included Dad's essays on his reasons for leaving the army and a couple of short stories he wrote. On its cover, framed by some Native American symbol above and his blue combat infan-tryman's medal below, was the epitaph inscribed on his grave.

At the program's end, the families were instructed to bring a metal stand holding a certificate showing the honored veteran's name, dates of service, birth and death, and photograph to a specified section of the wall. I entered the walkway with my family and headed toward the designated section. We walked slowly, with a large crowd of others, all there for the same purpose. Always respectful of the Wall, I walked mostly in silence, reflecting on its meaning. I knew how important it was to veterans, I knew that it honored those who had died, and I knew that it told of the great tragedy of war. But for some reason, I had never completely *felt* all of this meaning before.

Finally, I placed the tripod stand against the Wall snugly between two others, and someone put the book in front of it. Everything was in place. Then, it came over me, not gradually but certainly. As I looked at the familiar picture of Dad's smiling face, I realized the weight of what we had done, not for us, but for him. I thought of the poster of the four soldiers erecting the flag on his office door; I saw the white tee-shirt depicting the Wall with red lettering that read, "We will never forget." I felt the way I always had when hearing Dad speak of the Wall: not entirely understanding what he said but being awed by his passion and even a bit frightened. Again I felt the indescribable emotion that had filled me when hearing him talk about Donald Yarrington, his commanding officer and friend, who had died not thirty feet from him in Viet Nam. I understood the importance of looking Yarrington up on the wall and how much that had meant to Dad. When I looked again at the Native American symbol and his medal on the cover of his book, I felt as if my whole body smiled. I walked away, content. This was right; this was so right for Dad.

He deserved it. This was universal justice. This was exactly the right place for Dad to be.

We have seen that veterans suffer in part because of their war experiences and in part because of their treatment upon homecoming. They also suffer because of the contrast between the truth of war and the illusions our society has about it. Hillman emphasizes that PTSD is "a specific syndrome suffered by *American* veterans . . . occurring within the wider syndrome: the endemic numbing of the American homeland and its addiction to security." [4] As he implies, we could significantly alleviate the suffering of our veterans and minimize their disabilities by attending to the societal dimensions of PTSD. We could thereby also increase the number of contributing citizens, stop the pain of war from echoing down the generations, and create a warrior class that could offer lifelong service and help us immeasurably in reducing our preoccupation with violence.

In Native American societies, no one would dare wear an eagle feather, a sash, or a warrior's charm or shirt that he had not earned by trial. To do so would have brought dishonor to the young warrior and to his elders. In sharp contrast, our entertainment-driven consumer society markets empty icons of the war experience. We turn camouflage into a clothing style and sell toy replicas of advanced weaponry. Teenagers wear "I'm a veteran and proud of it" hats and tee-shirts and sport combat ribbons on their jackets. Millions play graphic war video games, some designed and now marketed by the military. While we shun war's truth, we graft it onto popular culture and produce a consumer patriotism in which uninitiated people unconsciously partake.

We would be wise not to market movies and computer war games that co-opt the war experience for its adrenalin rush in the place of real rites of passage that are challenging, productive, and creative. We owe it to the soldiers who risk their lives in our name to reserve honors for those who have earned them and to teach what those honors represent. When the media relates war stories, it must tell them in ways that educate the public regarding war's realities, rather than numb them or seduce them into its frenzy.

Two of what Prof. Leroy Rouner has called "the high holy days of American civil religion"—Memorial Day and Veterans' Day—are meant to help us cope with war's aftermath.[5] They could serve our nation as public rituals for healing from war, but they do not.

May 30 was first set aside toward the end of the Civil War by Southern women, led by Cassandra Oliver Moncure of Virginia, to commemorate soldiers killed on both the Union and the Confederate sides. Its original ritual was the decorating of soldiers' graves. Since then, the holiday has evolved into a day of remembrance for soldiers killed in all wars.

On the eleventh hour of the eleventh day of the eleventh month in 1918, World War I ended. A year later, Woodrow Wilson proclaimed this day, November 11, Armistice Day in the hope that it would be associated with the quest for world peace. An act of Congress in 1954 changed the name of Armistice Day to Veterans' Day.

During the thirty-six years between the creation of Armistice Day and its renaming, the world witnessed the Great Depression and the Spanish Civil War. World War II followed— the costliest war in history, with more than twenty-two million dead and thirty-four million wounded. We developed and used atomic weapons for the first time. The Korean War soon followed. The modern era proved itself a time not of world peace but of massive disillusionment. The War Department was renamed the Department of Defense, a change seeming to reflect our modern confusion in which we aggressively pursue military action but always justify it as a matter of necessary self-defense. We are apparently convinced we will always need the military and thus always create veterans. The name and intention of Armistice Day has faded from memory, and the holiday on November 11 has become a time, not to meditate on the end of war, but to thank those who fought.

To be sure, memorials for the dead and celebrations for the safe return of the living are necessary public rituals. But the purpose of both holidays has been reduced to the lauding of patriotism. Many veterans go into hiding on "their" holidays. Owen Germain, a navy veteran of the Normandy invasion who survived the sinking of his ship, blurted out in response to an inquiry about participating in Veterans Day:

> November 11 is *Armistice* Day! They should never have changed the name. Armistice Day is when World War I was declared over. Veterans' Day is just an excuse for a parade. They're always boys, too, eighteen- or nineteen-year-olds. I voted for Eisenhower. He'd won battles, but at what cost? How many men died under his leadership? Nobody talks about that. I didn't think about these things when I was younger, but now I just can't let it go. Anything I let go is gonna slide right into my son's lap.

Restoring the original meanings of Memorial Day and Armistice Day would be a step toward healing our nation and those who have sacrificed for it.

"The human soul is God's candle," Proverbs tells us. Many traditions light memorial candles on the death anniversaries of loved ones or on annual holidays marked as special times of remembrance. How many memorial candles might we light on Memorial Day to remember all those killed in our modern wars and dead in war's aftermath? We could close the shopping malls and open our churches, synagogues, and mosques. We could invite the public to cemeteries to light candles and pray together. We could institute national rituals, such as reading the names of the war dead, and honoring their widows and their orphans, to guide us into our collective but secret grief, fear, and hunger for hope.

Veterans could benefit, too, from restoring the original meaning of Armistice Day. As Germain and many other veterans long for, we could open our religious, civic, and educational institutions for gatherings of communities in public rituals of shriving—making public confession regarding participation in war and its pains, losses, and sufferings. Veterans Day could become Armistice Day again, at least in spirit, by inviting genuine thanksgiving and shriving such as Lincoln led at Gettysburg, or King David inspired through some of his psalms, or Pericles invoked in his famous Funeral Oration honoring all Athenian war dead at the end of the first year of the Peloponnesian War. This holiday could again become inspirational, helping cleanse veterans' souls and restore the dream of the end of war and coming of peace. It is this dream, ultimately, that most veterans want to have served.

Fifteen

INITIATION AS A WARRIOR

Joe limped into my office leaning heavily on his cane. He was a broad, burly man with hair in a military cut. He wore a black Harley Davidson tee-shirt with its fierce eagle in bright colors across his chest. Serving on aircraft carriers rather than in combat during the Vietnam War, Joe felt personally responsible for the men who had died. He felt as if he had neither helped his brothers nor been tested.

"I went into the service to live out the John Wayne story," he said. "I wanted my father's approval. I wasn't becoming a man in his eyes and had no acceptance at home." But Joe was selected to be a flight mechanic because he was skilled with his hands. "A chicken-shit job," he said. "It denied me the chance to prove myself."

Nonetheless, Joe endured rocket attacks while in Viet Nam briefly "without even a gun in my hands to protect myself." On his carrier, he recovered wounded and dead men from returning aircraft. He also witnessed deaths on shipboard from accidents. And yes, he lost friends.

Several times, he requested a transfer to the combat zone. It was denied. "I'm still angry about it," he says. As a result of his harsh childhood and disappointing war experience, Joe lived a life of alienation, mistrust, and hostility. He could not get along with authority, was often accused of being paranoid, and had an unstable employment history. He was obsessed with fantasies of doing violence and felt he could barely control his impulses. "I've been penned up my whole life. Even if violence doesn't solve anything, at least I'd get it out. At least I'd feel better."

Joe had not been validated for his service by his country or his peers. Instead, he felt the culture in which he was reared had given him a false and distorted vision of masculinity. He had accepted that vision, but then felt denied the chance to prove himself in combat. Simultaneously, he felt betrayed by our government for making his generation fight a brutal and unjust war. The final betrayal had been the public scorn that veterans, including Joe, had received upon their return from Viet Nam.

Joe held out little hope for reconciliation with our country, but he did want to reconcile with combat vets. In his eyes, they were the only men of stature. He wanted them to declare him a worthy peer, forgive him for not being by their side in the bush, and validate his manhood.

"Everything you say resonates with the ancient tradition of warriorhood," I said to him. "That's what you believe in! It isn't John Wayne you want to emulate. It's Achilles and Lancelot and Geronimo. That's the kind of honor, brotherhood, and validation you seek."

Joe leaned forward and looked at me wide-eyed. "I didn't think anyone could understand," he smiled. "I know I'm a warrior inside. That's why I wear this tee-shirt. I don't give a damn about Harleys. I'm wearing the eagle!"

"You want the eagle to be the emblem on your shield. You want to stand tall with your feathers flying and let the world see the proud warrior."

"Exactly! I feel as if I was born in the wrong century. I went to Viet Nam to be a knight errant. I didn't know it wasn't a crusade. I didn't know there were no knights or warriors left in the world. I didn't know I'd be scraping the guts of good men out of flying tin cans."

No matter what men did in or instead of the Vietnam War, many of that generation, like Joe, experienced failed rites of passage. Huge numbers found, as they moved into adulthood, that they felt weak and incomplete—that their inner warrior, in other words, was inadequately trained and developed. Many veterans felt disordered and dishonored. Many nonveterans avoided the warrior concept entirely. Vets and nonvets, moreover, were afraid of each other, rarely discussed the war together, and had no sense of shared history. But every man's inner warrior needs to be called forth and honored by a tribe. A need does not disappear just because the culture does not evoke it.

The final step in the long road home for the veteran is completing this initiation as a warrior. A veteran does not become a warrior merely for having gone to war. A veteran becomes a warrior when he learns to carry his war skills and his vision in mature ways. He becomes a warrior when he has been set right with life again. A warrior's first priority is to protect life rather than destroy it. He serves his nation in peace as well as in war making and dissuades his people from suffering the scourges of war unless absolutely necessary. He uses the fearlessness he has developed to help keep sanity, generosity, and order alive in his culture. A warrior disciplines the violence within himself. Internally and externally, he stares violence in the face and makes it back down. A warrior serves spiritual and moral principles, which he places higher than himself. The role of warrior has a high, noble, and honorable status. In Plains societies, on the hunt, when camp was being moved, and in times of activity or trouble, it was the warriors who were responsible for making sure all the people were safe and cared for.

As a nation, we recognize no such role. We have a great many veterans, but very few warriors. To be sure, we do have high-ranking professional soldiers. But we could more accurately describe many of them as corporate executives of our military industrial complex. When they betray truth, forsake honor, follow immoral orders, or propagate policies based upon falsehoods or ignorance, they fail the virtues of warriorhood.

Throughout history, there have been presidents, premiers, kings, and dictators who have fostered blind patriotism or allegiance. They have demonstrated hunger for military victory, political or economic power, or territorial expansion disguised as a pursuit of moral and spiritual principles. This kind of leadership is an expression of what Jungians call the shadow warrior. It is a twisted version of warriorhood that comes from an immature psyche still trying to prove itself in a world it fears. It is characterized, as Robert Moore summarizes, by lack of control of aggression, insensitivity to relatedness, desire for vengeance, enjoyment of carnage and cruelty, scorn toward the vulnerable, hostility toward the feminine and everything soft, and compulsive and workaholic tendencies.[1] No matter what the public image or "spin," any leader manifesting these qualities or pursuing policies that encourage them is, in fact, not a true warrior but the shadow of one.

We need a class of noble citizen-warriors who know the cost of war and who speak about it before the nation and world. We need people who are awake to human suffering and are willing to guide us in alleviating it. We need those who can serve fearlessly, confronting threat without resorting to needless violence in order to return matters to life-affirming order again.

Consider the example of Hugh Thompson. As a helicopter pilot in the Vietnam War, Thompson was hovering his craft low over My Lai trying to draw enemy fire. But there wasn't any. Surveying the hamlet, he saw not a battle but a massacre. "This wasn't war," he later recalled. Thompson landed his chopper between the marauding GIs and cowering Vietnamese villagers, confronted the GIs, and ordered them to stand off. Then he and his crew rescued four adults and six children, including one badly wounded young boy, and flew them to safety. Thompson returned to combat at a later date and was even shot down and survived. He did not refuse his duty as a warrior, but his actions during My Lai demonstrated the moral stand a warrior must take, even during war, to protect life, minimize destruction, and differentiate between war and oppression.

"You could not discover the limits of soul," Heraclitus taught, "even if you traveled every road to do so; such is the depth of its meaning."[2] Though war threatens life, the experience of war, when understood as the opportunity for profound deepening, can be aligned with the natural movement of soul. Forced to descend into the abyss of human and earthly nature, the young warrior learns that which he or she did not want to know—the brevity of life and love, our human capacity for destruction, our smallness and helplessness against existential forces. The Trojan warrior Glaukos in the *Iliad* expressed this fragility in saying, just as he and the Greek Diomedes were facing off in hot combat, "Very like the generations of leaves upon this earth are the generations of men."[3] Today, Robert Moore stresses the clearness of thought and intensity of experience that come from "living with the awareness of [one's] own imminent death."[4] In retrospect, the mature warrior might say that one high purpose of his venture into warfare had been to attain such wisdom.

But this sanguine view depends upon the culture guiding the soldier's return from war's Underworld spiritually as well as physically. Traditional peoples understood this need. For instance, many Native American tribes, the Lakota, Cheyenne, Apache, Commanche, and Iroquois nations among them, enacted initiation ceremonies for every stage of warriorhood, from joining a war party for the first time to serving the people as a wise elder. The warrior's path was a path through life. A man knew what he needed to do to walk it. He was accompanied by his companions and community every step of the way.

In stark contrast, and in the absence of that communal structure, our veterans remain uninitiated and stuck in the death passage. Instead of being reborn into a new identity of the warrior, they suffer the myriad symptoms of PTSD. Indeed, modern warfare, as we have seen, aborts the testing of manhood and is antithetical to true initiation on the battlefield. Ironically, even Native American soldiers in the U.S. forces discovered this difference. After World War I, Sioux veterans who were already members of the American Legion sought admission to their tribe's warrior societies. But the old keepers of the orders resisted their claims. "They considered that killing men with rifle fire was no qualification for standing as warriors." Such warfare, they said, is "just shooting."[5]

Nonetheless, modern men and women experience the spiritual motivation that calls them onto the warrior's path. The initiatory route that leads to the full level of maturity this path offers can and must be rediscovered, even in the twenty-first century. The war survivor must accept and finally affirm his or her war experiences. The veteran must grow a new identity large enough to surround and carry those traumatic experiences. And he or she must call the soul back into service as the community's witness not only to horror but also to love.

"To know war we must enter its love," James Hillman has written.[6] A warrior is one who knows the love of war. This does not mean he loves destruction and killing. Rather, through this love a warrior embraces the beauty and fragility of life and the compassion of extreme comradeship. He has earned the wisdom and humility that come from having once served Ares, and he takes on the commitment now to be an instrument of justice and healing for humanity as a servant of Athena. His soul is recomposed, regenerated. It becomes again an agent of creative vision, civilization, beauty, and charity. It becomes a protector and nurturer rather than a destroyer.

During the Papago Indians' ceremony of a warrior's return, an elder warrior questions the new young "enemy slayer" each night of sixteen days of purification. "Verily, who desires this experience?" the elder asks again and again regarding the initiate's attitude toward having killed. "Do you not desire it? Then you must endure its many hardships."[7] The ceremony cannot proceed and the initiate remains in isolation until he is able to say "Yes, I desire it."

Here we view one of the mysteries of initiation. If we want the status of warrior, we must be willing to accept the challenges and difficulties that go with it. The Papago ceremony teaches the profound truth that the way for a soul to return to life and the world is by way of consent: I had this experience, we must say, and I accept it. I have taken the long, difficult road. I have been initiated. I am now a warrior and will serve the code and embody the qualities of a warrior all my days. It is by this spiritual acceptance that the soul lost in war may return.

Today, much of the veteran's resistance to this kind of assent originates in his alienation from the government and country that he feels betrayed him. It is difficult to affirm an experience that robbed you of health, sanity, and normalcy; it is perhaps more difficult to set aside your anger toward the leadership who sent you into that experience. Until a veteran finds the depth of character to negotiate this resentment—to grieve his lost ideals and innocence, to say yes to the new difficulties, to live for himself and all his dead comrades, to make meaning out of the entire matrix—he or she remains stuck in a lonely inner world, just as the Papago initiate remained in his isolation hut. Many veterans' organizations counsel the public to "Honor the warrior, not the war." In similar fashion, veterans can be guided in honoring the inner warrior even while questioning the purpose for which they fought.

The warrior archetype seems to be hard-wired into us. It not only drives young people who seek initiation into service; it also surfaces under combat conditions, and veterans often spontaneously enact its dictates, live by its values, and perform its rituals. The archetype can act like a map of unknown and difficult terrain, showing the returned soldier the way towards full warriorhood.

Keith Forry was a grunt serving in the Iron Triangle near the Cambodia border during the Vietnam War. One day, deep in the jungle, Keith found the skull of a canine-like animal. He pulled some teeth out of its lower jaw and added them to the necklace he wore with a cross and peace sign on it that he had fashioned. "I called the energy of the animal to be with me," Keith told me. He thought of the teeth as wolf's teeth, unconsciously invoking the symbology used by the Norse berserks and the Indo-European warrior society initiations, for which "the test of courage [was] resistance to physical suffering, followed by magical transformation into a wolf." In these initiations, the transformation into the animal spirit happened through "ritual donning" of its parts, which "constituted the essential moment of initiation into a men's secret society." The initiate "assimilated the behavior of the wolf . . . became a wild-beast warrior, irresistible and invulnerable."[8] Similarly, Keith thought of the "wolf teeth" he wore as a sign that the animal's spirit was simultaneously protecting him and giving him the powers he needed to succeed in combat.

It is important that therapists who work with veterans be educated in the warrior tradition and its rituals in order to recognize and help veterans identify this surfacing of warrior traits. Veterans often keep their stories of such experiences secret, treasuring them for the power they once held but also guarding them against a secular profession and society that is not willing to recognize their spiritual significance. Ignoring these traits is harmful to the veteran, for then the inner warrior remains invisible. Pathologizing the traits is also harmful, for then the vet is further wounded by reductionist interpretations that may minimize their importance to him, treat them as symbolic of something other than a primary experience, or empty them of spiritual potency.

After decades alone with his experiences, Keith finally found a therapist who was experienced with trauma and could aid his further evolution as a warrior. Interestingly, Keith had spent only a few months with this new therapist before he was bitten by a dog. The bite triggered the memory of an event that had occurred when he was in Viet Nam: machine gun in hand, Keith had stood up in the middle of a firefight and declared, "Nobody lives forever!" He described his feelings of that day as carefree and exuberant. As his unit was being surrounded, he had looked at his comrades and thought, "What are you waiting for?" To live, they would have to "punch through the enemy."

This incident, too, mirrors the universal warrior experience. Remember the Lakota warriors' famous battle cry, "It is a good day to die!" Keith's stand was not a suicidal gesture, such as desperate fighters sometimes make during combat. His was a warrior's affirmation, an acceptance and a declaration of his alignment with life's brevity, his duty to save his comrades, and the presence of the wolf spirit that could help him act fiercely enough to "punch through."

The dog bite took on several meanings for Keith. The event of the bite itself seemed rather unusual. He didn't think he had gotten too close to the dog; it just struck without provocation, and then it stayed where it was. Afterward, Keith had what he called a "peculiar mindset." He accepted the bite as the return of the wolf—it brought the wolf's spirit back into him. Keith said, "I think the dog bite was a way to trigger my rage. It was a wild card. Who knew what it would reveal? But in fact, I'm fine now." The dog bite became for Keith a measure of his initiation into warriorhood. Through it he demonstrated that he had finally mastered his impulsive training to strike back against what hurt him. "Before, I would have strangled the dog before it had a chance to bite me," he said, but he hadn't even raised a hand. His mind and spirit now transcended his gut instinct and military experience. He could take pain without causing it in return. He was transforming from a disabled veteran into a warrior of honor.

Keith concluded his reflections on this experience by declaring, several times, that "Life is a fabulous journey." After decades of silence and secrecy, he said "Yes!" to his wartime experiences, to his old affinity with the wolf spirit, to the difficult wisdom of life's brevity, and to a warrior's duty.

Keith's story shows us that, even in the absence of culturally-led rituals, initiation into warriorhood can sometimes still occur on a personal level. Aware therapists can help, as can sensitivity such as Keith's to the symbolic meaning of events. As Mircea Eliade observes, "Initiations of warriors and shamans are individual; and in their scenarios we can still trace the archetypal scenarios revealed by myths." [9]

We have said much about the character of the mature warrior, whose role is ultimately to serve values greater than themselves. What, then, are some examples of mature warriors in this kind of service?

A mature warrior exercises restraint even on the battlefield. Hugh Thomson, as we heard, achieved this moral level even in the midst of gunfire when he rescued rather than killed villagers at My Lai. As Thomson did, the mature warrior stays conscious that it is other human beings he is fighting and strives not to dehumanize his own or his antagonist's people. He uses force only when he has absolutely no other choice. Eighty-year-old Nguyen Van Tam, known as "Mr. Tiger," a veteran of thirty years of war against the Japanese, French, and Americans, voiced this wisdom as he warmly welcomed American veterans to his Mekong Delta farm. He explained, "I didn't fight Americans. I fought the enemy. The enemy is anyone who invades your home and tries to take it from you."

When a soldier is able to resist dehumanization even in the combat zone, he is less likely to be scarred by the experience. Vietnam War veteran and poet Yusef Komunyakaa said, "I never used the words 'gook' or 'dink' in Viet Nam.... There is a certain kind of dehumanization that takes place to create an enemy, to call up the passion to kill this person. I knew something about that growing up in Louisiana."[10] North Vietnamese soldier Nguyen Duy said that though it was "easier to kill" and he knew the fleeing GI would have turned his M16 on *him*, Duy used all his strength to restrain his trigger finger, telling himself, "Save him, it's harder."[11] And Terry Miltner, a combat zone dog handler, tells of meeting an armed enemy combatant on a dark road late at night. The two men's eyes met, they nodded, and each walked past the other without raising a weapon.

Then there is the famous Buddhist story of a samurai ordered to kill the assassin of his lord. He hunted the assassin for a long time and finally found him. The samurai swung his sword overhead and was about to execute the man when the other spit in his face. The samurai sheathed his sword and walked away, leaving the assassin free. And why? Because the samurai was personally offended by the spitting and had become angry. His training was never to kill when flooded with emotion or for personal reasons. The teaching was that when violence is mixed with anger, it becomes egoistical and dehumanizes us as well as our enemy. So he let the man go.

After returning from combat, mature warriors may serve their communities in a variety of ways. They know, as Phil Ochs sang in protest during the Vietnam War, that "there but for fortune go you or I." We see this awareness in veterans who, both privately and through organizations, care for their wounded comrades with great loyalty and effectiveness. They understand the hideous distortions of body and psyche that PTSD, disease, and death can cause as others do not. Thus Jack became a volunteer aid to his wheelchair-bound and tube-fed veteran neighbor. And the members of the Tom Paine Chapter of Veterans for Peace immediately mobilized—meeting with lawyers, politicians, city planners, and VA officials and threatening public demonstrations—as soon as they heard that regional disabled veterans were to be evicted from a halfway house in a city's attempt to "upgrade" a neighborhood.

Veterans often serve their community in policing roles as well. Reid Mackey, a helicopter crew chief in Viet Nam, became a state trooper, then a town sheriff, then a White House security guard, all the while practicing Native American spirituality. The police force, fire department, conservation corps, and various security officer forces tend to attract veterans, replicating the policing and restraining functions that warriors filled in traditional societies. Kathy, a domestic abuse survivor, reports that after many false tries in psychotherapy, it was the counsel she received from a former prisoner of war that finally helped her. "He had been there," she said, "so he was the one who understood the mentality of my abuser and could coach me on how to get out of his clutches without being killed."

Another function of the mature warrior is to serve the state in political capacities. They sometimes sound as voices of restraint and reason when politicians and other citizens are swept away in war frenzy. Late in life, Generals Eisenhower and MacArthur made all but unknown antiwar speeches. In the public sector, from our local communities to the floor of Congress, survivors are in the unique position to say to us all: Beware of war and violence. If you choose its path of destruction, be sure you are willing to pay the price. We know; we have seen its horrors.

This awareness reveals the helpful and constructive side of PTSD. It is not only a form of suffering. If understood in its mythic context and social functions, it is an alarm system sounding a warning through survivors that the social order is breaking down and the savage breaking through. As the ancient poet Pindar of Thebes wrote, "War is sweet to those who have not tried it. The experienced man is frightened at the heart to see it advancing."

In his novel, *Hermanos!,* William Herrick, a veteran of the Abraham Lincoln Brigade of the Spanish Civil War, told this story: Jake Starr was an idealistic young American who fought in Spain and joined the Communist party, believing it would reform the world's ills. To consolidate power, the Communists turned against their own allies. Starr's allegiance was tested. He was ordered to witness the execution of a peasant resistance group leader. The peasant looked at Starr and thought, "I will marry him, as every victim marries his executioner." His final request was that Starr pull the trigger, because, he said, ". . . the American, he is gentler. I prefer him to marry me." [12]

The idea of killing as creating a sacred bond may startle, but the truth is that war is an intimate act. Whether we intend it or not, we achieve a permanent shared history with those we battle. In the grand arena, no matter who wins or loses, nations that go to war shape each other's cultures and politics. On the personal level, every participant is affected for generations. Since violence is an intrusion into another's intimate space, it is the inverse of love, a forced interpenetration. We cannot separate the history of the conquering of this continent from the history of the Iroquois or the Navajo or the Cheyenne people. We also cannot separate the history of the modern era from that of Nazi Germany, or the course of events in the United States from Korea or Viet Nam. We are all, in the Spanish peasant's sense of the word, "married" through our mutual violence.

Given the fact that we and our enemies have wounded each other so deeply, how can we fulfill the widespread dream of becoming all one nation, one tribe, one planet? How do we restore oneness when each war, every war, yields not just wounds of body and soul to individuals, not just countless damaged for each nation involved, but a millennia-old world history of fragmentation?

These hard questions bring us to a final characteristic of mature warriors—for most often it is they, knowing firsthand the cost of divisiveness, who throughout history have had a vision of oneness and shown us the path toward it.

In 472 BCE, Aeschylus, who fought the Persians at Marathon and whose brother was killed there, penned *The Persians*. Seth Benardete, in the introduction to his translation, says that the tragedy portrayed Athens' greatest enemy as "having started an unjust war and suffering a deserving defeat . . . not as criminals but rather as great and noble, dying deaths that are as much to be pitied as the deaths of Athenians."[13] Writing about his adversaries as well as his own people, Aeschylus declared that the common soldiers suffered "the lowest depths of woe" as "payment for [their king's] pride and godless arrogance."[14] Daring to sympathize with the enemy, Aeschylus affirmed belonging to a larger society than that of just one's ethnic group or nation.

To heal our veterans, we must take Aeschylus' cue and restore humanity to those against whom we have warred. We must enter into a new identity that transcends nationalism and shares war's aftereffects. As mature warriors have always done, we must develop the wisdom that our rightful tribe is the entire human race and that we owe allegiance to all life, gaining witness from and bearing sympathy for each side.

Nonveterans whose lives have been devastated by war sometimes demonstrate largess of vision to a remarkable degree. Elie Weisel, who survived Auschwitz as a teenager, used his career as writer, educator, and activist to witness to the holocaust, serve as a prophet warning against its recurrence, and help preserve the Eastern European Jewish culture he experienced as targeted with annihilation. Later, to witness and protest the recurrence of genocide, this time against other peoples, he visited the Cambodian border during that country's self-genocide and visited the Serbian concentration camps during the Balkans Wars.

Another example: On the island of Crete are large German military cemeteries holding the remains of thousands of paratroopers killed during the Nazi invasion. The people of the island still regularly oversee and tend to these cemeteries of their former enemies. As the Cretan custodian of one military cemetery tells us,

> At dusk, you can often see a poignant sight; black-dressed old Cretan women lighting candles on the graves of past adversaries. When you ask them why, they reply: "They, too, have a mother, and she is far away or dead. We also lost our sons. . . . We know how a mother feels. Now, we are their mothers." [15]

Another civilian who fulfills the role of mature warrior is an elderly woman named Bianca. A hospice volunteer, she approached me after a recent meeting at which I had addressed the hospice group on how to work with dying veterans. "When the bombs fall on Baghdad, I feel them right here," she whispered in an Italian accent as she patted her chest. Then she placed her hands over her womb. "When they torture prisoners at Abu Ghraib, I feel it here."

Bianca had been just a child in Sicily when the Allies invaded during World War II. "I hated America for destroying my home and village, but I loved you for liberating us. Now I again hate this country I love. Can't you stop torturing us?"

Viewed only from the psychological perspective, Bianca might be declared pathologically hypersensitive and a victim of PTSD. However, from the spiritual perspective, her sensitivity did not mark her as dysfunctional. To the contrary, Bianca was feeling exactly as she should during another time of war. Over the years, she had clearly developed into full warriorhood; it was evident in her gaze, her proud gait even in her older age, and her determination to speak about old pain and protest new war. In the context of her elder's role in relation to her society, her sensitivity was an asset. It allowed her to serve others who had suffered with a compassion that was healing. It had become a moral sensitivity.

Earlier we heard of George, the World War II Italian-American who could not forgive himself for attacking his own ancestral people during the Allies' invasion of Italy. George was a patient at the hospice where Bianca volunteered. After our conversation, I referred her to the team helping George. Thus a woman who survived the invasion of Italy and a dying veteran grieving over his part in it were able to serve one another in the quest for peace and forgiveness at life's end.

Veterans themselves sometimes strive to achieve the mature warrior's vision of reconciliation by traveling to the places where they fought, visiting distant war cemeteries of their comrades, and providing charitable services to those they have hurt, such as many do today in Afghanistan and Viet Nam. We can also create encounters with former antagonists at home. With careful preparation, I have had Vietnamese refugees attend veterans' therapy group meetings.[16] Air force vet Jim Helt, who has suffered Agent Orange–related diseases, says about the Vietnamese who similarly suffer, "I feel so close to the Vietnamese victims of Agent Orange; we share a bond that will last forever." Jim, as well as other veterans, works with American and Vietnamese advocates to create educational and health services for these victims. As Mr. Tiger tells all his veteran visitors, "Nationality has nothing to do with who we are. We are brothers and sisters because we all survived the same hell."

Incidents of PTSD among Vietnamese do exist. Bao Ninh's *The Sorrow of War* provides a powerful fictionalized account based upon his personal experience.[17] Also, journalist Morley Safer on his return to Viet Nam uncovered reports on the suffering of both veterans and civilians. He met with Dr. Duong Quynh Hoa, one of the founders of the Viet Cong and later director of a maternity clinic. Said Dr. Duong, "The veterans feel forsaken, abandoned. They are poor; they cannot find jobs; they have the most serious psychological problems. They abuse their wives and their children. Many lost their wives during the war."[18]

Nevertheless, Vietnamese veterans suffer a far lower incidence of PTSD than do American veterans, with fewer instances of nightmares, depression, alienation, and dysfunction. Yet during the war, far more Vietnamese, both civilians and military, were exposed to combat conditions than were Americans. This anomaly suggests that the severity, incidence, and aftermath of PTSD increase or decrease according to the surrounding social context. Though PTSD may be an inevitable effect of the battlefield, the host society can ameliorate the condition.

One way for our own nation to do so is to acknowledge the grief we share with the world. We can honor and grieve each other's dead. On a 2002 visit to Viet Nam, Bob Cagle prayed in a small cemetery near his former firebase for the Viet Cong dead as well as on the old fields of battle for his own. The much larger Trung Son cemetery lies deep in the jungle of the old demilitarized zone and holds the remains of over a hundred thousand Vietnamese who worked the Ho Chi

Minh trail. When air force colonel Frank Houde, who had flown reconnaissance missions over the area, visited this cemetery in 2000, he said, "Unlike the grunts, I thought I had no home base on Vietnamese soil to which I could return. But I found my base right here, because I helped cause this."

Frank's reconciliation with the country where he had fought had begun several years earlier. In 1998, on his first visit to Viet Nam since the war, Frank found himself sitting around a table with Vietnamese officials. It was a stiff, formal meeting discussing politics and governmental relations, monitored by officials and dependent upon a translator for communications. Frank looked across the table at a gray-haired Vietnamese man who appeared to be about his same age. Introductions had been limited, but Frank's eyes met those of the gray-haired man. Something was communicated.

Frank held out his arms like mock airplane wings, swerved and steered them up and down, then pointed to himself and to the sky, communicating through mime that he had been a pilot during the war.

His counterpart across the table put his hands together. Pointer fingers extended, he moved them back and forth and said, "Ack ack!" His miming indicated that he had been an anti-aircraft gunner.

The men stared at each other for a moment, each realizing that they once had been enemies trying to bring about the other's death. Then Frank turned to their translator and said, "Please tell my friend that we respected him and were frightened. He was good!"

The translator spoke. The former gunner's face beamed a smile. The entire company around the table from both sides broke into laughter. From then on, the meeting was easy, personal, and informal. The former enemies exchanged handshakes and saluted in mutual honor.

On another occasion, I arrive with my group of veterans and their spouses at the small thatched home and gardens of Mr. and Mrs. Tam Tien in the Mekong Delta of Viet Nam. Mr. Tien, a former Viet Cong soldier, rushes to our veterans, grabs their hands, and welcomes them. He lifts his shirt and points to three large scars that pock his chest and abdomen. "Look!" he laughs, "Here, here, here. You almost killed me during the war. How funny! If I had died we would not have had this wonderful opportunity to meet again and become friends."

Mrs. Tien joins us. They lead us to their table, feast us on tea and fruit, and insist on hearing every American's war story. Then they invite us to stay as their guests and "dream on our pillows in peace."

The numbers of Vietnamese people killed, wounded, missing, displaced, homeless, and disabled during the Vietnam War far exceeded ours. Their ecology and infrastructure were ravaged, while ours was untouched. How disarming it is, then, for Americans to find Vietnamese welcoming them as honored guests and offering friendship and forgiveness—while many at home still quake in terror of how we might be treated around the world.

Viet Nam is a society characterized by a tight and complex kinship system. While American veterans have no such system at home, the Vietnamese welcome everyone, even American veterans. No one is blamed. All are forgiven. Mr. Tiger, Mr. and Mrs. Tien, and many like them receive our veterans as lost brothers and sisters with whom they share history and their most influential life experiences. It is in such company, and before such audiences, where relationship and honor are significant, that initiation is recognized and healing occurs. It is here that the vision of the mature warrior is fulfilled.

Sixteen

WAR IN RELIGION AND SPIRITUALITY

War is built into the nature of both the psyche and the cosmos as competition and strife. It is inherent in our blueprints for the ordering of society and in our rites of passage to adulthood. As a strategy, it is built into the ways human social groups, from roving street gangs to competing tribes to small and great nations, meet their survival needs, bond, and seek to accomplish their political and ideological ends. Across epochs, war has caused untold numbers of people to enact vengeance upon one another. It is a very old story that, if sanity and compassion ruled, would long ago have become obsolete. But for all these reasons and more, war remains.

On the surface, worship, belief, and the search for meaning seem contradictory to war making. In fact, they are not. War and religion have been linked since the beginning of time. Each is a primary expression of our relations with each

269

other, the cosmos, and the Divine. Each constitutes a primary expression of mythology and its workings. And each has been used to further the cause and justify the practice of the other. War has fostered religion, and religion war.

We must revisit what both religion and mythology teach about war. We have reached the limits of this age-old relationship between belief and violence. The overwhelming destructiveness of modern warfare demands that we reconsider the interworkings of religion and war; the well-being of humanity and the earth itself require it. We cannot control the existential truths of life or the influence of the archetypes, but we can change our interpretations of them and the way their mythic stories unfold in our lives. It is time we reconsider the lessons about war embedded in our religious and spiritual traditions and recreate them according to the conditions necessitated by modern techno-war. To do so, we would do well to go back to the beginning.

The word *akedah* in Hebrew means "binding." It is the name given to the biblical story, told in Genesis, of Isaac lying on Mt. Moriah under the knife of his father Abraham, bound and waiting to be sacrificed to God. Earlier, we heard of Don's oath to not proceed with his own life until he had helped end war, which was a modern expression of binding to God. Medieval crusaders, modern suicide bombers, Muslim terrorist cell leaders, and Christian presidents have all claimed to know the will of God. As they have all shown, whenever people go to war "to rid the world of evil" and take vows regarding their own or their followers' lives, the binding is no different. We bind ourselves with an oath before God when we want the resolve to be absolute. This level of vow is known seemingly to every culture around the world.

The poet Wilfred Owen, while recuperating from shell shock in a World War I hospital, wrote a war parable based on the biblical *akedah*. In this infantry officer's poem, "Abram" and Isaac journey to Mt. Moriah and their story unfolds as in Genesis—Abram is ordered to sacrifice his son and proceeds with the preparations. However, in his modern version Owen writes: "Then Abram bound the youth with belts and straps, / and builded parapets and trenches there."[1]

In essence, war is always a sacrificial altar. The father raises the knife and his child awaits it. He may be slain and his loved ones made to live with unbearable loss. Or he may survive and endure, filled with disillusionment and despair, knowing that his "father"—officers, rulers, homeland—tried to slay him. Owen felt this despair on the front lines. In his poem, as in Genesis, an angel intercedes. In Owen's telling, however, the angel announces that the Creator wants the sacrifice not of the son but of the father—the generals, presidents, and "masters of war." "Offer the Ram of Pride instead of him," Owen's angel says. Navy veteran Dr. Robert Wickiewicz once interpreted the meaning of this line as being that to free the sacrificial children, we must slay our inordinate love of country in their place. Owen, however, concludes his poem with a bitter reflection on reality: "The old man would not so, but slew his son, / and half the seed of Europe, one by one."

While divine command ordered Isaac's sacrifice, Abraham banished his other son, Ishmael, to the wilderness where he might easily die. Sacrifice or banishment—Abraham's treatment of his two sons is metaphor for what we do to our children whenever we give them war. In Genesis, both sons are saved only by divine intervention. This accurately reflects how survivors often feel—"not by my hand but by Thine."

This imagery of slaying the beloved son applies to all wars, ancient and modern, in which people are sacrificed en masse rather than valued as individuals and preserved.

Dr. Stephen Sabom, a combat veteran and psychotherapist, discovered that he, too, inherited Isaac's situation: "Vietnam is Moriah, the mountain of Genesis 22, place of sacrifice, where all bets are off, emotionality is eliminated, and one's belief system is emptied of understood moral sanction."[2] The message of Owen's angel, however, holds true: In all modern wars and situations of sacrifice, morality must be challenged rather than assumed. And the more absolutist the morality in the name of which a leader dictates violence as God's choice, the more severely that morality must be questioned. Human beings cannot know divine will; they can only interpret it.

One of the most difficult aspects of healing from PTSD is in accepting that the tremendous destructive powers we encounter in war are evidence of God's might. It is God's benevolent, loving side we seek to know, not God's power to destroy. Yet both are far beyond human comprehension. As the Voice out of the Whirlwind challenged Job, "Where were you when I laid the foundations of the earth?"[3] All religions and mythologies contain this same vision: The supreme god power, whether we conceive of it as one or many, whether we name it Zeus, Odin, Allah, or Jehovah, governs over life and death—and over war.

In the Russian trenches of World War I, Saul Tchernikovsky, a great Hebrew writer and translator, was a physician operating in an underground surgery. After he failed to save the life of one wounded soldier, he sadly wrote, "I erased a living being from my page." But Tchernikovsky had had a revelation in the death glance of that suffering soldier. He had seen that the light flickering out in the man's eye was the same as the light in the fires of the bullets, mortars, and bombs. And he saw that those lights and God's holy light are one and the same. He declared to the Divine:

Yet in that very spark of the fading eye,
In the light that absorbs light before it dims forever;
Yet in that very flash of scorching, lacerating light,
In the fire that summons fire, ordering misery and
    persecution—
You were in them; Your glory overwhelmed me.[4]

This is the essential witness of modern war, and perhaps of all war and sacrifice. What this good doctor saw was a vision of God's power, the power that creates and destroys worlds and all their creatures, the power that creates and destroys us. The great forces of creation and destruction are of God's realm. God's power is the light created on the first day of creation, before the sun and stars. It is also the fire that Moses saw in the burning bush. There, it was contained, gentle, and given by the Divine to call Moses to his destiny. But what happens to the power of that fire when we human beings seek to posit it in our own hands?

In an interview held shortly before his death in 1967, J. Robert Oppenheimer, leader of the team that developed the first atomic bomb, confessed that as he viewed the first explosion he recalled a passage from the Hindu scripture, the Bhagavad Gita. It describes the god Krishna's appearance to the warrior Arjuna on the battlefield before the great contest between opposing armies began: "If the radiance of a thousand suns were to burst at once into the sky, that would be like the splendor of the Mighty One. . . . I am become death, the Shatterer of Worlds."

In war, the divine fire is released not by God but in unrestrained ways by the hands and tools of the small human animal who should merely worship at the altar. Afterward, the survivor cannot return to a state of pre-holocaust innocence.

Lot's wife was turned to a pillar of salt when she looked upon God's destruction of Sodom. We can see that pillar as a metaphor for post-traumatic stress disorder: Before God's power, we are petrified in terror; our tears solidify. Our beliefs, of necessity, are shattered when we perceive "the fire that summons fire." To avoid turning to a pillar of salt, the survivor must reshape his or her identity from the experience in a way that affirms the vision of that fire, no matter how difficult. For one thing, the survivor has learned that such fire is far beyond our human capacity to control, and thus he or she strives to stay forever humble. And, in both action and the meaning of PTSD, the survivor warns us all against "playing with fire."

The writers of the Bible had experienced both natural and human disasters. They knew the overpowering dimensions of God's fire and what could happen when humans took it into their own hands. Thus they tried to provide guidance as to how and when we might utilize it. The Sixth Commandment is not, "Thou shalt not kill," but rather, "Thou shalt not murder." It forbids unauthorized homicide, blood vengeance, and ending a life out of hatred and malice. However, it does not prohibit war or capital punishment. The Old Testament seems to conclude that sometimes there are reasons for people to kill each other and, furthermore, that human nature tends toward the savage and so needs civilizing dictates to help limit destructiveness.

The giving of life and the taking of life are sacred acts. Whenever we participate in these processes, we intrude on powers beyond our own, powers before which we must be utterly humble and which we must approach with utmost care. If and when we take life, our reasons must be transcendent, so completely in line with a higher moral and spiritual purpose that they do not cause us to break the original meaning of the Sixth Commandment. Bill, the World War II bombardier we met at the beginning of our inquiry who "felt like a mass murderer," was never convinced that helping to stop Hitler justified firebombing European cities. Almost all the veterans with whom I have worked, regardless of the purpose of the war in which they were involved, have agonized over the question of whether the killing they did was or was not murder.

If the Bible accepts war as a reality, what does it say about whether and when to make war? Another episode from the life of Abraham is helpful here. During the War between Nine Kings described in Genesis,[5] Abraham avoids going to war for the sake of gaining land, power, or natural resources. But when his nephew Lot is taken captive, Abraham fights for and frees him. When offered booty, Abraham refuses it, accepting for his men only replacements for those goods they had lost during the fighting. Thus, from its beginning the Judeo-Christian tradition has taught that it is wrong to wage war for power or riches, but it may be necessary to fight for the survival of loved ones.

Not forbidding war but strictly forbidding violence for personal ends, the Old Testament attempts to guide us in limiting war's destructiveness. Millennia before the Geneva Convention, Deuteronomy 20 put forth laws to regulate the practice of warfare. The purpose was to put a humane limit on war's barbarity and to bring even warfare under the highest moral guiding spirit. These rules are easily summarized: First, rely on faith rather than advanced weaponry for strength in battle. Second, exempt from service new home builders and farmers, the newly married, and those unduly afraid. Third, offer humane treatment for cities that yield or surrender. Finally, prohibit deforestation or the destruction of food sources. In other words, make war against other soldiers, but not against a people or an ecological system.

Needless to say, people have been violating these regulations since ancient times. Our own country has violated them repeatedly, from the European conquest of this continent up through and including our most recent wars. The newly married and the frightened are sent. Old, proud, densely populated cities with irreplaceable antiquities are put under siege with modern techno-weaponry that annihilates citizens, property, and soldiers without distinction. Modern warfare practices the scorched-earth policy, destroying forests, waters, food supplies, homes, hospitals, civilian transportation systems, and everything that grows. And though we profess faith in our religions, we rely on advanced weaponry to win our battles. As we have seen, one reason veterans suffer from PTSD is that they became witnesses and agents in the practice of total war, where all humane limits are regularly surpassed. PTSD, in addition to its other sources, may be the moral defeat of our nation internalized in its veterans.

The ancient Greek tradition also offered guidelines regarding the distinction between murder and killing, whether and when to kill, and how to respond to our own guilt afterward. Soon after King Agamemnon returned home from the Trojan War, his queen, Clytemnestra, murdered him, taking revenge for his sacrifice of their daughter to the gods ten years earlier in exchange for favorable winds to take his fleet to war. Orestes, their son, killed Clytemnestra in turn. As a result, he was pursued by the Furies, whom we can see as the inner forces of a veteran's suffering. The Furies are the powers of psychological and spiritual torture we feel after surviving war and killing. They are the spirit of soldier's heart, of what today, without the poetry that provides soul, we call PTSD.

As Orestes voiced it, "These are no fancies of affliction. They are clear, / and real; the bloodhounds of my mother's hate."[6] They pursued him until he arrived in Athens, where he threw himself at the goddess Athena's feet, begging relief. The Furies arrived before Athena as well, declaring that war and murder are governed by the return of blood for blood and pain for pain. They averred that all violent crimes are equal, that a tortured conscience witnesses to the betrayal of truth, and that death is just punishment. They announced their own power to scatter wits, infuse frenzy and fear, hurt the heart, and bind the brain. And they declared that through the raw agony of the real they "diminish into the ground . . . men's illusions in their pride."[7]

However, it is Athena, "without work of her spear," rather than the Furies, who presided over Orestes' fate. She declared an end to the cycle of "an eye for an eye," ordered Orestes to stand trial, and acted as judge. If the Furies represent our most primitive impulses, which prompt us to vengeance, Athena embodies our highest. She uses reason to preserve and protect civilization.

To fairly judge Orestes, Athena chose a jury of Athens' best citizens, creating the first trial in Western civilization and establishing "a court for all time to come." She ruled that, forevermore, trials rather than blood feuds should settle disputes. Citizens shall revere laws and not pollute them with misinterpretations or twists to make them fit their wishes. Forevermore, adjudication "shall be untouched by moneymaking" so that it remains a fair and impartial sentry of civilization. In the stead of the Furies' vengefulness, Persuasion shall take "her sacred place."

Conrad Silke, who had suffered much in Viet Nam and afterwards, at a critical moment in his healing decided to embrace the meaning of this myth in his own life and abandon his hunger for revenge against the state that had wronged him. Approaching fifty years of age, he registered to vote for the first time. And for the first time since the dissolution of his early troubled marriage, he felt safe and in control enough to live with another being. He adopted a homeless kitten and named her Athena.

To reiterate, we see that the two spiritual traditions at the roots of Western civilization, the biblical and the Greek, offer regulations and socialization processes to restrain the primitive forces that lead to war. Thus, the West's oldest sources of spiritual and moral wisdom call for us to transcend the savage in human nature by uniting reason and compassion and by resorting to persuasion to redress wrongs. If we fail at this task, we may meet the fate long ago forewarned by Norse mythology. Though the Norse deities, protectors of civilization, struggle mightily for eons, they are finally defeated by the forces of chaos and destruction. They warn us that we must never forsake or fail the marriage of judgment with mercy. We must rely on rationality at all times; we must revere all beings, especially those who differ from us in ways that threaten us; and we must remain humble before those powers that should never be under our fallible control.

The World Court, not world war. The council chamber, not the war council. The appeal to reason, not the power of force. Compassion and redress for everyone's pain and suffering, not revenge for one's own. Only when the mind pulls the heart up from vengeance do we become strong enough to resist the downward pull; only then do we become spiritual warriors and not the berserk. Keith Forry, whose story we previously heard, achieved that strength through a dog bite, thirty-seven years after combat. And recall Art, whose story of soul loss opened our investigation. By the end of his psychotherapy, Art no longer looked to empty space to hear from his soul, and he no longer expected his old blue chair from the war zone mess tent to explode around him. Art's healing manifested as new self-control and respect. His PTSD symptoms reduced significantly. He successfully fought the harassment he had experienced at work. He overcame much alienation and participated in the veteran community with dignity and honor. Art finally achieved a significantly healed relationship with his soul. It has come a long way home to his body and to the present.

Clearly, in its overpowering destructiveness and debilitating long-term consequences to people and the planet alike, war has become anachronistic. The mythology that prompts us to war making still arises in us, but given the devastating forces of modern technology, the *reality* of war is no longer tenable—if it ever was.

One Palestinian mother-turned-suicide bomber stated, "I always wanted to be the first woman to carry out a martyr attack, where parts of my body fly all over. That is the only wish I can ask God for."[8] As long as any culture indoctrinates its followers with ancient warrior myths such as this woman believed in that promulgate violence and death over the preservation of life, we will live blood-encrusted and terrified.

It is time for us to imagine, create, and tell new myths, or to focus on the old myths that counsel dispassionate moderation over the lust for control—the way of Athena, that is, not Ares. The coalition the first President Bush mustered in the Gulf War demonstrated that the world can indeed marshal vast military force for a singular political objective. But we must use it solely to restrain violence rather than indulge in it. The necessity for this imperative was recognized after World War I and written into the Covenant of the League of Nations. Echoing Athena's mythic declaration of the substitution of persuasion for conflict, the nations of the world declared that "resort to war would henceforth be as unjust as it had always been for a private person . . . the only just war would be the use of international force to subdue the recalcitrant nation."[9]

Some old myths are best understood as incomplete, and we can develop new conclusions for them. We can imagine, for example, reconciliation between those two angry and alienated brothers, the forefathers of the Jewish and Muslim people, Isaac and Ishmael.

We can also study the old teaching of "an eye for an eye" and transform its meaning. A group of veterans and I visited with Mr. Tam in the Mekong Delta of Viet Nam. He was the brother of Kim Phuc, the girl who became famous for the cover photograph of her running naked and burning from napalm. Tam had been caught in the same bombing raid. He welcomed my vets into his home, served us coffee and fruit, and introduced his daughters. He proudly showed us the artificial eye that North American benefactors had given him. "An eye for an eye" once meant revenge. But Tam was given a prosthesis. His gift in return is his open-heartedness, which helps our veterans find forgiveness. When we discover ourselves living out old myths, we can give them new endings. We can reinterpret "an eye for an eye" to mean not revenge but restitution.

We can develop new adventures and ordeals that satisfy the heroic, that challenge us while promoting peace and healing, and offer these to our youth as rites of passage. We must discover what William James calls "the moral equivalent of war: something heroic that will speak . . . as universally as war does and yet will be as compatible with their spiritual selves as war has proven itself to be incompatible."[10] We can support humanitarian projects in former places of combat, such as many of our veterans from the Afghanistan and Vietnam Wars are undertaking, to clear mines, build medical clinics, and help war orphans and the disabled.

While, as described previously, my group of veterans and I were visiting the former Viet Cong soldier Mr. Tien and his wife, Mrs. Tien told us her story. When she was a child, American forces bombed and destroyed her school. She was one of the few survivors. Her teacher helped dig out the living children and then said, "We must do what we can to stop this violence against our people. Who will come with me into the jungle?" It was then, at age ten, that she became Viet Cong.

The morning after our visit with the Tiens, our group proceeded to another Mekong Delta island to dedicate a school whose building we had funded. Eight American veterans—nurses, grunts, a chaplain, and a soldier who had laid mines—as well as dozens of veterans and civilians had spent three years raising the money to build a nursery school and kindergarten for this impoverished river community.

That morning, we walked happily through the jungle the vets had once feared. Where they had once been on guard for ambushes, we were greeted by adults and children from behind trees and in dykes and paddies. Where once they had dreaded being overrun, parents, teachers, and children came running to the clearing of the new school. Dozens of bright-eyed children welcomed us. Teachers from distant schools arrived to thank us. The green jungle opened upon the new school, painted a bright yellow, lined with locally made flowered tiles. Our war veterans, some of whom had fought and killed just miles away from the site, helped dedicate the school. The children sang for them. The parents beamed. No longer were these Americans the boogey-men of their nightmares. Children passed out gifts not to frightening armed white giants but to their benefactors from the other side of the world, friends who had worked hard to build them a school and bring them books and give them a future.

Then, smiling joyously, eight American veterans—who no longer feared that they were hunted enemies, who now slept peacefully during their in-country nights—also broke into song. For two dozen laughing Vietnamese children, they danced and sang, "I've been working on the railroad . . ."

The resolution achieved by the school project has been so profound that some of these veterans no longer have PTSD. Those who do report fewer and less-severe symptoms. Bill Keyes, an engineer, has made a second trip back to Viet Nam and now serves as vice president of his Veterans for Peace post. Beth Marie Murphy, a combat zone nurse who trembled involuntarily, relied on medications, and could not sleep before her first trip back, has now made five return trips, adopted a Vietnamese foster child, learned the Vietnamese language, and become a leader of her own reconciliation journeys. Rev. Jackson Day, Jim Helt, Bob Cagle, and others have provided money for emergency medical services, as well as money to purchase new animals for peasants whose livestock was devastated by the bird flu. In Hanoi, twenty-four-year-old Vuong Toan Nam, who is sent to school by Americans and whose father was saved with brain surgery funded by thirty American vets and civilians, says that he now has many uncles and aunts throughout the country that was formerly his country's enemy.

Post-traumatic stress symptoms, then, can diminish or disappear when we reconcile with our deepest moral and spiritual convictions about the sacredness of life. The eight American veterans, too, practiced "an eye for an eye." And they too gave the ancient law new meaning. Take an eye. Return an eye. Bomb a school. Build a school. Restore what we have taken. Give it back. Give back life and a chance at a good life. This new meaning to the old law restores the soul and heals the self and the planet.

CONCLUSION

We crave war in its mythic dimension. We crave war *because* we crave the mythic dimension, and war and religion are the collective forces that propel us there. But the reality of war is horrible and deadly. When we try to turn the myth of war into reality to satisfy our craving for meaning and passion, we risk our own destruction as well as that of each other and even meaning and reality themselves. PTSD is the soul illness suffered by individuals and cultures as a result.

These ancient concerns are with us to this day. The Holocaust is not behind us. Dith Pran, the photographer whose story of miraculous survival during Cambodia's genocide of its own people is told in the movie *The Killing Fields,* said that the Holocaust did not happen just to the Jewish people. It did not happen just to his people. Rather, the Holocaust is an evil force visiting now one, now another people as it creeps like an international plague around the planet.

We might wish to disagree. We might wish the twentieth-century genocide against the Armenians, or Hitler's genocide against the Jews, the gypsies, the gays, and the disabled were the end of it. But the daily news reports of this new millennium tell us differently. And I have spent a quarter century listening to Holocaust survivors and to survivors of numerous wars large and small tell me of scorched earth and of burning children and homes. In the past decade, similar stories have slowly emerged from the shocked lips of Gulf War veterans. In the last several years, I have treated some Bosnian refugees and their children, newly arrived in this country, who are survivors of Serbian concentration camps. They, too, are in the stupor of Job thrown onto the dung heap of history.

Service to these survivors, whether it is witnessing to the horror they experienced or helping to relieve its brutal psychological and spiritual impact, is no less than the Jewish practice of *tikkun olam*, which means "repairing the world." Not only in our large-scale efforts at social justice or world peace but also, and perhaps especially, in our deep, slow, one-on-one efforts with individuals, the tears in our world may be repaired. As the ancient rabbinical sage Hillel said, "Whoever saves one person, it is as if they have saved the entire world."

During the last year, I have been sitting with a young Bosnian man, a Muslim, listening to his stories of capture, torture, slave labor, and the murders of his friends. At one moment, this young man turned to me and asked, "You seem to know what this suffering is about. You seem to have been there yourself. How can you sit with me through all this pain and understand it like it is your own?"

I answered this Muslim concentration camp survivor, "I am a Jew. In a previous generation it was my people in the camps. I, too, lost family there. This terrible thing, this Holocaust that visited both our people, makes us brothers."

For the first time, this Muslim man smiled at his Jewish therapist over our mutual struggle in the fire that summons fire.

This is one example of our efforts to repair the tears in our world. We must not deny or deaden our feelings about war. Rather, we must remember war and its lessons. We must say our prayers for peace and remember the pain and losses war has caused us. We must learn to walk through hell with our hearts wide open. If we do not, we deaden ourselves while abandoning the victims past and present to hopeless suffering.

Words hold secrets. Tears that rend and tears that fall are homonyms. We must melt the salt pillar of Lot's wife that dwells in each of our hearts and, contemplating destruction, release our fountain of tears. Especially regarding war and its healing, the tears in our world are repaired with our tears.

On one reconciliation journey to Viet Nam, my group briefly met with Mr. Tiger, the eighty-year-old man living on a small bonsai farm in the Mekong Delta who regularly councils American veterans. Though Mr. Tiger is a veteran himself of thirty years of warfare against three invaders, he does not have PTSD. In contrast, he beams with joy, health, and loving welcome. He welcomes our veterans and all Americans into his home, addresses and feeds them, and offers forgiveness and the universal brotherhood of people who have survived hell. How, we wonder, is it possible for the soul of a man three decades at war to beam with love toward his former enemies?

The soul at war is characteristically distorted along all its essential functions: how it locates itself in the cosmos and identifies with moral and spiritual principles, how it views the everyday workings of the world and processes and evaluates experiences, and what its relationship is to its own instincts and to the ultimate principles of life and death. War stamps the soul with an indelible imprint and makes it its own. The soul that once went to war is forever transformed.

This transformation need not be to disability and debilitation. Yet to facilitate health instead, we must first tell the difficult, painful truth, keep our hearts open, and listen and affirm without denial. Then, with the truth in hand, we can turn toward learning the world's warrior tradition. We can study the myths and use them as roadmaps. We can access spiritual energies to sustain and guide us. We can embrace the life-affirming and protective capacities of the warrior spirit and practice a living spirituality. We can restore relations with former enemies and with the dead and witness to the suffering caused by war and violence. We can find new and meaningful forms of service that atone for former actions and contribute to the healing of our own veterans and those we harmed. We can perform sacred ceremonies and rituals for ourselves, others, and the dead. All this, hand-in-hand with the truth about war, can lead to a spiritual transformation in which the soul grows again.

Our goal is not just to awaken the soul; that is what childhood religious and secular education is meant to do. Rather, our goal is to *grow* the soul large enough, to help it become wise and strong enough, so that it can surround the dominating wound we call trauma. When we do this, PTSD can evaporate and we can have people like Mr. Tiger, devoted to the peaceful cultivation of the earth and to international friendship and reconciliation.

The formula for healing the war-wounded soul is simple: surround trauma with soul. Its application may be the most difficult and important work we ever undertake.

One day during a reconciliation visit to Viet Nam, our group arrived at a Cao Dai temple in Tay Nynh. With us was Bob Cagle, the vet who was haunted by the memory of the fourteen-year-old Viet Cong boy he had killed. Bob waited while the others disembarked from the bus and disappeared into the temple, and I waited for him. Immediately off the bus, he grabbed me while tears exploded from his eyes.

"I saw them all," he cried, "as we drove through the rice paddies. All those ghosts of the people I lost and the people I killed."

"I've seen them for years," he continued. "In my nightmares. In my day dreams. When I'm supposed to be working or with my family. There they are, behind the living, staring at me, wanting something from me. I know where their souls are! But I don't know where mine is!"

I held Bob's face. I made him look into my eyes.

"My soul," he repeated. "It's gone. I've been without a soul since the war. I killed innocent people. I killed a boy. I did wrong. I can't feel a thing."

I took Bob's hand and raised it to his face. I made his fingers touch and wipe his own tears. "What are these?" I asked.

"Tears," he said.

"And what do tears mean?

"Feelings," he said. "My God! I'm feeling and don't even know it."

"And which part of us feels?" I asked.

He stumbled over the words, but answered, "My heart and soul."

"And who sees the souls of the dead? Which part of us can see souls?"

"Only the soul," he said. Then his tears burst forth again. We hugged beneath a simple tree in the dusty hot parking lot of a Cao Dai temple. Bob cried tears that had been awaiting release for decades. I cried with him. Finally he laughed and said, "I guess I do still have a soul. Now it's time to make friends with it again."

Later that afternoon, our group climbed to the Buddhist temple atop Nui Ba Den, Lady Black Mountain, a scene of terrible fighting during the war but today a place of beauty and peace crowned with a Buddhist pagoda. There, with the help of the resident priest, Bob conducted prayers for the soul of the boy he had slain. His grief continued washing through him as he poured out prayers for this boy. He cried and prayed, cried and prayed, as the monk chanted prayers for the dead. Finally, after decades of nightmares, Bob saw the boy's spirit smile at him. The soul of the boy, who would forever be fourteen years old in Bob's mind, offered the aging American veteran peace and the promise that from now on he would be Bob's spiritual ally, his helper and friend.

Homer's *Iliad* detailed the traumatizing combat of war, and his *Odyssey,* the physical and spiritual return. Bob's military service in Viet Nam was his *Iliad,* and his return journeys, his *Odyssey.* On this second return, seeking his way home, armed with courage and love and willing to slay his old identity through encounters with spirits, former enemies, and decades of internalized pain, Bob replicated the mythic descent into the Underworld. Odysseus fled the Underworld because there were too many disembodied spirits, too many losses. But Bob took the *Odyssey* a great step further. He stayed in his Underworld, and he returned again and again, to make friends and exchange devotions.

Bob's nightmares are no more. Where once the war dominated his consciousness, now he carries it in peace. Now he says, "It's just my story."

In all of humankind's efforts at war making—in our recruitment and training of the vulnerable young, in our indoctrination of our populations on every side of the globe, in our politics and arms manufacture, and especially in our crusades that mimic the crusades of the past—we are in search of the mystic warrior. But no matter how much we aspire to be the cultural hero who performs the great tasks of civilization in the name of divinity, modern warfare cannot engender the mystic warrior. It can only create the latest and most techno-logical version of what Buffy Sainte-Marie's song called the universal soldier—the one from every race, religion, culture, of all sizes, shapes, and colors, who will do the killing he or she is bidden to do.

We must return our charges — our children and our veterans, our deeds and our dreams, our soldiers and our adversaries—to the path of the mystic warrior. And we must do so in the name of healing, reconciliation, and restoration. We must make the pursuit of peace as mythic as the pursuit of war has been. The fate of our world depends upon how successfully we undertake and carry through this great task.

Notes

CHAPTER 1: War, Trauma, and Soul

1. Khe Sanh was a heavily fortified U.S. military base in the north-western corner of South Viet Nam. During 1967, the U.S. fought heavy hill battles with North Vietnamese regulars who controlled the surrounding countryside. From January to April 1968, huge numbers of Vietnamese troops laid siege to the U.S. base to distract our military while they prepared the Tet Offensive. The ruse worked and the U.S. responded with heavy supplies, fortifications, bombardments, and resistance. Destruction and casualties on both sides were immense. Khe Sanh was one of the most brutal, sustained, and controversial battles of the war.

2. "Gook" was a derogatory term used by American GIs to refer to Vietnamese. In this meeting, as can commonly occur when veterans discuss their combat experiences, Art switched from a respectful use of "Vietnamese" to derogatory military slang as he became more animated and his war memories took control of his expression. In later chapters, we will examine the meaning of such derogatory terms as forms of the dehumanization of the enemy common to war making and the necessity to rehumanize the other as part of the healing process.

3. Heraclitus, Fragment 43, in Philip Wheelwright, *Heraclitus* (New York: Atheneum, 1968), 53.

4. Aristotle, *De Anima*, in W. D. Ross, *Aristotle Selections* (New York: Scribner, 1955), 199, 205.

5. I gratefully acknowledge my wife, Kate Dahlstedt, for instigating the following section on the traits of soul. Kate contends that concepts that were once numinous have become so emptied of meaning

291

that we must carefully elucidate them again in order to restore their significance and make them usable in our contemporary hyperempirical climate.

6. Albert Camus, *Selected Essays and Notebooks*, ed. and trans. Philip Thody (Middlesex, England: Penguin, 1967), 237.

7. Gustav Hasford, *The Short Timers* (New York: Bantam, 1980).

8. Plato, *Phaedrus*, in *The Works of Plato,* trans. B. Jowett (New York: Tudor, n.d.), 3:403.

9. William Faulkner, "Upon Receiving the Nobel Prize for Literature, 1950," *Essays, Speeches and Public Letters*, ed. James B. Meriwether (New York: Random House, 1965), 119–120.

10. Andrew Jacobs, Ariel Hart, Eric Schmitt, Abby Goodnough, "Extended Tours in Iraq Dash Hopes and Raise Fears Among Troops' Families," *New York Times,* April 16, 2004.

11. Slavenka Drakulic, *The Balkan Express: Fragments from the Other Side of War* (New York: W. W. Norton, 1993), 39.

12. Ibid., 4.

13. "American Deaths," *Boston Globe,* April 15, 2004.

14. "Soldier's Family to Bring Body Home from Albany Airport," *Times Union,* April 14, 2004.

CHAPTER 2: The Mythic Arena of War

1. David Nichols, ed., *Ernie's War: The Best of Ernie Pyle's World War II Dispatches* (New York: Touchstone, 1986), 81.

2. Norman Mailer, *The Naked and the Dead* (New York: Rinehart, 1948), 566.

3. Edward Tick, *Sacred Mountain: Encounters with the Vietnam Beast* (Santa Fe, NM: Moon Bear Press, 1989), 31–32.

4. Wilfred Owen, "Apologia Pro Poemate Meo," *The Collected Poems of Wilfred Owen*, ed. C. Day Lewis (New York: New Directions, 1963), 39.

5. Heraclitus, frag. 25, Wheelwright, *Heraclitus,* 29 (see chap. 1, n. 3).

6. The Greeks believed that the gods lasted for a very long time but

not forever. Like everything else, they must eventually disappear under the greater cosmic forces of necessity and eternal transformation. For example, Wheelwright (see above) records that Heraclitus wrote: ". . . nothing abides" (frag. 20); "The universe has not been made by any god . . . " (frag. 29); "God undergoes transformations." (frag. 121).

7. Heraclitus, frag. 26, Wheelwright, *Heraclitus,* 29.

8. Joseph T. Shipley, *Dictionary of Word Origins* (Towota, NJ: Littlefield, Adams, 1982), 385.

9. Later philosophical thought moved away from specific deities toward general principles. Eris became the principle of strife itself. That she was once a goddess personifying strife, and in such figures as the avenging Furies, the warrior Amazons, and the gorgons, ancient Greek mythology recognized the feminine dimensions of aggression and conflict and did not oversimplify violence as an expression of the masculine.

10. Homer, *Iliad,* bk. 4, lines 444-45, trans. Robert Fitzgerald (Garden City: Doubleday, 1974), 103.

11. Not a direct fragment but recorded by Philodemus, Wheelwright, *Heraclitus,* 35.

12. Homer, *Iliad,* bk. 13, lines 74 and 82, Fitzgerald, pp. 301-2.

13. Habakkuk 3:12.

14. Isaiah 25:2.

15. Exodus 15:3-4, 6.

16. Deuteronomy 9:1, 3.

17. Deut. 9:5.

18. Patricia Terry, trans., *Poems of the Vikings* (Indianapolis: Bobbs-Merrill, 1980), 5.

19. Mircea Eliade, *Rites and Symbols of Initiation: The Mysteries of Death and Rebirth,* trans. Willard R. Task (Woodstock, CT: Spring Publications, 1995), 81-83.

20. *Ynglinga Saga,* quoted in H. R. Ellis Davidson, *Gods and Myths of Northern Europe* (New York: Penguin, 1979), 66.

21. Ibid., 71

22. Jacob Neusner and William Scott Green, *Dictionary of Judaism in the Biblical Period* (New York: Macmillan Library Reference, 1996), 666. While this reference elucidates the characteristics of Holy Wars as portrayed in the Bible, we see that the same characteristics apply cross-culturally and throughout history.

23. Quoted from Romans 13:1-4.

24. St. Augustine, *Contra Faust,* sec. 22, line 75, as quoted by St. Thomas Aquina, *The Summa Theologica,* Section 2, Part 2, Question 40, second and revised edition, translated by Fathers of the English Dominican Province, 1920.

25. Ibid., 74.

26. Chris Hedges, *War is a Force That Gives Us Meaning* (New York: Anchor, 2003).

27. James Hillman, *A Terrible Love of War* (New York: Penguin Press, 2004), 17. Hillman reports that this massive number of wars only includes those that had a decisive outcome. There were many more wars with large-scale slaughter uncounted by the scholars he cites because they had no decisive results.

28. George W. Bush, television address to the nation, March 20, 2003.

29. Homer, *Iliad*, bk. 17, lines 228–29, Fitzgerald, p. 414.

CHAPTER 3: War as a Rite of Passage

1. Eliade, Rites and Symbols of Initiation, x, xii (see chap. 2, n. 19).

2. Robert Jay Lifton, *Home from the War: Vietnam Veterans, Neither Victims Nor Executioners* (New York: Simon and Schuster, 1973), 28.

3. Mary Renault, *The Bull From the Sea* (New York: Vintage, 1975).

4. William James, *Varieties of Religious Experience* (New York: Collier, 1971), 290-91.

5. Ibid.

6. Peter Matthiessen, *Under the Mountain Wall: A Chronicle of Two Seasons in the Stone Age* (New York: Ballantine, 1972), 10-11.

7. Stanley Vestal, *Sitting Bull: Champion of the Sioux* (Norman, OK and London: University of Oklahoma Press, 1989), 11.

8. Hartley Burr Alexander, *The World's Rim: Great Mysteries of the North American Indian* (Lincoln, NE and London: University of Nebraska Press, 1967), 188–89.

9. John's story is exemplary. I have worked with or interviewed hundreds of noncombatant veterans and civilian males who report similar negative self-judgments, lack of vitality, potency, confidence, and senses of failure and inadequacy from not having experienced combat or passed some form of initiatory ritual akin to its demands.

10. Retold from Tick, *Sacred Mountain*, 91–93 (see chap. 2, n. 3).

11. Quoted in Alexander, *The World's Rim,* 193.

CHAPTER 4: **Ancient Myth and Modern War**

1. See, for example, Matthiessen, 10–11: "A single death on either side would mean victory or defeat. And yet that death—or two or three—was the end purpose of the war" (see chap. 3, n. 6).

2. Quoted in Richard A. Gabriel, *No More Heroes: Madness and Psychiatry in War* (New York: Hill and Wang, 1987), epigraph, xi.

3. Owen, "Parable of the Old Man and the Young," *The Collected Poems of Wilfred Owen,* 42 (see chap. 2, n. 4).

4. Edward Tick, "Casualties of the Vietnam War," *Utne Magazine*, January–February 2005, 75. It is telling that I could not find as complete an account of the human, environmental, and economic costs of the Vietnam War such as this one anywhere. It took many years and a search through sources worldwide to compile this list. In general, Viet Nam reports American as well as their own casualties and losses to a far greater degree than the United States reports Vietnamese. Further, some American losses are only reported by the press or veterans' advocacy groups rather than by official sources. A partial list of sources include Disabled American Veterans; *New York Times;* Daniel Hallock, *Hell, Healing and Resistance: Veterans Speak* (New York: Plough Publishing Company, 1998); Steven A. Leibo, *East, Southeast Asia, and the Western Pacific, 2004* (Harpers Ferry, WV: Stryker-Post Publications, 2004); Marilyn B. Young, John J. Fitzgerald, and A. Tom Grunfeld, *The Vietnam War: A History in Documents* (New York: Oxford University Press, 2002); and *Webster's New World Dictionary of the Vietnam War.* Sources

in Viet Nam include information gathered at The Army Museum, Ha Noi; Hong Ngoc (Rosy Jade) Humanity Center, Sao Do; Research Center for Gender, Family, and Environment in Development, Ha Noi; Women's Museum, Ha Noi; War Remnants Museum, Ho Chi Minh City.

5. Report of the Veterans Benefits Administration Office, cited by Dr. Doug Rokke, "Gulf War Casualties," Truprock Peace Center.

6. Human Rights Watch: Federal Republic of Yugoslavia, World Report, 2000.

7. Human Rights Watch: Human Rights Backgrounder, "Cluster Bombs in Afghanistan," October 2001.

8. Vlada Alekankina, "Afghanistan Post-Conflict Environmental Assessment Report," United Nations Environment Programme in collaboration with the Afghanistan Transitional Authority, January 30, 2003.

9. Research of Connie Frisbee Houde, visits to Afghanistan in February 2003 and March–April 2004. Connie is a photojournalist documenting indigenous peoples and their struggles to survive worldwide. View her work at www.globalvillagephotographer.com.

10. United Nations Children's Fund, *Childhood Under Threat,* December 2004, reported in Celia Dugger, "Unicef Says a Billion Children Now Suffer Deprivation Worldwide," *New York Times*, Dec. 10, 2004.

11. Gabriel, *No More Heroes,* 88.

12. Ibid., xi.

13. Ibid., 87.

14. William Manchester, *Goodbye, Darkness: A Memoir of the Pacific War* (New York: Dell, 1980), 447.

CHAPTER 5: The Soul in Slaughter

1. George Orwell, *1984* (New York: Penguin Plume, 1983).

2. Johann Wolfgang von Goethe, *Faust*, trans. Bayard Taylor (New York: Washington Square Press, 1967), 163.

3. Secretary of State Albright made this remark on the *Sixty Minutes* television news show in 1996. In fairness, I should add that, in response to a protest when she spoke at the University of Southern

California in October 2001, she stated that she should not have said it and regretted doing so. Still, its impact was felt and revealed the moral dimensions of leadership during the time of the sanctions.

4. G. M. Gilbert, *Nuremberg Diary* (New York: Signet, 1961), 255–56.

5. Evan S. Connell, *Son of the Morning Star: Custer and Little Bighorn* (San Francisco: North Point Press, 1984), 134.

6. Ibid.

7. Ibid., 100.

8. Drakulic, *The Balkan Express,* 3 (see chap.1, n.11).

9. Ibid., 142.

10. Reproduced in George Armstrong Custer's *My Life on the Plains* and quoted in Connell, *Son of the Morning Star,* 132.

11. Testimony of Lt. William Calley at his court-martial, 1970.

12. Many texts on child development support this understanding of moral and intellectual development. See the classic Jean Piaget, *The Moral Judgment of the Child* (New York: Free Press, 1997). In testing, see the *California Social Competency Scale* or the social/emotional section of the *Brigance Inventory.* See *Revised Brigance Diagnostic Inventory of Early Development* by Albert H. Brigance (1978, 1991), section on curriculum development, such as "Pushing for Autonomy" at age five. At around age four-and-one-half on the scale, the child has a sense of "good" and "bad" behavior, either of himself or of others. The scale also lists milestone skills by developmental age. Appendix D states that the child under age four "seeks detailed explanations with frequent use of why." I am grateful to Joan Nelson, CSW, for her research assistance on this topic.

13. Calley court-martial testimony.

14. Hedges, *War is a Force,* 22 (see chap. 2, n. 26).

15. On this topic see, for example, Sam Keen's exhaustive study, *Faces of the Enemy: Reflections of the Hostile Imagination: The Psychology of Enmity* (New York: HarperCollins, 1991).

16. Hedges, *War is a Force,* 21.

17. Quoted in Lt. Col. David Grossman, *On Killing: The Psychological Cost of Learning to Kill in War and Society* (Boston: Little, Brown, 1995), 190.

18. Erich Marie Remarque, *All Quiet on the Western Front*, trans. A. W. Wheen (Boston: Little, Brown, 1929), 22–23.

19. Nguyen Duy, "Stop," *Distant Road*, trans. Kevin Bowen and Nguyen Ba Chung (Willimantic, CT: Curbstone Press, 1999), 83.

20. Johann Pfefferkorn, verbal testimony in C. Hadjipateras and M. Fafalios, eds. *Crete 1941 Eyewitnessed* (Athens: Efstathiades Group, 1999), 147.

21. Drakulic, *The Balkan Express,* 64 (see chap. 1, n. 11).

22. Dith Pran, compiler, Kim DePaul, ed, *Children of Cambodia's Killing Fields: Memoirs by Survivors* (Chiang Mai, Thailand: Silkworm Books, 1997), 183.

23. Homer, *Iliad*, bk. 21, various lines 103–133, Fitzgerald, pp. 496–97 (see chap. 2, n. 10).

24. Mari Sandoz, *Crazy Horse: The Strange Man of the Oglalas* (Lincoln: University of Nebraska Press, 1961), 204.

25. Jonathan Shay, *Achilles in Vietnam: Combat Trauma and the Undoing of Character* (New York: Atheneum, 1994) various pp., but see esp. 98.

26. Bill Karpowicz, "I Shouldn'ta Done It," *Voices: the Art and Science of Psychotherapy*, 25:4 (Winter 1989): 38–39.

27. Kate Dahlstedt, "Wave," *Oriel,* no. 20 (1999): 53–54.

CHAPTER 6: Inside PTSD: Identity and Soul Wound

1. J. D. Salinger, "For Esme—With Love and Squalor," *Nine Stories* (New York: Bantam, 1971), 109. This paraphrased portrait is from Salinger's short story. Recent biographies document that Salinger was himself a traumatized combat veteran and wrote such portraits from personal experience. See Paul Alexander, *Salinger: A Biography* (New York: Renaissance, 2000) and Margaret A. Salinger, *Dream-Catcher: A Memoir* (New York: Washington Square Press, 2001).

2. Remarque, *All Quiet on the Western Front,* 88 (see chap. 5, n. 18).

3. Paul Fussell, *Doing Battle: The Making of a Skeptic* (Boston: Little, Brown, 1996), 105.

4. Gabriel, *No More Heroes,* 57 (see chap. 4, n. 2).

5. Sidney and Samuel Moss, *Thy Men Shall Fall* (Chicago: Ziff-Davis, 1948), 184.

6. Anonymous, from George Hill, disabled marine, in "Sharing the Struggles of a Friend," *The Gainesville Sun*, Nov. 10, 1993, quoted in Hansel, Steidle, Zacek, and Zacek, eds., *Soldier's Heart: Survivor's View of Combat Trauma* (Lutherville, MD: Sidran, 1995), xiii.

7. Remarque, *All Quiet on the Western Front,* 18.

8. Tick, *Sacred Mountain*, 90 (see chap. 2, n. 3).

9. A July 2004 study showed significant degrees of major depression, generalized anxiety, or PTSD after duty in Iraq (15.6 to 17.1 percent) or Afghanistan (11.2 percent). Only 23 to 40 percent sought mental health care. See Charles W. Hoge, M.D., Carl A. Castro, Ph.D., Stephen C. Messer, Ph.D., Dennis McGurk, Ph.D., Dave I. Cotting, Ph.D., and Robert L. Koffman, M.D., M.P.H., "Combat Duty in Iraq and Afghanistan, Mental Health Problems, and Barriers to Care," *New England Journal of Medicine*, 351:1, July 1, 2004, 13–22.

 More recent Army studies show one in six soldiers, both combatants and noncombatants, in Iraq experiencing PTSD during service. Military experts estimate that the rate will rise to at least one in three over time and upon return home. See Scott Shane, "A Flood of Troubled Soldiers is in the Offing, Experts Predict," *New York Times,* Dec. 16, 2004. This means that at least several hundred thousand individuals will suffer from PTSD along with millions of family members, greatly increasing the supposedly low casualty rates reported to the public. And these are the characteristically low rates offered during wartime. They always increase over time.

10. Gabriel, *No More Heroes,* 16, 43–44.

11. Shay, *Achilles in Vietnam* (see chap. 5, n. 25).

12. Erik Erikson, *Childhood and Society* (New York: Norton, 1963), 42.

13. Judith Herman, M.D., *Trauma and Recovery* (New York: Basic Books, 1992).

14. Peter Levine, *Waking the Tiger: Healing Trauma* (Berkeley: North Atlantic Books, 1997).

15. William Sloane Coffin, Jr., "Sanctuaries for Men of Conscience," *Union Seminary Quartery Review* 22, no. 2 (Winter 1968): 183.

16. Edward Tick, "Satori in the Hut." *Pilgrimage: Psychotherapy and Personal Exploration* 19, no. 3, (Summer 1993): 24–26.

17. Shane, "A Flood of Troubled Soldiers . . . " *New York Times* (see n. 9).

18. Lifton, *Home from the War,* 37 (see chap. 3, n. 2).

19. Craig Nelson, "Genocide Haunts a Tormented Land," *Times Union,* April 4, 2004.

20. *The Fog of War: Eleven Lessons from the Life of Robert S. McNamara,* film documentary by Errol Morris, (Sony Pictures Classics, 2004).

21. Coffin, "Sanctuaries for Men of Conscience," 184.

22. Peter Marin, "Living in Moral Pain" first published in *Psychology Today*, 1981. Anthologized in *Freedom and Its Discontents: Reflections on Four Decades of American Moral Experience* (South Royalton, VT: Steerforth Press, 1995), 119–136.

23. Ibid., 136.

24. For the degree to which minority veterans felt conflicted about fighting "a white man's war" against other oppressed and impoverished peoples, see especially Wallace Terry, *Bloods: An Oral History of the Vietnam War by Black Veterans* (New York: Random House, 1984).

25. Marin, "Living in Moral Pain," 136.

26. Michael Blake, *Dances With Wolves* (New York: Fawcett, 1990), 269. The novel portrays Dunbar with the Comanche people, the movie with the Lakota. At the end of the novel, Dunbar remains with his adoptive tribe; at the end of the movie, he returns with his wife to white society to attempt to represent the Native American cause.

CHAPTER 7: Eros and Aesthetics in Hell

1. Thomas Hardy, "The Man He Killed," *Story Poems,* Louis Untermeyer, ed. (New York: Washington Square Press, 1964), 85–86.

2. Deena Metzger, "The Woman Who Slept with Men to Take the War Out of Them," *Tree: Essays and Pieces* (Berkeley: North Atlantic Books, 1997), 101.

3. Grossman, *On Killing*, 136 (see chap. 5, n. 17).

4. Robert A. Cagle, *One Veteran Speaks* (privately printed, 2004), 76–77.

5. Quoted in Lifton, *Home from the War,* 271 (see chap. 3, n. 2).

6. Hedges, *War is a Force,* 25 (see chap. 2, n. 26).

7. Penny Cupp, "They Also Serve Who Only Stand and Wait," *Voices: the Art and Science of Psychotherapy*: 27: no. 1 and 2, (Spring/Summer 1991), 93–102.

8. Hillman, *A Terrible Love of War,* 145–46 (see chap. 2, n. 27).

9. *Helen,* trans. Richard Lattimore in *Euripides,* vol. 3 of *The Complete Greek Tragedies,* ed. David Grene and Richard Lattimore (Chicago: University of Chicago Press, 1992), 422, 441, 446.

10. George Seferis, *Collected Poems, 1924–1955,* trans. Edmund Keeley & Philip Sherrard (Princeton, NJ: Princeton University Press, 1971), 188.

CHAPTER 8: Relations with the Missing and the Dead

1. Paraphrased reporting of Jordan Carleo-Evangelist, "Family, Neighbors Bring a Fallen Son Home," *Times Union*, Dec. 7, 2004.

2. George W. Bush, second inaugural address, January 20, 2005.

3. See Robert Jay Lifton, *History and Human Survival* (New York: Random House, 1970), *Home from the War* (see chap. 3, n. 2), and elsewhere.

4. Siegfried Sassoon, "Dead Musicians," in *The War Poems* (London: Faber and Faber, 1983), 102.

5. William Crapser, *Remains: Stories of Viet Nam* (Old Chatham, NY: Sachem Press, 1988), 83–85.

6. Charles Hanley, Sang-Hun Choe, and Martha Mendoza, *The Bridge at No Gun Ri,* (New York: Henry Holt, 2001), 1.

7. Mailer, *The Naked and the Dead,* 640 ff (see chap. 2, n. 2).

8. Vestal, *Sitting Bull,* 37 (see chap. 3, n. 7).

9. Book 11 of Homer's *Odyssey*, which relates Odysseus's descent to the Underworld and visit with the shades, is one of the most important documents a survivor or trauma therapist can study to aid the healing journey.

10. James Hillman, *The Dream and the Underworld* (New York: Harper and Row, 1979).

11. Bao Ninh, *The Sorrow of War*, trans. Phan Thanh Hao (London: Minerva, 1994), 83–84.

12. Ibid., 82.

13. Iakovos Kambanellis, *Mauthausen*, trans. Gail Holst-Warhaft (Athens, Greece: Kedros, 1995), 163, 318.

14. *Antigone*, trans. David Grene, in *Sophocles*, vol. 2 of *The Complete Greek Tragedies*, ed. David Grene and Richard Lattimore (Chicago: University of Chicago Press, 1992), 202.

15. Hanley, *The Bridge at No Gun Ri*, 1.

16. Cagle, *One Veteran Speaks*, 52 (see chap. 7, n. 4).

CHAPTER 9: The Soul of the Nation

1. Eric Schmitt, "The Gulf War Veteran: Victorious in War, Not Yet at Peace," *New York Times*, May 29, 1995.

2. Mark Baker, *Nam: The Vietnam War in the Words of the Men and Women Who Fought There* (New York: William Morrow, 1981), 33. This quote is notable not for its uniqueness but for its commonality. Echoed by a vast majority of Vietnam War veterans, it is a mantra of a media generation. Wayne's importance as a role model and the impact of the entertainment industry must not be underestimated by claiming that Wayne was just a movie star or movies are "not real."

3. *Time*, June 29, 1970.

4. Moss, *Thy Men Shall Fall*, 220 (see chap. 6 n. 5).

5. Fussell, *Doing Battle*, 215, 182 (see chap. 6, n. 3).

6. *Fahrenheit 9/11*, film documentary directed by Michael Moore (IFC Films, Fellowship Adventure Group, Lions Gate Films, 2004).

7. I worked with a man who was a religious conscientious objector during World War II and spent several years in federal prison rather than serve in the military. Though shunned by his peers both in and out of prison, his experience set this man on a course of moral steadfastness that served him throughout adulthood in his career as an administrator resisting the deterioration of our educational system.

8. Mailer, *The Naked and the Dead*, 176 (see chap. 2, n. 2). As the pre-

sent book went to press, the first case of fragging in the Iraq War was reported to the public. An American soldier, Sgt. Alberto Martinez, was accused of killing two of his own officers with a mortar attack disguised as an enemy action.

9. George Bush, "Presidential Diaries," quoted in Herbert Parmet, *George Bush* (New York: Scribner's, 1997), 479.

10. Schmitt, "The Gulf War Veteran."

11. Report of the Research Advisory Committee on Gulf War Veterans' Illnesses, Nov. 15, 2004.

12. For a fuller treatment of the symptoms and consequences of such neglect, see Edward Tick, "Neglecting Our Vietnam Wounds." *Voices: the Art and Science of Psychotherapy* 22, no. 1 (Spring 1986), 46-56.

13. For an early yet definitive examination of the Agent Orange problem, see Fred A. Wilcox, *Waiting for an Army to Die: The Tragedy of Agent Orange*, (New York: Vintage, 1983). For a recent review of the problem thirty years after the war, see Tick, "Fallen Leaves, Broken Lives," *Utne Magazine* (January/February, 2005), 72-77.

14. W. H. Capps, *The Unfinished War: Vietnam and the American Conscience*, (Boston: Beacon Press, 1982).

15. Daniel William Hallock, *Hell, Healing and Resistance* (Farmington, PA: Plough Publishing, 1998).

16. David J. Morris, "Fratricide Reflects Need for More Training," *Times Union*, Mar. 26, 2004. Morris is author of *Storm on the Horizon* (New York: Free Press, 2004) documenting the battle of Khafji in the first Gulf War.

17. Al Gore, speech at New York University, reported in James Barron, "The 2004 Campaign: The Former Vice President; Citing a 'Shamed America,' Gore Calls for Rumsfeld, Rice, Tenet, and Three Others to Resign," *New York Times*, May 27, 2004.

18. Philip Kenicott, "A Wretched New Picture of America: Photos from Iraq Prison Show We Are Our Own Worst Enemy," *Washington Post*, May 5, 2004.

CHAPTER 10: Warrior or Soldier, Hero or Waste?

1. Robert Moore and Douglas Gillette, *The Warrior Within: Accessing*

the Knight in the Male Psyche (New York: William Morrow, 1992), 75. Much of the ensuing discussion of the development of the warrior archetype in the human life cycle is based on Moore's work.

2. Vestal, *Sitting Bull,* 97 (see chap. 3, n. 7).

3. Martin Luther King, Jr., Sermon, "Declaration of Independence from the War in Viet Nam," 1967.

4. Many combat veterans, from the pain of having killed, declare that all killing is wrong. The distinction between justifiable killing and criminal murder has been debated and legislated throughout the ages. This debate is critical to understanding the warrior archetype and what harms it. In later chapters we will examine some of the distinctions religious and legal doctrines have drawn between different kinds of killing and their applications today.

5. Fussell, *Doing Battle,* 145 (see chap. 6, n. 3).

6. In the United States, veterans are imprisoned for criminal behavior at a rate two to three times their proportion to the general population.

Chapter 11: The Soul's Homeward Journey

1. Edward Tick, *The Practice of Dream Healing* (Wheaton, IL: Quest Books, 2001), 12.

2. Jonathan Shay, *Odysseus in America* (New York: Scribner, 2002).

3. Robert Moore, *Facing the Dragon*, ed. Max J. Havlick (Wilmette, IL: Chiron Publications, 2003), 30.

Chapter 12: Purification and Cleansing

1. This reframing is a cornerstone of Hillman's method, helping demonstrate that the archetypes are expressing their universal lives through us. See especially *Re-visioning Psychology* (New York: Harper and Row, 1975).

2. Peter Marin, *Freedom and Its Discontents*, see especially 135–36 (see chap. 6, n. 22).

3. While all Frankl's work deserves study, his best known book, *Man's Quest for Meaning* (New York: Pocket, 1997), should be required reading for all those seeking to heal from war, violence, and atrocity. Also recommended are the writings by Dr. Jim Lantz, one of Frankl's students, who was a combat medic in Viet Nam and later became a distinguished psychotherapist. Jim used Frankl's teachings first to heal himself and later masterfully to help survivors of extreme trauma recover, find meaning, and rebuild lives of service. He was one model for the vision of the transformed returned warrior of honor presented in this book. See esp. Lantz, *Existential Family Therapy: Using the Concepts of Viktor Frankl*, (New York: Jason Aronson, 1993). Jim died during the writing of this book. I honor and salute his memory and service.

4. Steven Silver, "Lessons from Child of Water," *Report of the Working Group on American Indian Vietnam Era Veterans*, (Washington, DC: Readjustment Counseling Services, Dept. of Veterans Affairs, 1992), 17.

5. Stephanie Mines, *Sexual Abuse, Sacred Wound: Transforming Deep Trauma* (Barrytown, NY: Station Hill Openings, 1996), 239–278.

CHAPTER 13: The Healing Power of Storytelling

1. Deena Metzger, *Entering the Ghost River* (Topanga, CA: Hand to Hand, 2002), 9.

2. Ibid., 8–9.

3. Aeschylus, "Epitaph," trans. Richard Lattimore, in *Aeschylus*, vol. 1 of *The Complete Greek Tragedies*, ed. David Grene and Richard Lattimore (Chicago: University of Chicago Press, 1992), 1.

4. Euripides, *The Trojan Women*, in *Three Greek Plays*, trans. Edith Hamilton (New York: W. W. Norton, 1937), 48.

CHAPTER 14: Restitution in the Family and the Nation

1. King Henry V, in *The Histories, Sonnets, and Other Poems*, vol. 2 of *The Annotated Shakespeare*, ed. A. L. Rowse (New York: Clarkson N. Potter, 1978), 4.1.139–140 and 150–153. References are to act, scene, and line.

2. Vestal, *Sitting Bull,* 60 (see chap. 3, n. 7).

3. Thus Veterans Administration evaluations of PTSD pay much attention to homecoming experiences. But these are personal and do not extend to our larger political system. Many veterans typically rage for life at our government that, in its turn, never responds with the needed *mea culpa.*

4. Hillman, *A Terrible Love of War,* 31, italics added. (See chap. 2, n. 27).

5. Leroy S. Rouner, "Civil Religion, Cultural Diversity, and American Civilization," *The Key Reporter* 64, no.3 (Spring 1999): 1-6.

Chapter 15: Initiation as a Warrior

1. Robert Moore and Douglas Gillette, *King, Warrior, Magician, Lover: Rediscovering the Archetypes of the Mature Masculine* (New York: HarperCollins, 1990), see especially 88-95.

2. Heraclitus, frag. 42, Wheelwright, *Heraclitus,* 58 (see chap. 1, n. 3).

3. Homer, *Iliad,* bk. 6, lines 48-49, Fitzgerald, p. 146 (see chap. 2, n. 10).

4. Moore, *King, Warrior, Magician, Lover,* 82.

5. Vestal, *Sitting Bull,* 59-60 (see chap. 3, n. 7).

6. James Hillman, *A Blue Fire*, ed. Thomas Moore (New York: Harper & Row, 1989), 180.

7. Silver, "Lessons from Child of Water," *Report of the Working Group on American Indian Vietnam Era Veterans,* 17 (see chap. 12, n. 4). There is a small but potentially very important body of professional writing supporting the use of traditional Native American rituals such as the inipi with veterans. See the entire report cited above. See also Steven M. Silver and John P. Wilson, "Native American Healing and Purification Rituals for War Stress," in Wilson et al, eds., *Human Adaptation to Extreme Stress From the Holocaust to Vietnam,* (New York: Plenum, 1988).

8. Eliade, *Rites and Symbols of Initiation,* 82-83 (see chap. 2, n. 19).

9. Eliade, Ibid., 66.

10. Chris Hedges, "A Poet of Suffering, Endurance and Healing," *New York Times,* July 8, 2004.

11. Nguyen Duy, "Stop," (see chap. 5 n. 19).

12. William Herrick, *Hermanos!* (New York: Simon and Schuster, 1969), 255. Herrick is one of the great American writers on the experiences of modern war and the manipulation of violence for political ends. Many of his books are worthy of study on this topic. See especially, *Shadows and Wolves* (New York: New Directions, 1980), *Love and Terror* (New York: New Directions, 1981), and *Kill Memory* (New York: New Directions, 1983). Herrick was asked throughout his elder years whether he was Jake Starr and had committed the assassination. In his memoir, *Jumping the Line* (Madison, WI: University of Wisconsin Press, 1998), he clarified that he did witness executions in Spain but did not commit any. This scene from *Hermanos!* demonstrates how fact can be fictionalized in order to emphasize lessons. Herrick wanted the world to learn this lesson of intimacy necessarily achieved through violence. William Herrick died at the age of eighty-nine during the writing of this book, a bullet from the Spanish Civil War still embedded in his neck. I honor his memory and salute his contributions, including all he taught me as a writer, witness, and mentor.

13. Seth Benardete, "Introduction to *The Persians*," trans. Seth Benardete, in *Aeschylus*, vol. 1 of *The Complete Greek Tragedies*, 216 (see chap. 13, n. 3).

14. Aeschylus, *The Persians*, lines 806-7. Ibid., 249.

15. Hadjipateras and Fafalios, *Crete Eyewitnessed*, 18. (see chap. 5, n. 20).

16. Edward Tick, "Healing among Common Victims of War: Vietnamese Refugees in a Combat Veterans Therapy Group," *Voices: the Art and Science of Psychotherapy* 31, no. 2 (Summer 1995): 37–42.

17. Bao Ninh, *The Sorrow of War* (see chap. 8, n. 11).

18. Morley Safer, *Flashbacks: On Returning to Vietnam* (New York: St. Martin's Paperbacks, 1990), 62-63.

CHAPTER 16: War in Religion and Spirituality

1. Wilfred Owen, *The Collected Poems of Wilfred Owen*, 42 (see chap. 2, n. 4).

2. W. Stephen Sabom, "Judgment at Catecka," *Voices: The Art and Science of Psychotherapy* (Fall 1987): 54.

3. Job 38:2.

4. Saul Tchernikovsky, "As I Stood," *The Penguin Book of Hebrew Verse,* ed. and trans. T. Carmi (Middlesex, England and New York: Penguin, 1981), 516. Carmi's translation is in prose; I have restored the original line sequence.

5. Genesis 14.

6. Aeschylus, *The Libation Bearers*, trans. Richard Lattimore, in *Aeschylus*, vol. 1 of *The Complete Greek Tragedies,* 131 (see chap. 13, n. 3).

7. Aeschylus, *Eumenides.* Ibid., 147.

8. Ibrahim Barzak, "Hamas Uses Female Bomber," *Times Union,* January 15, 2004.

9. Telford Taylor, *Nuremberg and Vietnam: An American Tragedy* (Chicago: Quadrangle Books, 1970), 68.

10. James, *Varieties of Religious Experience,* 290 (see chap. 3, n. 4).

Selected Bibliography

*S*ince war is as old as civilization, it is impossible to offer a complete record of all the works and sources that witness to its effects. This bibliography indicates the substance and range of reading upon which I have formed my ideas. I offer it as a guide for those who wish to pursue the subject further.

Aeschylus. *Agamemnon*. Translated by Richard Lattimore. In vol. 1 of *The Complete Greek Tragedies*, edited by David Grene and Richard Lattimore. Chicago: University of Chicago Press, 1991.

———. *Eumenides*. Ibid.

———. *The Libation Bearers*. Ibid.

———. *The Persians*. Translated by Seth Benardete. Ibid.

Alexander, Hartley Burr. *The World's Rim: Great Mysteries of the North American Indian*. Lincoln, NE and London: University of Nebraska Press, 1967.

Arendt, Hannah. *Eichmann in Jerusalem: A Report on the Banality of Evil*. New York: Penguin Books, 1994.

Baker, Mark. *Nam: The Vietnam War in the Words of the Men and Women Who Fought There*. New York: William Morrow, 1981.

Blake, Michael. *Dances with Wolves*. New York: Fawcett, 1990.

Campbell, Joseph. *The Hero with a Thousand Faces*. Cleveland and New York: Meridian Press, 1968.

Capps, W. H. *The Unfinished War: Vietnam and the American Conscience.* Boston: Beacon Press, 1982.

Clauswitz, Carl von. *On War.* London: Penguin Classics, 1982.

Coffin, William Sloane, Jr. "Sanctuaries for Men of Conscience." *Union Seminary Quarterly Review* 13 (1968): 2.

Connell, Evan S. *Son of the Morning Star: Custer and Little Bighorn.* San Francisco: North Point Press, 1984.

Crapser, William. *Remains: Stories of Viet Nam.* Old Chatham, NY: Sachem Press, 1988.

Davidson, H. R. Ellis. *Gods and Myths of Northern Europe.* New York: Penguin Books, 1979.

Drakulic, Slavenka. *The Balkan Express: Fragments from the Other Side of War.* New York: W. W. Norton, 1993.

Duy, Nguyen. *Distant Road.* Translated by Kevin Bowen and Nguyen Ba Chung. Willimantic, CT: Curbstone Press, 1999.

Eliade, Mircea. *Rites and Symbols of Initiation: The Mysteries of Death and Rebirth.* Translated by Willard R. Task. Woodstock, CT: Spring Publications, 1995.

Euripides. *Helen.* Translated by Richard Lattimore. In vol. 3 of *The Complete Greek Tragedies,* edited by David Grene and Richard Lattimore. Chicago: University of Chicago Press, 1991.

———. *The Trojan Women.* In *Three Greek Plays*, translated by Edith Hamilton. New York: W. W. Norton, 1937.

Faulkner, William. "Upon Receiving the Nobel Prize for Literature, 1950." In *Essays, Speeches & Public Letters*, edited by James B. Meriwether. New York: Random House, 1965.

Frankl, Victor. *Man's Quest for Meaning.* New York: Pocket Books, 1997.

Fussell, Paul. *Doing Battle: The Making of a Skeptic.* Boston: Little, Brown and Co., 1996.

———. *The Great War and Modern Memory.* New York and Oxford: Oxford University Press, 1975.

Gabriel, Richard A. *No More Heroes: Madness and Psychiatry in War.* New York: Hill and Wang, 1987.

Gilbert, G. M. *Nuremberg Diary.* New York: Signet, 1961.

Golding, William. *Pincher Martin.* New York: Capricorn, 1956.

Grass, Gunther. *The Tin Drum.* Translated by Ralph Manheim. Greenwich, CT.: Fawcett Crest, 1965.

Grossman, Lt. Col. David. *On Killing: The Psychological Cost of Learning to Kill in War and Society.* Boston: Little, Brown and Co., 1995.

Hadjipateras, C. and M. Fafalios, eds. *Crete 1941 Eyewitnessed.* Athens: Efstathiades Group, 1999.

Hallock, Daniel. *Hell, Healing and Resistance: Veterans Speak.* New York: Plough Publishing Company, 1998.

Hanley, Charles, Sang-Hun Choe, and Martha Mendoza. *The Bridge at No Gun Ri.* New York: Henry Holt, 2001.

Hansel, Arah, Ann Steidle, Grace Zaczek, and Ron Zaczek, eds. *Soldier's Heart: Survivor's View of Combat Trauma.* Lutherville, MD: Sidran Press, 1995.

Hasford, Gustav. *The Short Timers.* New York: Bantam, 1980.

Hedges, Chris. *War is a Force That Gives Us Meaning.* New York: Anchor, 2003.

Hemingway, Ernest. *A Farewell to Arms.* New York: Charles Scribner's Sons, 1957.

———. *For Whom the Bell Tolls.* New York: Charles Scribner's Sons, 1940.

Herman, Judith. *Trauma and Recovery.* New York: Basic Books, 1992.

Herrick, William. *Hermanos!* New York: Simon and Schuster, 1969.

———. *Kill Memory.* New York: New Directions, 1983.

———. *The Last to Die.* New York: Simon and Schuster, 1971.

———. *Love and Terror.* New York: New Directions, 1980.

———. *Shadows and Wolves.* Ibid.

311

Hillman, James. *A Terrible Love of War.* New York: Penguin Press, 2004.

Homer, *Iliad.* Translated by Robert Fitzgerald. Garden City: Doubleday, 1974.

———. *Odyssey.* Translated by Robert Fitzgerald. Garden City: Doubleday, 1963.

Huong, Duong Thu. *Novel without a Name.* Translated by Phan Hay Duong and Nina McPherson. New York: Penguin Books, 1996.

Kambanellis, Iakavos. *Mauthausen.* Translated by Gail Holst-Warhaft. Athens, Greece: Kedros, 1995.

Keegan, Paul. *The Face of Battle.* New York: Penguin Books, 1978.

———. *The Mask of Command.* New York: Penguin Books, 1987.

Keen, Sam. *Faces of the Enemy: Reflections of the Hostile Imagination: The Psychology of Enmity.* New York: HarperCollins, 1991.

King, Martin Luther, Jr. *A Testament of Hope: The Essential Speeches and Writings of Martin Luther King, Jr.* Edited by James M. Washington. New York: HarperCollins, 1991.

Kovic, Ron. *Born on the Fourth of July.* New York: Pocket Books, 1997.

Langer, William. *The Mind of Adolf Hitler: The Secret Wartime Report.* New York: Basic Books, 1972.

Leibo, Steven A. *East, Southeast Asia, and the Western Pacific, 2004.* Harpers Ferry, WV: Stryker-Post Publications, 2004.

Levine, Peter. *Waking the Tiger: Healing Trauma.* Berkeley, CA: North Atlantic Books, 1997.

Lifton, Robert Jay. *History and Human Survival.* New York: Random House, 1970.

———. *Home from the War: Vietnam Veterans, Neither Victims Nor Executioners.* New York: Simon and Schuster, 1973.

———. *The Nazi Doctors: Medical Killing and the Psychology of Genocide.* New York: Basic Books, 2000.

———. *Thought Reform and the Psychology of Totalism.* New York: W. W. Norton, 1969.

Lorenz, Konrad. *On Aggression.* Translated by Marjorie Kerr Wilson. New York: Bantam, 1971.

Mailer, Norman. *The Naked and the Dead.* New York: Rinehart and Co., 1948.

Manchester, William. *Goodbye, Darkness: A Memoir of the Pacific War.* New York: Little, Brown and Co., 1980.

Marin, Peter. *Freedom and Its Discontents.* S. Royalton, VT: Steerforth Press, 1995.

Matthiessen, Peter. *Under the Mountain Wall: A Chronicle of Two Seasons in the Stone Age.* New York: Ballantine, 1972.

Metzger, Deena. *Entering the Ghost River.* Topanga, CA: Hand to Hand, 2004.

———. and Michael Ortiz Hill. *Sacred Illness, Sacred Medicine.* Salt Lake City: Elik Press, 2004.

Miller, David Humphreys. *Custer's Fall: The Native American Side of the Story.* New York: Meridian, 1992.

Mines, Stephanie. *Sexual Abuse, Sacred Wound: Transforming Deep Trauma.* Barrytown, NY: Station Hill Openings, 1996.

Moore, Robert and Douglas Gillette. *King, Warrior, Magician, Lover: Rediscovering the Archetypes of the Mature Masculine.* New York: HarperCollins, 1990.

———. *The Warrior Within: Accessing the Knight in the Male Psyche.* New York: William Morrow, 1992.

Moore, Robert. *Facing the Dragon.* Edited by Max J. Havlick. Wilmette, IL: Chiron Publications, 2003.

Morris, David J. *Storm on the Horizon.* New York: Free Press, 2004.

Moss, Sidney and Samuel Moss. *Thy Men Shall Fall.* Chicago: Ziff-Davis, 1948.

Napolean, Harold. *Yuuyaraq: The Way of Being Human.* Fairbanks, Alaska: Center for Cross-Cultural Studies, 1991.

Nichols, David, ed. *Ernie's War: The Best of Ernie Pyle's World War II Dispatches.* New York: Touchstone, 1986.

Niehardt, John G. *Black Elk Speaks: Being the Life Story of a Holy Man of the Oglala Sioux*. New York: Pocket Books, 1973.

Ninh, Bao. *The Sorrow of War*. Translated by Phan Thanh Hao. London: Minerva, 1994.

Oakes, Maud and Joseph Campbell. *Where the Two Came to Their Father: A Navajo War Ceremonial Given by Jeff King*. Princeton: Bollingen, 1969.

Orwell, George. *1984*. New York: Penguin Plume, 1983.

———. *Homage to Catalonia*. Orlando, FL: Harvest, 1980.

Owen, Wilfred. *The Collected Poems of Wilfred Owen*, ed. C. Day Lewis. New York: New Directions, 1963.

Pran, Dith, comp. and Kim DePaul, ed. *Children of Cambodia's Killing Fields: Memoirs by Survivors*. Chiang Mai, Thailand: Silkworm Books, 1997.

Pressfield, Steven. *Gates of Fire*. London and New York: Doubleday, 1999.

Remarque, Erich Maria. *All Quiet on the Western Front*. Translated by A. W. Wheen. Boston: Little, Brown and Co., 1929.

Department of Veterans Affairs. *Report of the Working Group on American Indian Vietnam Era Veterans*. Readjustment Counseling Service. Washington, D.C.: Dept. of Veterans Affairs, 1992.

Sabom, W. Stephen. "Back from Moriah: Moral Trauma and the Vietnam Veteran." *Pastoral Psychology* 36, no. 3 (Spring 1988): 172–186.

———. ed. *Healing a Generation: The Vietnam Experience*. Special issue of *Voices: the Art and Science of Psychotherapy* 27, nos. 1 and 2 (Spring/Summer 1991). New York and London: Guilford Press, 1991.

———. "Judgment at Catecka." *Voices: the Art and Science of Psychotherapy* 23, no. 3 (Fall 1987): 51–64.

Safer, Morley. *Flashbacks: On Returning to Vietnam*. New York: St. Martin's Paperbacks, 1990.

Sajor, Indai and Le Thi Nham Tuyet. *Agent Orange: Impact of Chemical Warfare on the Reproductive Rights of Women and Men in*

Vietnam. Phillipines: Asian Centre for Women's Human Rights and Ha Noi, Viet Nam: Research Centre for Gender, Family and Environment in Development, 2000.

Sandoz, Mari. *Crazy Horse: The Strange Man of the Oglalas.* Lincoln: University of Nebraska Press, 1961.

Sassoon, Siegfried. *The War Poems.* London: Faber and Faber, 1983.

Shakespeare, William. *Julius Caesar.* In *The Annotated Shakespeare,* vol. 3: *The Tragedies,* edited by A. L. Rowse. New York: Clarkson N. Potter, 1978.

———. *King Henry V.* In *The Annotated Shakespeare,* vol. 2: *The Histories, Sonnets, and Other Poems.* Ibid.

Shay, Jonathan. *Achilles in Vietnam: Combat Trauma and the Undoing of Character.* New York: Atheneum, 1994.

———. *Odysseus in America.* New York: Scribner, 2002.

Shirer, William L. *The Rise and Fall of the Third Reich.* New York: Touchstone, 1980.

Silko, Leslie Marmon. *Ceremony.* New York: Viking Penguin, 1987.

Sophocles. *Ajax.* Translated by John Moore. In *The Complete Greek Tragedies,* vol. 2: *Sophocles,* edited by David Grene and Richard Lattimore. Chicago: University of Chicago Press, 1991.

———. *Antigone.* Translated by David Grene. Ibid.

Taylor, Telford. *Nuremberg and Vietnam: An American Tragedy.* Chicago: Quadrangle Books, 1970.

Terry, Patricia, trans. *Poems of the Vikings.* Indianapolis: Bobbs-Merrill, 1980.

Terry, Wallace. *Bloods: An Oral History of the Vietnam War by Black Veterans.* New York: Random House, 1984.

Tick, Edward. "Fallen Leaves, Broken Lives," and "Casualties of the Vietnam War." *Utne Magazine,* no. 127 (Jan.–Feb. 2005): 72–77.

———. *The Golden Tortoise.* Granada Hills, CA: Red Hen Press, 2005.

———. "Healing among Common Victims of War: Vietnamese Refugees in a Combat Veterans Therapy Group." *Voices: the Art and Science of Psychotherapy* 31, no. 2 (Summer 1995): 37–42.

———. *The Practice of Dream Healing: Bringing Ancient Greek Mysteries into Modern Medicine.* Wheaton, IL: Quest Books, 2001.

———. *Sacred Mountain: Encounters with the Vietnam Beast.* Santa Fe: Moon Bear Press, 1989.

Tolstoy, Leo. *War and Peace.* Translated by Ann Dunnigan. New York: New American Library, 1968.

Tran, Emperor Thai Tong, *Lessons in Emptiness.* Translated by Thich Nhat Hahn. *Zen Keys.* New York: Doubleday Image, 1995.

Tritle, Lawrence A. *From Melos to My Lai: War and Survival.* London and New York: Routledge, 2000.

Tzu, Sun. *The Art of War.* Translated by Ralph D. Sawyer. Boulder, Colorado: Westview Press, 1994.

United Nations Children's Fund. *Childhood under Threat.* New York: United Nations Children's Fund, 2004.

Vallejo, Cesar. *Spain, Take This Cup from Me.* Translated by Clayton Eshleman and Jose Rubia Barcia. New York: Grove Press, 1974.

Vestal, Stanley. *Sitting Bull: Champion of the Sioux.* Norman, OK and London: University of Oklahoma Press, 1989.

Wiesel, Elie. *Night.* Translated by Stella Rodway. New York: Bantam, 1982.

Wilcox, Fred A. *Waiting for an Army to Die: The Tragedy of Agent Orange.* New York: Vintage, 1983.

Wilson, John P., Zev Harel, and Boaz Kahana, eds. *Human Adaptation to Extreme Stress from the Holocaust to Vietnam*. New York: Plenum, 1988.

Xenophon. *The Anabasis.* Translated by Rev. J. S. Watson. London: Henry G. Bohn, 1859.

Young, Marilyn, John J. Fitzgerald, and A. Tom Grunfeld. *The Vietnam War: A History in Documents.* New York: Oxford University Press, 2002.

Index of Cited Veterans and Survivors

Anonymous:

First Names:

Full Names:

General Index